THE LIBRARY BOOK

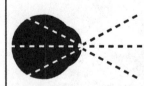

THE LIBRARY BOOK

SUSAN ORLEAN

THORNDIKE PRESS
A part of Gale, a Cengage Company

Farmington Hills, Mich • San Francisco • New York • Waterville, Maine
Meriden, Conn • Mason, Ohio • Chicago

Copyright © 2018 by Susan Orlean.
Thorndike Press, a part of Gale, a Cengage Company.

ALL RIGHTS RESERVED
Thorndike Press® Large Print Popular and Narrative Nonfiction.
The text of this Large Print edition is unabridged.
Other aspects of the book may vary from the original edition.
Set in 16 pt. Plantin.

LIBRARY OF CONGRESS CIP DATA ON FILE.
CATALOGUING IN PUBLICATION FOR THIS BOOK
IS AVAILABLE FROM THE LIBRARY OF CONGRESS

ISBN-13: 978-1-4328-5646-5 (hardcover)

Published in 2018 by arrangement with Simon & Schuster, Inc.

Printed in Mexico
1 2 3 4 5 6 7 22 21 20 19 18

The Los Angeles Public Library

For Edith Orlean, my past
For Austin Gillespie, my future

Memory believes before knowing remembers.

— William Faulkner, *Light in August*

And when they ask us what we're doing, you can say, We're remembering.

— Ray Bradbury, *Fahrenheit 451*

I have always imagined Paradise as a kind of library.

— Jorge Luis Borges, *Dreamtigers*

1.

Stories to Begin On (1940)
By Bacmeister, Rhoda W.
X 808 B127

Begin Now — To Enjoy Tomorrow
(1951)
By Giles, Ray
362.6 G472

A Good Place to Begin (1987)
By Powell, Lawrence
Clark 027.47949 P884

To Begin at the Beginning (1994)
By Copenhaver, Martin B.
230 C782

Even in Los Angeles, where there is no shortage of remarkable hairdos, Harry Peak attracted attention. "He was very blond. Very, very blond," his lawyer said to me, and then he fluttered his hand across his forehead, performing a pantomime of Peak's heavy swoop of bangs. Another lawyer, who questioned Peak in a deposition, remembered his hair very well. "He had a lot of it," she said. "And he was very definitely blond." An arson investigator I met described Peak entering a courtroom "with all that hair," as if his hair existed independently.

Having a presence mattered a great deal to Harry Omer Peak. He was born in 1959, and grew up in Santa Fe Springs, a town in the paddle-flat valley less than an hour southeast of Los Angeles, hemmed in by the dun-colored Santa Rosa Hills and a looming sense of monotony. It was a place that offered the soothing uneventfulness of conformity, but Harry longed to stand out. As a kid, he dabbled in the minor delinquencies and pranks that delighted an audience. Girls liked him. He was charming, funny, dimpled, daring. He could talk anyone into anything. He had a gift for drama and invention. He was a storyteller, a yarn-spinner, and an agile liar; he was good at fancying up facts to make his life seem less plain and mingy. According to his sister, he was the biggest bullshitter in the world, so quick to fib and fabricate that even his own family didn't believe a word he said.

The closeness of Hollywood's constant beckoning, combined with his knack for performance, meant, almost predictably, that Harry Peak decided to become an actor. After he finished high school and served a stint in the army, Harry moved to Los Angeles and started dreaming. He began dropping the phrase "when I'm a movie star" into his conversations. He always said "when" and not "if." For him, it was a statement of fact rather than speculation.

Although they never actually saw him in any television shows or movies, his family was under the impression that during his time in Hollywood, Harry landed some promising parts. His father told me Harry was on a medical show — maybe *General Hospital* — and that he had roles in several movies, including *The Trial of Billy Jack.* IMDb — the world's largest online database for movies and television — lists a Barry Peak, a Parry Peak, a Harry Peacock, a Barry Pearl, and even a Harry Peak of Plymouth, England, but there is nothing at all listed for a Harry Peak of Los Angeles. As far as I can tell, the only time Harry Peak appeared on screen was on the local news in 1987, after he was arrested for setting the Los Angeles Central Library on fire, destroying almost half a million books and damaging seven hundred thousand more. It was one of the biggest fires in the history of Los Angeles, and it was the single biggest library fire in the history of the United States.

Central Library, which was designed by the architect Bertram Goodhue and opened in 1926, is in the middle of downtown Los Angeles, at the corner of Fifth Street and Flower, on the downslope of a rise once known as Normal Hill. The hill used to be higher, but when it was chosen as the site of the library, the summit was clawed off to make it more buildable. At the time the library opened, this part of downtown Los Angeles was a busy neighborhood of top-heavy, half-timbered Victorians teetering on the flank of the hills. These days, the houses are gone, and the neighborhood consists of dour, dark office towers standing shoulder to shoulder, casting long shafts of shade across what is left of the hill. Central Library is an entire city block wide, but it is only eight stories high, making it sort of ankle-height compared to these leggy office towers. It projects a horizontality that it probably didn't in 1926, when it debuted as the high point in what was then a modest, mostly four-story-tall city center.

The library opens at ten A.M., but by daybreak there are always people hovering nearby. They lean against every side of the building, or perch half on and half off the low stone walls around the perimeter, or array themselves in postures of anticipation in the garden northwest of the main entrance, from which they can maintain a view of the front door. They watch the door with unrewarded vigilance, since there is no chance that the building will open earlier than scheduled. One recent warm morning, the people in the garden were clustered under the canopy of trees, and beside the long, trickling watercourse that seemed to emit a small breath of chilled air. Rolling suitcases and totes and book bags were stashed here and there. Pigeons the color of concrete marched in a bossy staccato around the suitcases. A thin young man in a white dress shirt, a hint of sweat ringing his underarms, wobbled on one foot, gripping a file folder under his arm while trying to fish a cell phone out of his back pocket. Behind him, a woman with a sagging yellow backpack sat on the edge of a bench, leaning forward, eyes closed, hands clasped; I couldn't tell if she was napping or praying. Near her stood a man wearing a bowler hat and a too-small

15

T-shirt that revealed a half-moon of shiny pink belly. Two women holding clipboards herded a small, swirling group of kids toward the library's front door. I wandered over to the corner of the garden, where two men sitting by the World Peace Bell were debating a meal they'd apparently shared.

"You have to admit that garlic dressing was good," one of the men was saying.

"I don't eat salad."

"Oh, come on, man, everyone eats salad!"

"Not me." Pause. "I love Dr Pepper."

Between each volley of their conversation, the men cast glances at the main entrance of the library, where a security guard was sitting. One of the doors was open, and the guard sat just inside, visible to anyone passing by. The open door was an irresistible conversation starter. One person after another approached the guard, and he deflected them without even blinking an eye:

"Is the library open yet?"

"No, it's not open."

Next: "Ten A.M."

Next: "You'll know when it's time."

Next: "No, not open yet."

Next: "Ten A.M., man" — shaking his head and rolling his eyes — "ten A.M., like it says on the sign."

Every few minutes, one of the people ap-

16

proaching the guard flashed an identifica-
tion badge and was waved in, because the
library was actually already in gear, humming with staff members who were ready-
ing it for the day. The shipping department
had been at work since dawn, packing tens
of thousands of books into plastic bins.
These were books requested at one of the
city's seventy-three libraries, or that had
been returned to one in which they didn't
belong and were being repatriated, or they
were brand-new books that had been just
cataloged at Central Library and were now
on their way to one of the branches. Security
guards are at the library around the clock;
the guards on duty had started their shift at
six A.M. Matthew Mattson, who runs the
library's website, had been at his desk in
the basement for an hour, watching the
number of website visits surge as the morning advanced.

In each of the eight subject departments
throughout the building, librarians and
clerks were tidying shelves, checking new
books, and beginning the business of the
day. The reading tables and carrels were
empty, each chair tucked under each table,
all enfolded in a quiet even deeper than the
usual velvety quiet of the library. In the History Department, a young librarian named

Llyr Heller sorted through a cart of books, weeding out the ones that were damaged or deeply unloved. When she finished, she pulled out a list of books the department wanted to order, checking to make sure they weren't already in the collection. If they passed that test, she would look at reviews and librarian tip sheets to make sure they warranted buying.

In the Children's Department, children's librarians from around the city were gathered in the puppet theater for their regular meeting. The topic being discussed was how to run an effective story time. The thirty full-size adult humans who were wedged into the tiny seats of the theater listened to the presentation with rapt attention. "Use an appropriate-sized teddy bear," the librarian running the session was saying as I walked in. "I had been using one I thought was the size of a baby, but I was wrong — it was the size of a very premature baby." She pointed to a bulletin board that was covered with felt. "Don't forget, flannel boards are wonderful," she said. "You may want to use them for things like demonstrating penguins getting dressed. You can also hide things inside them, like rabbits and noses."

Upstairs, Robert Morales, the library's budget director, and Madeleine Rackley, the business manager, were talking about money with John Szabo, who holds the job of Los Angeles city librarian, in charge of all the libraries in Los Angeles. Just below them, the main clock clicked toward ten, and Selena Terrazas, who is one of Central Library's three principal librarians, stationed herself at the center axis of the lobby so she could keep watch over the morning rush when the doors officially opened.

There was a sense of stage business — that churn of activity you can't hear or see but you feel at a theater in the instant before the curtain rises — of people finding their places and things being set right, before the burst of action begins. The library entrances have been thrown open thousands of times since 1859, the year that a public library first existed in Los Angeles. Yet every time the security guard hollers out that the library has opened, there is a quickening in the air and the feeling that something significant is about to unfold — the play is about to begin. This particular morning, Selena Terrazas checked her watch, and the head of security, David Aguirre, checked his as well, and then Aguirre radioed the guard at the entrance to give the all-clear. After a moment, the guard clambered off his stool and pushed the door open, letting the buttery light of the California morning spill into the entry.

A puff of outside air wafted in and down the hall. Then, in an instant, people poured in — the hoverers, who bolted from their posts in the garden, and the wall-sitters, and the morning fumblers, and the school groups, and the businesspeople, and the parents with strollers heading to story time, and the students, and the homeless, who rushed straight to the bathrooms and then made a beeline to the computer center, and the scholars, and the time-wasters, and the readers, and the curious, and the bored — all clamoring for *The Dictionary of Irish Artists* or *The Hero with a Thousand Faces* or a biography of Lincoln or *Pizza Today* magazine or *The Complete Book of Progressive Knitting* or photographs of watermelons in the San Fernando Valley taken in the 1960s or *Harry Potter* — always, *Harry Potter* — or any one of the millions of books, pamphlets, maps, musical scores, newspapers, and pictures the library holds in store. They were a rivering flow of humanity, a gush, and they were looking for baby-name guides, and biographies of Charles Parnell, and maps of Indiana, and suggestions from a librarian for a novel that was romantic but not corny; they were picking up tax information and getting tutored in English and checking out movies and tracing their family history. They were sitting in the library, just because it was a pleasant place to sit, and sometimes they were doing things that had nothing to do with the library. On this particular morning, in Social Sciences, a woman at one of the reading tables was sewing beads onto the sleeve of a cotton blouse. In one of the carrels in History, a man in a pin-striped suit who had books on his desk but wasn't reading held a bag of Doritos under the lip of the table. He pretended to muffle a cough each time he ate a chip.

I grew up in libraries, or at least it feels that way. I was raised in the suburbs of Cleveland, just a few blocks from the brick-faced Bertram Woods branch of the Shaker Heights Public Library system. Throughout my childhood, starting when I was very young, I went there several times a week with my mother. On those visits, my mother and I walked in together but as soon as we passed through the door, we split up and each headed to our favorite section. The library might have been the first place I was ever given autonomy. Even when I was maybe four or five years old, I was allowed to head off on my own. Then, after a while, my mother and I reunited at the checkout counter with our finds. Together we waited as the librarian at the counter pulled out the date card and stamped it with the checkout machine — that giant fist thumping the card with a loud *chunk-chunk,* printing a crooked due date underneath a score of previous crooked due dates that belonged to other people, other times.

Our visits to the library were never long enough for me. The place was so bountiful. I loved wandering around the bookshelves, scanning the spines until something happened to catch my eye. Those visits were dreamy, frictionless interludes that promised I would leave richer than I arrived. It wasn't like going to a store with my mom, which guaranteed a tug-of-war between what I wanted and what my mother was willing to buy me; in the library I could have anything I wanted. After we checked out, I loved being in the car and having all the books we'd gotten stacked on my lap, pressing me under their solid, warm weight, their Mylar covers sticking a bit to my thighs. It was such a thrill leaving a place with things you hadn't paid for; such a thrill anticipating the new books we would read. On the ride home, my mom and I talked about the order in which we were going to read our books and how long until they had to be returned, a solemn conversation in which we decided how to pace ourselves through this charmed, evanescent period of grace until the books were due. We both thought all of the librarians at the Bertram Woods Branch Library were beautiful. For a few minutes we would discuss their beauty. My mother then always mentioned that if she could have chosen any profession at all, she would have chosen to be a librarian, and the car would grow silent for a moment as we both considered what an amazing thing that would have been.

When I was older, I usually walked to the library myself, lugging back as many books as I could carry. Occasionally, I did go with my mother, and the trip would be as enchanted as it was when I was small. Even when I was in my last year of high school and could drive myself to the library, my mother and I still went together now and then, and the trip unfolded exactly as it did when I was a child, with all the same beats and pauses and comments and reveries, the same perfect pensive rhythm we followed so many times before. When I miss my mother these days, now that she is gone, I like to picture us in the car together, going for one more magnificent trip to Bertram Woods.

■ ■ ■

My family was big on the library. We were very much a reading family, but we were a borrow-a-book-from-the-library family more than a bookshelves-full-of-books family. My parents valued books, but they grew up in the Depression, aware of the quicksilver nature of money, and they learned the hard way that you shouldn't buy what you could borrow. Because of that frugality, or perhaps independent of it, they also believed that you read a book for the experience of reading it. You didn't read it in order to have an object that had to be housed and looked after forever, a memento of the purpose for which it was obtained. The reading of the book was a journey. There was no need for souvenirs.

By the time I was born, my parents' financial circumstances were comfortable, and they learned how to splurge a little, but their Depression-era mentality adhered stubbornly to certain economies, which included not buying books that could be gotten very easily from the library. Our uncrowded bookshelves at home had several sets of encyclopedias (an example of something not convenient to borrow from the library, since you reached for it regularly and urgently) and a random assortment of other books which, for one reason or another, my parents had ended up buying. That included a few mild sex manuals (*Ideal Marriage: Its Physiology and Technique* is the one I remember best, because of course I read it whenever my parents were out of the house). I assume my parents bought the sex books because they would have been embarrassed to present them at the checkout desk of the library. There were also some travel guides, some coffee table books, a few of my father's law books, and a dozen or so novels that were either gifts or for some reason managed to justify being owned outright.

When I headed to college, one of the many ways I differentiated myself from my parents was that I went wild for owning books. I think buying textbooks was what got me going. All I know is that I lost my appreciation for the slow pace of making your way through a library and for having books on borrowed time. I wanted to have my books around me, forming a totem pole of the narratives I'd visited. As soon as I got my own apartment, I lined it with bookcases and loaded them with hardcovers. I used the college library for research, but otherwise, I turned into a ravenous buyer of books. I couldn't walk into a bookstore without leaving with something, or several somethings. I loved the fresh alkaline tang of new ink and paper, a smell that never emanated from a broken-in library book. I loved the crack of a newly flexed spine, and the way the brand-new pages almost felt damp, as if they were wet with creation. I sometimes wondered if I was catching up after spending my childhood amid sparsely settled bookcases. But the reason didn't matter to me. I actually became a little evangelical about book ownership. Sometimes I fantasized about starting a bookstore. If my mother ever mentioned to me that she was on the waiting list for some book at the library, I got annoyed and asked why she didn't just go buy it.

Once I was done with college, and done with researching term papers in the stacks of the Harold T. and Vivian B. Shapiro Undergraduate Library, I sloughed off the memory of those wondrous childhood trips to the Bertram Woods branch, and began, for the first time in my life, to wonder what libraries were for.

It might have remained that way, and I might have spent the rest of my life thinking about libraries only wistfully, the way I thought wistfully about, say, the amusement park I went to as a kid. Libraries might have become just a bookmark of memory more than an actual place, a way to call up an emotion of a moment that occurred long ago, something that was fused with "mother" and "the past" in my mind. But then libraries came roaring back into my life unexpectedly. In 2011, my husband accepted a job in Los Angeles, so we left New York and headed west. I didn't know Los Angeles well, but I'd spent time there over the years, visiting cousins who lived in and around the city. When I became a writer, I went to Los Angeles many times to work on magazine pieces and books. On those visits, I had been to and from the beach, and up and down the canyons, and in and out of the valley, and back and forth to the mountains, but I never gave downtown Los Angeles a second thought, assuming it was just a glassy landscape of office buildings that hollowed out by five o'clock every night. I pictured Los Angeles as a radiant doughnut, rimmed by milky ocean and bristling mountains, with a big hole in the middle. I never went to the public library, never thought about the library, although I'm sure I assumed there was a public library, probably a main branch, probably downtown.

My son was in first grade when we moved to California. One of his first assignments in school was to interview someone who worked for the city. I suggested talking to a garbage collector or a police officer, but he said he wanted to interview a librarian. We were so new to town that we had to look up the address of the closest library, which was the Los Angeles Public Library's Studio City branch. The branch was about a mile away from our house, which happened to be about the same distance that the Bertram Woods branch was from my childhood home.

As my son and I drove to meet the librarian, I was flooded by a sense of absolute familiarity, a gut-level recollection of this journey, of parent and child on their way to the library. I had taken this trip so many times before, but now it was turned on its head, and I was the parent bringing my child on that special trip. We parked, and my son and I walked toward the library, taking it in for the first time. The building was white and modish, with a mint green mushroom cap of a roof. From the outside, it didn't look anything like the stout brick Bertram Woods branch, but when we stepped in, the thunderbolt of recognition struck me so hard that it made me gasp. Decades had passed and I was three thousand miles away, but I felt like I had been lifted up and whisked back to that time and place, back to the scenario of walking into the library with my mother. Nothing had changed — there was the same soft *tsk-tsk-tsk* of pencil on paper, and the muffled murmuring from patrons at the tables in the center of the room, and the creak and groan of book carts, and the occasional papery clunk of a book dropped on a desk. The scarred wooden checkout counters, and the librarians' desks, as big as boats, and the bulletin board with its fluttering, raggedy notices were all the same. The sense of gentle, steady busyness, like water on a rolling boil, was just the same. The books on the shelves, with some subtractions and additions, were certainly the same.

It wasn't that time stopped in the library. It was as if it were captured here, collected here, and in all libraries — and not only my time, my life, but all human time as well. In the library, time is dammed up — not just stopped but saved. The library is a gathering pool of narratives and of the people who come to find them. It is where we can glimpse immortality; in the library, we can live forever.

So the spell libraries once cast on me was renewed. Maybe it had never really been extinguished, although I had been away long enough that it was like visiting a country I'd loved but forgotten as my life went galloping by. I knew what it was like to want a book and to buy it, but I had forgotten what it felt like to amble among the library shelves, finding the book I was looking for but also seeing who its neighbors were, noticing their peculiar concordance, and following an idea as it was handed off from one book to the next, like a game of telephone. I might start at Dewey decimal 301.4129781 (*Pioneer Women* by Joanna L. Stratton) and a few inches later find myself at 306.7662 (*Gaydar* by Donald F. Reuter) and then 301.45096 (*Dreams from My Father* by Barack Obama) and finally 301.55 (*The Men Who Stare at Goats* by Jon Ronson). On a library bookshelf, thought progresses in a way that is logical but also dumbfounding, mysterious, irresistible.

Not long after my son interviewed the librarian, I happened to meet a man named Ken Brecher who runs the Library Foundation of Los Angeles, the nonprofit organization that champions the city's libraries and raises money for extra programming and services. Brecher offered to give me a tour of Central Library, so a few days later, I drove downtown to meet him. From the highway, I could see the quiver of dark skyscrapers in the center of the city that surrounded the library. The summer and fall had been rainless. The landscape around me was bright and bleached, blasted, with an almost ashy pallor. Even the palm trees seemed sapped of color, and the reddish rooftops were whitened, as if dusted with sugar.

I felt new here, and the sheer breadth of Los Angeles still astonished me. It seemed like I could drive and drive and the city would just keep unfurling, almost as if it were a map of Los Angeles being unrolled as I drove over it, rather than a real city that started and stopped somewhere specific. In Los Angeles, your eye keeps reaching for an endpoint and never finds it, because it doesn't exist. The wide-openness of Los Angeles is a little intoxicating, but it can be unnerving, too — it's the kind of place that doesn't hold you close, a place where you can picture yourself cartwheeling off into emptiness, a pocket of zero gravity. I'd spent the previous five years living in the Hudson Valley of New York, so I was more used to bumping into a hill or a river at every turn and settling my gaze on some foreground feature — a tree, a house, a cow. For twenty years before that, I'd lived in Manhattan, where the awareness of when you are in or out of the city is as clear as day.

I expected Central Library to look like the main libraries I knew best. New York Public Library and the Cleveland Public Library are serious buildings, with grand entrances and a stern, almost religious aura. By contrast, the Los Angeles Central Library looks like what a child might assemble out of blocks. The building — buff-colored, with black inset windows and a number of small entrances — is a fantasia of right angles and nooks and plateaus and terraces and balconies that step up to a single central pyramid surfaced with colored tiles and topped with a bronze sculpture of an open flame held in a human hand. It manages to look ancient and modern at the same time. As I approached, the simple blocky form of the building resolved into a throng of bas-relief stone figures on every wall. There were Virgil and Leonardo and Plato; bison herds and cantering horses; sunbursts and nautiluses; archers and shepherds and printers and scholars; scrolls and wreaths and waves.

Philosophical declarations in English and Latin were carved across the building's face like an ancient ticker tape. Compared to the mute towers around it, the library seemed more a proclamation than a building.

I circled, reading as I walked. Socrates, cool-eyed and stony-faced, gazed past me. I followed the bustle of visitors to the center of the main floor, and then I continued past the clatter and buzz of the circulation desk and climbed a wide set of stairs that spilled me out into a great rotunda. The rotunda was empty. I stood for a moment, taking it in. The rotunda is one of those rare places that have a kind of sacred atmosphere, full of a quiet so dense and deep that it almost feels underwater. All the rotunda's features were larger than life, overpowering, jaw-dropping. The walls were covered with huge murals of Native Americans and priests and soldiers and settlers, painted in dusty mauve and blue and gold. The floor was glossy travertine, laid out in a pattern of checkerboard. The ceiling and archways were tiled with squares of red and blue and ocher. In the center of the rotunda hung a massive chandelier — a heavy brass chain dangling a luminous blue glass Earth ringed by the twelve figures of the zodiac.

I crossed the rotunda and walked toward

a large sculpture known as the Statue of Civilization — a marble woman with fine features and perfect posture and a trident in her left hand. I was so stirred by the library's beauty that when Brecher arrived to give me my tour, I was chattering like someone on a successful first date. Brecher is as thin as a pencil and has bright eyes, pure white hair, and a brisk, barking laugh. He began a running commentary about each fixture, each carving, each plaque on the wall. He also told me about his path to the library, which included stints living with a preliterate tribe of indigenous people in the Central Amazon and working for the Sundance Institute. He seemed electrified by everything he told me about the library, and between his electricity and my excitement, we must have made quite a lively pair. We inched along, stopping every few feet to examine another feature of the building, or to eyeball another shelf of books, or to hear about this or that person who had importance to the place. Everything about the library had a story — the architect, the muralist, the person who developed each collection, the head of each department, the scores of people who worked at the library or patronized it over the decades, many now long gone but still somehow present there, lingering in the wings, a durable part of its history.

We finally made our way to the Fiction Department and stopped near the first row of shelves. Brecher took a break from his commentary and reached for one of the books, cracked it open, held it up to his face, and inhaled deeply. I had never seen someone smell a book quite like that before. Brecher inhaled the book a few more times, then clapped it shut and placed it back on the shelf.

"You can still smell the smoke in some of them," he said, almost to himself. I wasn't quite sure what he meant, so I tried this: "They smell like smoke because the library used to let patrons smoke?"

"No!" Brecher said. "Smoke from the fire!"

"The fire?"

"The fire!"

"The fire? What fire?"

"The fire," he said. "The big fire. The one that shut the library down."

On April 29, 1986, the day the library burned, I was living in New York. While my romance with libraries had not been renewed yet, I cared a lot about books, and I am sure I would have noticed a story about a massive fire in a library, no matter where that library was. The Central Library fire was not a minor matter, not a cigarette smoldering in a trash can that would have gone without mention. It was a huge, furious fire that burned for more than seven hours and reached temperatures of 2000 degrees; it was so fierce that almost every firefighter in Los Angeles was called upon to fight it. More than one million books were burned or damaged. I couldn't imagine how I didn't know of an event of this magnitude, especially something involving books, even though I was living on the other side of the country when it occurred.

When I got home from touring the library with Brecher, I looked up the *New York Times* from April 29, 1986. The fire had started midmorning, Pacific time, which would have been early afternoon in New York. By then, the *Times* would have already published that day's paper. The front-page stories were the usual fare, including the postponement of mobster John Gotti's trial; a warning from Senator Bob Dole that the federal budget was in trouble; and a photograph of President Reagan and his wife, Nancy, waving goodbye as they embarked on a trip to Indonesia. On the right side of the front page, over a skinny, single-column story, was the headline SOVIET ANNOUNCES NUCLEAR ACCIDENT AT ELECTRIC PLANT / MISHAP ACKNOWLEDGED AFTER RISING RADIATION LEVELS SPREAD TO SCANDINAVIA. The next day, the headline on the follow-up story grew to panic size, announcing SOVIET, REPORTING ATOM PLANT "DISASTER," SEEKS HELP ABROAD TO FIGHT REACTOR FIRE with a place line of Moscow, U.S.S.R. There was also a special three-page section that began with NUCLEAR DISASTER: A SPREADING CLOUD AND AN AID APPEAL. By the second day, the fear about the accident at the Chernobyl nuclear plant triggered what was then the largest single-day point loss in the history of the American stock market.

The burning of Central Library in Los Angeles was finally mentioned in the *New York Times* on April 30, in a story that appeared on page A14. The story laid out the basic facts, mentioning that twenty-two people were injured in the blaze and that the cause of the fire was unknown. Another brief story provided a few more details on the fire and included interviews with residents of Los Angeles speculating about how it would feel to have the library closed indefinitely. There were no other stories about it in the *New York Times* that week.

The biggest library fire in American history had been upstaged by the Chernobyl nuclear meltdown. The books burned while most of us were waiting to see if we were about to witness the end of the world.

2.

The fire as seen from Fifth Street

*Fire!: 38 Lifesaving Tips for
You and Your Family* (1995)
  By Gibbons, James J.
  614.84 G441

Fire Behavior and Sprinklers
(1964)
  By Thompson, Norman J.
  614.844 T474

Fire: Friend or Foe (1998)
  By Patent, Dorothy Hinshaw
  X 634 P295-2

Fire! The Library Is Burning
(1988)
  By Cytron, Barry D.
  X 614 C997

April 28, 1986, was a peculiarly hot day in Los Angeles. Instead of the silky twinkle of spring, the day had a sullen, leaden feel. But by the next morning, April 29, the heat lifted. The air felt fresh. The sky was the bluest blue.

It had been a strange, sad year, beginning in January, when the *Challenger* spacecraft exploded, killing its crew of seven astronauts. The week of April 28 buckled under its own share of bad news. An earthquake rocked Central Mexico. Fires broke out in several British prisons, and scores of inmates escaped. The United States and Libya were in a tense standoff. Closer to the library, a bulldozer at a construction site in Carson,

California, sheared off a main sewer cap, and raw sewage was gushing into the Los Angeles River.

On April 29, Central Library opened as usual at ten A.M., and within minutes it was humming. About two hundred employees were already in place around the building, from the shipping docks to the circulation desks to the stacks. Glen Creason, a reference librarian who'd worked at Central since 1979, was at his desk in the History Department. Sylva Manoogian, a World Languages librarian, had just gotten a new car, so she parked it with extra care in the library lot before coming in for her shift. Two hundred or so patrons were inside, browsing the shelves or settling in at the reading tables. Four docents herded a large, giggly group of schoolkids on a tour of the building. Elizabeth Teoman, the head librarian at Central, was in her office with Norman Pfeiffer, a New York City architect who'd been hired to renovate and expand the building. Pfeiffer was thrilled about the commission. He loved the Goodhue Building — "The first time I saw it, I thought I had died and gone to heaven," he told me — and was eager to get to work renovating it and adding a large new wing. The construction plan was the result of almost

41

twenty years of debate about what to do with Central Library, which was over sixty years old, dilapidated, and too small for the city's needs. Pfeiffer's drawings were spread on Teoman's desk. He draped his suit jacket, with his hotel and rental car keys in the pocket, on a chair at the back of the room.

At the time, the library's fire prevention consisted of smoke detectors and handheld fire extinguishers. There were no sprinklers. The American Library Association, known informally as the ALA, always advised against sprinklers, because water damage was even worse for books than fire damage. In 1986, however, the ALA reversed its position and began advising libraries to install sprinklers. That morning, in fact, down the hall from Elizabeth Teoman's office, a colleague of Pfeiffer's, Steven Johnson, was meeting with the fire department to discuss how the sprinklers could be placed inconspicuously in the library's historic rooms. The library was built before the development of fire-resistant doors, which are now standard in all large buildings because they halt the spread of fire from one section of the building to another. Fire doors are so effective that new buildings all have them, and older buildings are usually retrofitted with them; they are required by law in most states. Funds for putting them in the library had been in the city budget for more than five years, but somehow, they kept getting overlooked; finally, that day, workers were getting around to installing them.

For years, the library had been written up repeatedly for multiple fire code violations. At this particular moment, there were twenty violations waiting to be resolved. Most were "operational," including blocked exits, exposed lightbulbs, frayed electrical cords, and the missing fire doors, rather than structural problems with the building. New violations were brought to the fire department's attention all the time. A number of architectural preservationists suspected that someone was exaggerating the violations to bolster the argument for demolishing the building and replacing it. Even if they were slightly overstated, the building's problems were real. Twenty years earlier, in 1967, a fire department report had concluded that the probability of a major fire at the library was "very high." A few years later, the *Los Angeles Times* called the library "part temple, part cathedral, and part fire hazard." When Elizabeth Teoman was in library school, she wrote a paper

43

outlining the building's problems, saying the library was seriously overcrowded but that the large number of fire and safety hazards was even more troubling. She got an A on the paper.

Things are always coming in and going out of a library, so it's impossible to know what it contains on any given day. By 1986, Central Library's contents were valued, for insurance purposes, at roughly $69 million. That included at least two million books, manuscripts, maps, magazines, newspapers, atlases, and musical scores; four thousand documentary films; census records dating back to 1790; theater programs of every play produced in Los Angeles since 1880; and telephone directories for every single American city with a population over ten thousand. It had America's finest assemblage of books on the subject of rubber, donated in 1935 by Mr. Harry Pearson, a noted rubber authority. It had a Shakespeare folio; a quarter million photographs of Los Angeles dating back to 1850; car repair manuals for every single make and model of automobile starting with the Model T; five hundred folk dolls from around the world; the only comprehensive patent collection in the western United States; and twenty-one thousand books about sports. It housed the largest collection of books on food and cooking in the country — twelve thousand volumes, which included three hundred on French cuisine, thirty on cooking with oranges and lemons, and six guides to cooking with insects, including the classic *Butterflies in My Stomach.*

A few minutes before eleven A.M. on April 29, a smoke detector in the library set off an alarm. The library telephone operator called the fire department dispatcher, saying, "Bells ringing at Central Library." Security guards spread out through the building, instructing patrons to leave. No one was particularly panicked. The library's fire alarm went off all the time, for all sorts of reasons — a cigarette tossed in a wastebasket, the occasional crackpot bomb threat, and, most often, for no reason at all except that it was an old, crotchety alarm system prone to spasms of hyperactivity. For the staff and regular patrons, the fire alarm had come to possess all the shock value of a clown horn. Packing up and leaving the building was so tiresome that some librarians were tempted to hide out in their workrooms and wait for the all-clear. Most of them left their personal belongings behind when they went out for the alarms, assuming they'd be right back.

When the alarm went off, Norman Pfeiffer began gathering his drawings and his jacket, but Teoman told him not to bother, since she was sure the interruption would be momentary. Some regular patrons also didn't bother to pack up when they cleared the building. That morning, a real estate broker named Mary Ludwig was in the History Department doing genealogy research. She'd just discovered she was related to a man in Vermont named Hog Howard when the alarm went off. Rather than disturb all her materials, she left them on the reading table, along with a briefcase containing two years' worth of research notes, and headed to the exit.

Patrons and staff headed out of the building with a minimum of jostling and rushing. The only person to report a disturbance was an elderly woman who told investigators that a young man with blond hair and a wisp of a mustache had bumped into her as he hurried by. She said he seemed agitated, but he stopped to help her get back on her feet before he dashed out the door.

The building emptied out in just eight minutes, and patrons and staff, a total of about four hundred people, clustered on the sidewalk outside. The sun was inching up in the sky and the pavement was warming. A few librarians used the occasion to light up a Chesterfield, the cigarette of choice among the staff. Sylva Manoogian decided to bide her time in the parking lot so she could keep an eye on her new car. Helene Mochedlover, a Literature librarian who is so devoted to the library that she likes to say she was left on the library doorstep as an infant, chatted with Manoogian and admired her car. Everyone watched with only mild interest as a fire truck rolled up and its crew entered the building on the Fifth Street side. The fire department's visits to Central Library were as fleeting as they were frequent. Usually, firefighters could take a look around and reset the alarm in a few minutes. Engine Company 10 — EC10, in fire department parlance — did the initial check, and one of the firefighters radioed to the incident chief that there was "nothing showing"; in other words, it was a false alarm. One of the firefighters went to the basement to clear the alarm system, but it refused to reset — it persisted in indicating that it detected smoke. The firefighter assumed the system was malfunctioning, but just to be sure, the crew decided to take another look around.

The firefighters didn't have a map of the building's snaky corridors and staircases, so they could only inch along. The library was organized around four book "stacks," a method of library storage invented in 1893 for the Library of Congress. The stacks at Central were narrow, freestanding vertical compartments — essentially, big concrete tubes — that ran from the basement to the ceiling of the second floor. Each stack was divided into seven tiers by shelving made of steel grating. The open weave of the shelves allowed air to circulate up and around the books, which was considered beneficial.

For human beings, though, the stacks were unwelcoming. They were dim and tomblike, as constricted as a chimney. Their walls were made of solid concrete. Each tier was less than half a floor high, so navigating them involved a lot of stooping and crouching. The ancient wiring couldn't handle anything brighter than a forty-watt bulb, leaving the stacks in perpetual twilight. Some of the librarians at Central used a handmade version of a miner's helmet — a hard hat with a flashlight taped to the brim — when they went looking for books in the stacks. Finding anything there was a challenge beyond just the lack of light. The library had been built to accommodate one million books. By this point, there were more than two million books in its collection, so books were piled in stairwells and crannies and corners and stuffed in any opening on the shelves.

Engine Company 9, EC9, also responded to the initial alarm, parking on the Hope Street side of the building. While waiting to hear that the building was clear and the alarm successfully reset, one of EC9's crew glanced up and noticed light smoke oozing from the east end of the roof. At that same moment, the firefighters from EC10, inside the building, reached the Fiction Department stacks in the northeast quadrant of the building. There they saw smoke threading along a shelf of books that started with a Robert Coover novel and ended with one by John Fowles. The smoke began to coil upward, drifting through the open grating of the shelves like a ghost. The firefighters tried to radio down to the command post to report the smoke, but the three-foot-thick concrete walls of the stacks blocked the radio signal. One of the firefighters finally clambered out of the stacks and found a telephone in the reading room and called down to the command post to report what they had found.

At first, the smoke in the Fiction stacks

was as pale as onionskin. Then it deepened to dove gray. Then it turned black. It wound around Fiction A through L, curling in lazy ringlets. It gathered into soft puffs that bobbed and banked against the shelves like bumper cars. Suddenly, sharp fingers of flame shot through the smoke and jabbed upward. More flames erupted. The heat built. The temperature reached 451 degrees and the books began smoldering. Their covers burst like popcorn. Pages flared and blackened and then sprang away from their bindings, a ream of sooty scraps soaring on the updraft. The fire flashed through Fiction, consuming as it traveled. It reached for the cookbooks. The cookbooks roasted. The fire scrambled to the sixth tier and then to the seventh. Every book in its path bloomed with flame. At the seventh tier, the fire banged into the concrete ceiling, doubled back, and mushroomed down again to the sixth tier. It poked around, looking for more air and fuel. Pages and book jackets and microfilm and magazines crumpled and vanished. On the sixth tier, flames crowded against the walls of the stacks, then decided to move laterally. The fire burned through sixth-tier shelves and then nosed around until it found the catwalk that connected the northeast stacks to the northwest stacks.

It erupted into the catwalk and hurried along until it reached the patent collection stored in the northwest stacks. It gripped the blocky patent gazettes. They were so thick that they resisted, but the heat gathered until at last the gazettes smoked, flared, crackled, and dematerialized. Wind gusts filled the vacuum made by the fire. Hot air saturated the walls. The floor began to fracture. A spiderweb of hot cracks appeared. Ceiling beams spalled, sending chips of concrete shooting in every direction. The temperature reached 900 degrees, and the stacks' steel shelves brightened from gray to white, as if illuminated from within. Soon, glistening and nearly molten, they glowed cherry red. Then they twisted and slumped, pitching their books into the fire.

The two fire companies inside the building connected their equipment to the standpipes and headed into the stacks, but their biggest hoses, swollen stiff with water, couldn't make the sharp turns in the tight stairways. Dean Cathey, one of the captains on duty, remembered tugging hoses that wouldn't budge. The firefighters traded them for smaller, more nimble hoses. The thinner stream of water from the small hoses sizzled and evaporated in the flames. In the stacks, with their open grid of shelving, the fire rose up while the water flooded down. Firefighters tossed salvage covers on the shelves, hoping to protect the books from the fury of fire and water.

The battalion chief, Donald Cate, alerted City Hall and the head of the fire department, Donald Manning, that an emergency was unfolding at the library. EC9 and EC10 were overwhelmed. Engine companies around the city were mustered. By eleven thirty A.M., an additional eight command officers and twenty-two fire companies in full firefighting turnouts and breathing apparatus assembled at Fifth and Flower. An ambulance parked on Hope Street. When the fire proved too much even for this larger team, Cate called for more help. Within an hour, the force grew to include sixty firefighter companies, nine ambulances, three helicopters, two emergency air units, 350 firefighters, and one arson unit — in total, more than half the fire department resources in the entire city of Los Angeles. Donald Manning arrived at the library. He worried that the department would be caught short if another major fire occurred in the city, so he asked the county fire department to field calls for the city while the library was burning. By this time the fire in the library was spreading fluidly, like spilled ink. The fire department spokesperson, Tony DiDomenico, watched from the sidewalk on Fifth Street. Talking to one reporter, he sounded worried: "Once that first stack got going, it was 'Goodbye, Charlie.' "

In the physics of fire, there is a chemical phenomenon known as a stoichiometric condition, in which a fire achieves the perfect burning ratio of oxygen to fuel — in other words, there is exactly enough air available for the fire to consume all of what it is burning. Such a ratio creates an ideal fire situation, which results in total, perfect combustion. A stoichiometric condition is almost impossible to create outside of a laboratory. It requires such an elusive, precise balance of fuel and fire and oxygen that, in a sense, it is more theoretical than actual. Many firefighters have never seen such a blaze and never will. Not long ago, I had coffee with a man named Ron Hamel. He is now an arson investigator, but at the time of the library fire, Hamel was a captain in the fire department. Although over thirty years have passed, he remains awed by what he saw that day at the library. He talked about it like someone might talk about seeing a UFO. In his decades with the department, Hamel fought thousands of fires, but he said he never experienced another that was as exceptional as the fire at Central Library. Usually, a fire is red and orange and yellow and black. The fire in the library was colorless. You could look right through it, as if it were a sheet of glass. Where the flame had any color, it was pale blue. It was so hot that it appeared icy. Hamel said he felt like he was standing inside a blacksmith's forge. "We thought we were looking at the bowels of hell," he said, tapping his coffee mug. "Combustion that complete is almost impossible to achieve, but in this case, it was achieved. It was surreal." Frank Borden, who now runs the Los Angeles Fire Department Museum, once said to me, "In every firefighter's career, there are those fires that are extraordinary and unforgettable. This was one of those."

The people on the sidewalk outside the library saw the hurried gathering of fire equipment and then noticed the smoke. The boredom of a false alarm was eclipsed by shock. Michael Leonard, who worked in the library's public relations department, ran to a nearby photography store and told the cashier he needed every roll of film in stock. Back at the library, he took pictures of the building and the smoke scrolling out of the upper windows, but he couldn't bring himself to take pictures of the librarians, who were watching the fire in anguish. Some of them were crying. Sylva Manoogian told me she could smell the syrupy odor of microfilm burning. She said that as she stood watching the building burn, a charred page floated down to the sidewalk, and she recalled that it was from a book called *God Is Judging You*. Norman Pfeiffer, the architect, dreading that the building might be a total loss, turned to Elizabeth Teoman and said, "This was the biggest opportunity of my career and it's going to burn down." Several members of the Board of Fire Commissioners arrived after they heard the news of the fire and stood with the bystanders on the sidewalk. The multinational oil company ARCO was headquartered in the skyscraper across the street; when employees saw the commotion, many came downstairs to see if they could help. Lodwrick Cook, the head of ARCO, was a supporter of the effort to save and renovate the old building. As soon as he saw the street jammed with fire trucks, he ordered coffee and food from the Bonaventure Hotel for the firefighters and anyone standing by.

Wyman Jones was not at Central Library that morning. Jones was in charge of all seventy-three libraries in the city as well as Central Library; his title was city librarian of Los Angeles and his office was on the fourth floor of the Goodhue Building. That morning, he was at the Hollywood branch library, speaking at the launch of a new literacy program. Jones had been city librarian since 1970. He was a tall, ornery Missourian, a jazz pianist, a skilled amateur magician, and the kind of person who liked to have two cigarettes going at the same time. He supervised the construction of more than a dozen new libraries at his previous posts. He came to Los Angeles hoping to tear down Central Library and replace it with a more modern structure, but he grudgingly agreed to renovate and expand it instead. He liked to say that California was a mess, and Los Angeles was a mess, and the library was a mess, but that somehow, he would make the best of it. As soon as the event at the branch in Hollywood ended, Jones left to head back to his office at Central Library. On the way to his car, he bought a chili dog from a street vendor to eat while driving downtown. He got behind the wheel of his car, turned on the radio, unwrapped his chili dog, heard the news that the library was on fire, threw the chili dog out the window, and sped downtown.

Police shut down a section of the Harbor Freeway, and Sixth, Fifth, Hope, Flower, and Grand Streets, and traffic knotted up around the city. The crowd in front of the library grew. Television and radio reporters lined up, waiting for any word. Inside, the fire was roaring into its third hour. The air in the building was blistering. Water sprayed on the fire boiled like a kettle put on for tea. The runoff from the hoses pooled in the basement and was already fifty inches deep. It was so hot in the building that firefighters couldn't bear it for long; they took breaks every few minutes so their core temperature could come back down to normal. Because they were breathing so heavily, their supplementary oxygen bottles, which ordinarily last an hour, were depleted in ten minutes. Steam from the boiling water percolated through the firefighters' heavy flameproof coats. Their ears and wrists and knees were scorched. Their lungs became crisp with smoke. Over the course of the day, fifty of them suffered burns, smoke inhalation, or respiratory distress so extreme that they were taken to a nearby hospital for treatment. One firefighter was removed by helicopter from the roof because he was too ill to go back through the fire to exit. All of the firefighters eventually recovered, but the number of casualties was the highest in a single incident that the city's Emergency Services Bureau ever handled.

As the day went on, it began to seem like the fire might eat the library alive. The compressed space of the stacks made it more like a ship fire than a building fire — it was suffocating, ferocious, feeding on itself. Chief Manning complained to a reporter, "The architect of this building may have been a great architect, but he didn't know his fanny from a hot rock when it came to fire protection." As the reports from firefighters inside the building grew more pessimistic, Manning admitted that it was the most difficult fire the department had ever faced, and it would take "every trick in the book to save this building." As a statement, it sounded like he was leaving open the possibility that every trick in the book might not be enough. One of Manning's deputies pulled Elizabeth Teoman aside and told her he didn't know if they could do anything more because the fire was so intense and the building was so hospitable to it, with the stacks acting as fireplace flues and the books providing so much fuel. He asked her to give him a list of the irreplaceable items in the building, in case that was all they could save. Teoman remembers this as the moment when she realized the fire was real and that it might destroy the entire library. She was so upset that she decided to focus on doing things that were useful, like describing the floor plan to firefighters and telling them what materials she hoped could be preserved.

Chief Manning briefed Wyman Jones, who'd just arrived, and then Manning left for City Hall to give Mayor Tom Bradley a briefing on the fire and to warn him of the possibility that the building could be lost. Bradley had been at a meeting in San Diego that morning, and while he'd flown back as soon as he heard about the fire, he was stuck in traffic near the airport.

By midday, reports of the fire were all over the local news. Patty Evans, an administrator at the city's Community Redevelopment Agency, had worked for almost two years to figure out how to finance the renovation of Central Library. The day of the fire, she was on jury duty, so she didn't have access to the news. When the court recessed for lunch, she called her office to check in. Her secretary told her to take a deep breath, then explained that the library was on fire. Evans ran back to the jury room and requested a sidebar with the judge, who agreed to let her leave. When she arrived at the library, she decided to circumvent city bureaucracy and gave an interview to the local television reporters, asking city residents to come downtown and volunteer once the fire was extinguished.

People in the rare-book world were paying special attention to the news from the library. Olivia Primanis, a book conservator with an expertise in mold and mildew, lived in Texas but happened to be in Los Angeles that week. When the head of paper conservation at the Los Angeles County Museum of Art heard about the fire, she called Primanis and said, "The library is on fire. You need to get there."

Even though a fire was storming inside, the library didn't look distressed if you viewed it from the street. The stucco was smooth and undisturbed. The limestone facing of the outer walls was cool as satin. The statuary gazed sightlessly into the middle distance. The windows glanced and glittered in the sunlight. It was quiet. Except for the pale trickle of smoke from the roof, you might not have known anything was amiss. Then, suddenly, with a bright, hard snap, the windows on the west side of the library exploded and the red arms of flame punched outward and upward, slapping at the stone facade. One of the library commissioners watching from the sidewalk burst into tears. The librarians recoiled. One said she felt like she was watching a horror movie. According to librarian Glen Creason, the breeze was filled with "the smell of heartbreak and ashes."

In the building, the air began to quiver with radiant heat. Crews trying to make their way into the stacks felt like they were hitting a barricade, as if the heat had become solid. "We could only stand it for ten, fifteen seconds," one of them told me. "Then we hotfooted out of there." The temperature reached 2000 degrees. Then it rose to 2500. The firefighters began to worry about a flashover, a dreaded situation during a fire in which everything in a closed space — even smoke — becomes so hot that it reaches the point of spontaneous ignition, causing a complete and consuming eruption of fire from every surface. As firefighters put it, it's the moment when a fire in a room is transformed into a room on fire. With the temperature as high as it was, there was a great potential for flashover, which would have made the chance of saving anything nearly impossible.

The main body of the fire moved on, traveling three hundred feet along the second floor of the library, then stopping to lap at the catwalk leading to the southeast stack. The crews attacked it from the west side, taking fifteen-minute turns on the hose lines, hitting the fire again and again with a heavy jet of water. A salvage team battered the walls with sledgehammers, breaching the stifling tube of the stacks. The super-heated air flooded out of the stacks into the reading rooms, like heat spilling out of an open oven door.

The sixth and seventh tiers of shelving in the northwest stacks collapsed.

The water dumped on the fire was now as much a problem as a solution. The librarians always worried more about floods than fire, and now they had both. Many of the books that hadn't burned were waterlogged. Their covers and pages bulged like balloons. Salvage crews pushed their way through the building in advance of the hose teams, throwing plastic sheeting over the shelves, doing their best to protect the books before the spraying began. On the third floor, Heavy Utility Company 27 jackhammered a series of eighteen holes through the concrete to vent some of the terrible heat.

Finally, after over five hours, the liquid

spill of flames slowed, yielding to the torrents of water and to the cool air that was wafting through the holes jackhammered through the ceiling and floors. The fire pulled back from the southeast section of the building and curled up in the northeast stacks, where it glowered angrily, feeding itself book after book, a monster snacking on chips. Fire crews punched more holes — in the third floor, in the walls of the stacks, in the roof. The fresh April air mingled with the smothering heat inside, easing the temperature down bit by bit. As the fire shrank, firefighters dug deeper and drenched it.

The flames in the northwest stacks withered and went out.

The fire in the northeast stacks, where it had begun, still smoldered, but it no longer had the fierceness it had earlier in the day: By this point it had burned through most of its fuel. The books in the northeast stacks were crumbles, ashes, powder, and charred pages heaped a foot deep. The last flags of fire fluttered, seethed, settled, and finally died. It had required 1,400 bottles of oxygen; 13,440 square feet of salvage covers; two acres of plastic sheeting; ninety bales of sawdust; more than three million gallons of water; and the majority of the city of Los Angeles's firefighting personnel and equipment, but the library fire was at last declared extinguished, "a knockdown," at six thirty P.M. on April 29, 1986. It had raged for seven hours and thirty-eight minutes.

3.

What Every Home Owner Needs to Know About Mold and What to Do About It (2003)
  By Lankarge, Vicki
  693.893 L289

The Preservation of Leather Bookbindings (1894)
  By Plenderleith, H. J.
  025.7 P725

A Splendor of Letters: The Permanence of Books in an Impermanent World (2003)
  By Basbanes, Nicholas A.
  085.1 B297

The Hoppin 'N' Poppin Popcorn Cookbook (1995)
  By Steer, Gina
  641.65677 S814

What was lost: A volume of *Don Quixote* from 1860, illustrated by French printmaker Gustave Doré. All of the books about the Bible, Christianity, and church history. All biographies of subjects H through K. All American and British plays. All theater history. All Shakespeare. Ninety thousand books about computers, astronomy, physics, chemistry, biology, medicine, seismology, engineering, and metallurgy. All of the unbound manuscripts in the Science Department. A book by architect Andrea Palladio from the 1500s. Five and a half million American patent listings dating from 1799, with drawings and descriptions. All Canadian patent material from approximately the same period. Forty-five thousand works of literature, authors A through L. A leaf from a 1635 Coverdale Bible, which was the first complete translation in modern English. The entire collection of the Jane's annuals for aircraft, dating back several decades. Nine thousand business books. Six thousand magazines. Eighteen thousand social science books. A first edition of Fannie Farmer's *Boston Cooking-School Cook Book* from 1896. Twelve thousand cookbooks, including six books of popcorn recipes. All of the art periodicals and every single art book printed on glossy paper, which dissolves into a gluey mush when exposed to water. Every ornithology book. Three quarters of all the library's microfilm. The information labels on twenty thousand photographs, which fell off when they got wet. Any book accidentally shelved in the sections that burned; we will never know what they were, so we cannot know what we are missing. In total, four hundred thousand books in Central Library were destroyed in the fire. An additional seven hundred thousand were badly damaged by either smoke or water or, in many cases, both. The number of books destroyed or spoiled was equal to the entirety of fifteen typical branch libraries. It was the greatest loss to any public library in the history of the United States.

The place stayed hot for five days. Little fires flared up here and there, ignited by the ambient heat. The temperature lingered close to 100 degrees, so firefighters continued to wear protective gear and breathing apparatus and needed to rotate out after ten minutes inside. Immediately after the main blaze was out, crews hurried to "dewater" the basement and main floor. So much water had collected that engineers worried the floors might collapse under the weight. The engineers wanted to cool down the building but couldn't risk damaging more books with water. They wanted to clear debris to break up hot spots, but Chief Manning instructed them to leave the site undisturbed, to preserve anything investigators might need to help determine what had set it off.

The librarians stayed at the library for the seven and a half hours that the fire blazed, and they stayed after it was put out. As soon as the fire department permitted it, almost all two hundred of them entered the building. Inside, it was filthy, smoky, and slick from water mixed with debris. The ash was ankle-deep. The melted shelving looked grotesque. Wyman Jones declared that the interior of the library looked "like an el cheapo movie set, done by scab special-effects men." Glen Creason and another librarian, Roy Stone, made their way into the stacks to get a sense of what had survived. They were also looking for Roy's wife's handbag; she was a librarian, too, and had left the bag behind when the alarm sounded. They didn't see the handbag, so Creason and Stone climbed out of the stacks and went to the Patent Room, where they came upon mounds of soot and a long row of molten typewriters. Billie Connor, a children's librarian, walked through the mess with Helene Mochedlover. Connor and Mochedlover are both retired now, but they still come to the library often, and one day we sat and talked about their experience of the fire. The room we were in happened to be one of the most badly burned and is now a handsomely appointed meeting room. They spoke about the fire as if it had happened earlier that morning. Connor said when they entered the building immediately after the fire, they felt like they'd died and gone to see if Dante knew what he was writing about. Mochedlover, who is birdlike and energetic, said she was as upset the day of the fire as she was the day of President Kennedy's assassination. Another senior librarian I interviewed that day told me that seeing the library in ruins so traumatized her that she didn't get her period for the next four months.

The books that survived the fire were in piles where they'd fallen or jammed with their sticky backs together on the shelves. Olivia Primanis, the book conservator, told Wyman Jones that they had to move quickly and freeze the books because mold spores begin to bloom within forty-eight hours after being activated by water. If the books got moldy, they would be unsalvageable.

That meant the staff would have to pack, move, and store seven hundred thousand damaged books somewhere cold before mold erupted.

By evening, news of the fire had spread around the city. Hundreds of volunteers came down to the library to help without even knowing what they could offer. There were only a handful of hard hats available and no boxes for the books and no place to store them. Wet books couldn't simply be put in a warehouse, either, because of the danger of mold. Some years earlier, the Bonaventure Hotel, near the library, had offered space in their restaurant freezer if a rare book got wet and needed to be frozen until a conservator could tend to it. However, the Bonaventure's freezer couldn't hold seven hundred thousand soggy books. Los Angeles has a multimillion-dollar fish-processing industry and one of the largest produce depots in the country, so there were huge freezers in town. Someone suggested contacting a few of those fish and produce companies. Though their freezers were full, the companies agreed to clear some space for the books.

The volunteers were sent home with instructions to come back at dawn. Radio and television stations put out a call for

70

more volunteers to come to the library the next day. The Junior League contacted its members and urged them to help out, warning, "This is an enormous and dirty job [that is] moderately to somewhat physical, so please dress accordingly." IBM gave its employees time off to volunteer. The next morning, close to two thousand people showed up at the library. Overnight, the city managed to procure thousands of cardboard boxes, fifteen hundred hard hats, a few thousand rolls of packing tape, and the services of Eric Lundquist, a mechanical engineer and former popcorn distributor who had reinvented himself as an expert in drying out wet things. The notion of putting the books in with groceries didn't faze Lundquist, since he'd freeze-dried his first salvaged books alongside a summer's worth of peas and carrots from his garden.

It was a huge job. The wet, smoky books needed to be removed, along with every other book in the library; the building had to be emptied so it could eventually be repaired. Wyman Jones decided not to publicly disclose where the books were being stored, in case the fire had been intentional and the arsonist was looking for them.

With Lundquist directing, the volunteers worked for the next three days around the clock. Most were strangers to each other, drawn together unexpectedly, and worked together for hours, diligently and peacefully. They formed a human chain, passing the books hand over hand from one person to the next, through the smoky building and out the door. It was as if, in this urgent moment, the people of Los Angeles formed a living library. They created, for that short time, a system to protect and pass along shared knowledge, to save what we know for each other, which is what libraries do every day.

The volunteers packed more than fifty thousand boxes, each of which held fifteen tightly packed books. Once the boxes were full, they were stacked on pallets — eventually, they filled more than eighteen hundred — and then loaded onto trucks. The dry, undamaged books were taken to a city depository. The wet and smoke-damaged books were taken in refrigerated trucks to the food warehouses, where they were stored on racks between frozen shrimp and broccoli florets at an average temperature of 70 below 0. No one really knew when the wrecked books would be thawed out or how many of them could be saved. Nothing on this scale had ever been attempted.

As the books were carted away, investigators combed through the building, taking note of the pattern of burn marks on the floor and the path of the flames. In spite of the fire code violations and the fact that a building full of books and bad wiring could have gone up in flames almost spontaneously, investigators believed almost from the beginning that the fire was intentional. This was a conservative assumption, because library fires in the United States are almost always what are known in fire terminology as "incendiary" — namely, a fire caused by human intervention. Most are the result of casual vandalism that gets out of hand.

Los Angeles employed nineteen arson investigators. Twenty agents from the Federal Bureau of Alcohol, Tobacco, and Firearms joined them on the case. The team's first concern was to find a clue to how the fire started — maybe a frayed wire that sparked, or a telltale spot of lighter fluid, or a match carelessly tossed near a magazine. The city posted a $20,000 reward for information about the fire's origin. The ATF added $5,000, and an anonymous donor put up $5,000 more.

After two days of studying the building, investigators weren't close to any conclusions, but the word "arson" began slipping into stories about the fire. The *Los Angeles Daily News* ran a story with the headline ARSON STRONGLY SUSPECTED IN FIRE AT CENTRAL LIBRARY. The *Los Angeles Herald Examiner* reported that library employees were being shown a composite drawing of a "stranger." On May 6, only a week after the fire, a story in the *Los Angeles Times* announced LIBRARY FIRE WAS ARSON, BRADLEY AND FIRE CHIEF SAY. Chief Manning was quoted saying, "Without any reservation . . . we can now tell you that it was an arson fire." According to Manning, they were looking for "a blondish man in his late twenties or thirties who was seen by several employees near the fire's point of origin . . . six feet tall, 165 pounds, with blue eyes, blond hair, a light mustache, and a rather thin face. He was wearing tennis shoes, jeans, and a casual shirt." A composite sketch was released. The man depicted in the sketch had a wide forehead and large eyes, an aquiline nose, the brushy mustache of a cartoon crook, and abundant blond hair that formed a soft corona around his head and winged out in half curls over his ears. You would not swear it was Harry Peak, nor would you swear it wasn't.

During the week, the nuclear accident at

Chernobyl dominated every newspaper around the world except for *Pravda,* which covered it briefly but managed to find ample room to report on the fire at Central Library. After that first terrifying week of Chernobyl passed, American papers found space to cover the library fire; around the country, there were stories with headlines like BLAZE DESTROYS VALUABLE BOOKS; FLAMES GUT L.A. LIBRARY; A CITY TRAGEDY; FIRE CHARS COLLECTION; UP IN SMOKE. The *Boston Globe* suggested the events in Chernobyl and in Los Angeles had a "ghostly symmetry" because each raised the primal fear of a fire that was beyond control, along with our dread of menacing and unmanageable power.

Central Library had been a busy place. Each year, more than nine hundred thousand books were loaned; six million reference questions were answered; and seven hundred thousand people passed through the doors. Two days after the fire, it was empty except for the powdery black remains of four hundred thousand destroyed books. The statuary was draped in white plastic tarps. The walls and ceilings were tarred and grimy, the reading rooms vacant. All the entrances were locked and beribboned with police tape. A few flattened boxes lay on the sidewalks on Fifth Street, near the entrance to the library, where someone had hung a handwritten sign that said: THANK YOU, L.A.! WE WILL BE BACK BIGGER AND BETTER.

4.

All about California, and the Inducements to Settle There (1870)*
*folded leaf of plates, maps
By California Immigrant Union
979.4 C1527

Migration and the Southern California Economy (1964)
By Southern California Research Council
330.9794 S727-7

San Jacinto Cemetery Inscriptions, 1888-2003 (2003)
By Hall, Dale
Gen 979.41 S227Ha

The Postman Always Rings Twice (1944)
By Cain, James M.

Harry Peak's sister, Debra, likes to describe their family as one with unending woes. She doesn't say this in a tone of self-pity or dismay but with the dispassion of an appraiser describing a universe where luck, fortune, tragedy, and disaster are meted out randomly. By Debra's accounting, this Peak unluckiness isn't shameful or stigmatizing; it's just a coin toss that landed the wrong way.

I met Debra because I was looking for Harry Peak; I wanted to figure out whether he really set the library on fire, and if he had, why he had done it. If he wasn't guilty, how did he end up accused? It wasn't easy to track Harry down. Finally, I came across a phone number for Harry Peak in the Los Angeles area, but it turned out to belong to Harry's father, who was also called Harry. Debra answered the phone when I called. Once we sorted out which generation of the family I had found, I explained why I was trying to locate her brother. Debra told me it was impossible, because Harry had passed away in 1993, seven years after the library fire. She went on to say she was glad I was going to write the story of what had happened to Harry. She invited me to visit, so I went the next day.

Debra is small and muscular, with pale

blue eyes and cottony blond hair and pretty dimples that show when she smokes or smiles. She could pass as a toughened teenager, but in fact, she is a grandmother in her mid-fifties. The day we met, she was wearing a small white undershirt and big, baggy jeans. Both articles of clothing looked like she might have borrowed them from people whose body types were very different from each other and from hers. Debra is widowed and her children are grown. She recently moved back in with her parents so she could help them with their afflictions and ailments and save on rent at the same time.

The Peaks have a modest ranch house in Hemet, a small town of modest ranch houses in the San Jacinto Valley. Hemet is about eighty miles east of downtown Los Angeles and about an hour from Santa Fe Springs, where the Peaks lived when their children were growing up. The day I visited Debra was blazing, blindingly hot. Hemet was treeless and still, and everything shimmered as if it were in a broiler. The road in front of the Peaks' house shimmered. Their lawn and sidewalk and driveway shimmered. When I drove over a patched section of pavement in front of their house, I could hear the sticky suck of melted tar on my tires.

"Well, you found us," Debra called out to me as I was parking. She stood near the front door and motioned me inside. In the living room, her father was snoring on the sofa, and her mother was dozing upright in an armchair. A television in the corner erupted with sharp blasts of applause and laughter from a game show. We walked out to the backyard and dragged two folding chairs into a sliver of shade cast by the lip of the roof. Debra opened a can of beer and then started talking about her brother — what he had been like, what a joker he had been. She laughed while she was talking, then segued into a phlegmy cough. She sipped her beer and caught her breath. After a moment, she started telling me how Harry brought trouble on himself all the time. For instance, she said, he grinned like a lunatic when he was released from jail after the fire, so all the pictures in the newspaper made him look like he thought the whole thing was a sitcom. "He was incredibly smart, but he didn't have sense. He tended to take things too far," Debra said. "He got in trouble because of it. He just didn't understand something like that and what a dumb move it was."

The Peaks didn't need more trouble; Debra said they had plenty of it. She began listing her burdens, which were plentiful: She almost succumbed to crib death as a baby and she now suffers from fibromyalgia, a painful neuromuscular condition. One of her nephews was murdered in a gang dispute and another nephew is severely autistic. Debra's husband, who weighed almost six hundred pounds, died of a massive stroke not long ago. Misfortune even reached back through the generations. Debra's maternal grandparents were killed in a car wreck a few years after they moved to California from Missouri. She had shown me a newspaper article about the accident when we'd walked through the house. The article was framed and displayed amid the bric-a-brac in a hall near the kitchen. I'd remarked that the accident sounded awful, but Debra had shrugged and said, "Well, they were drunk."

After finishing her accounting of the Peaks' troubles, Debra said, "I'll tell you one thing for sure, though." She paused for a moment, laughed, and then said, "We are *not* a boring family."

The Peaks came from Missouri in the 1940s, at a time when California was like a

Harry Peak

giant electromagnet tugging farm families
away from the prairies. California seemed
like a promise: a flawless golden abundance
in the rich space between the ocean and the
mountains and the desert. The places that
drew them were towns like Hemet and
Santa Fe Springs. The city of Los Angeles
— dirty, motley, teeming with immigrants
and actors — was only an hour away.
Notionally, it was the anchor of the region,
but it existed at such a spiritual and socio-
logical remove that it could have been on
the moon. Most likely, people settling in the
San Jacinto Valley hoped not to make their
way closer to Los Angeles but to make their
way farther from it. They aspired to more

space, fewer people, greater sovereignty, less commotion. In a sense, families like the Peaks tried to re-create the rural life they'd left behind in places like Missouri; they wanted to be in the California of chaparral, of scrub grassland, of ranchettes, and not in the fevered, extroverted, New York–inflected mess of L.A. It's as if the San Jacinto Valley were not really an outlying region of Los Angeles but just a tributary of the Great Plains that spilled westward, skipping over the big cities, and had its true terminus someplace remote and fierce, like, say, Alaska. Even where this part of California is paved over and packed with houses, it conveys a feeling of wintry desolation.

Harry and Debra's father was born in Missouri, but his family moved to California when he was young. He dropped out of high school and eventually became a sheet-metal mechanic, joining the thousands of men hired by the Southern California aerospace industry in the 1950s and '60s when it was swollen with postwar defense contracts and space-race money. He married young. In short order, he and his wife, Annabell, had four children — Debra, Brenda, Billy, and Harry.

The scratch farms and bare acreage around those aerospace factories were plowed and planted with rows of one-story, two-bedroom bungalows to accommodate all the young families like the Peaks. These instant neighborhoods were so uniform that they looked like they had been punched out of a kit, delivered by air, and installed as complete sets. Kids spilled out of every house. Little satellite towns popped up among the developments, featuring a confounding abundance of fast-food restaurants and mattress stores. Most mothers in the neighborhood stayed home with their children, but Annabell Peak worked as a cashier at a supermarket in what would be considered the wrong direction — the store was on the edge of Los Angeles. I told Debra that I lived in Los Angeles, and she thought I might be familiar with the supermarket. "It's the one near L.A., you know, that's owned by the Jew," she said. "You know that one, don't you?"

The four Peak children grew up in the 1960s. They were left on their own more than other kids because both of their parents worked nights and slept days. Unsupervised, they smoked pot and drank beer. They sometimes did things that could be viewed as either mischievous or borderline criminal. They were known to the police because they'd all been stopped at one time or another, though they weren't police station regulars.

When the whole family was at home, there was a lot of hollering and conflict. According to Debra's sister, Brenda Peak Serrano, their father was "a cruel, mean man." A month or so after visiting Debra, I called Brenda to talk to her about Harry. In the course of the conversation, she told me that her father had just died. I said I was sorry and then asked what had happened. "I was visiting him, and he was on the couch for a couple of hours," Brenda said. "When I spoke to him, he didn't answer, so I just assumed he was drunk and passed out." After several more hours, he still didn't move or respond. Brenda began to suspect something else was going on, so she rolled him off the sofa and got him to the hospital, where she was told he was comatose. He never regained consciousness. Right before his life support was turned off, Brenda said, she leaned over and whispered to him, "I don't know why you never loved me." She knew some people might think that was a harsh thing to do, but she told me that she was proud of herself for finally telling him how he made her feel.

The Peaks had a conventional life, as measured by the conventions of postwar prefab bedroom communities. They were not rich, not poor, not chasing after big ambitions; there was a quiet, inert assumption that the kids would stay close to home and slide into jobs at Lockheed or Rockwell or McDonnell Douglas when their time came. If you were to diagram the town anthropologically, the Peaks would be hard to place: In their case, the signifiers of status aren't clear. Perhaps they had a little less than some people; perhaps their mobility was more lateral than upward. Debra told me her father had built the space shuttle, so for a while I was under the impression that he was a mechanical engineer, a profession with a level of training that didn't fit with anything else I knew about the family and completely stumped my effort to place them sociologically. Later, Debra elaborated and explained that he'd worked on the assembly line at McDonnell Douglas, where part of the space shuttle was built, which made much more sense to me.

Neither Harry nor his siblings were prominent in school sports, the most valuable social currency in towns like Santa Fe Springs. Nor did they make themselves known academically — a somewhat less valuable social currency but a distinction nonetheless. Even though they were white, all of the Peaks except Harry ended up allied with the Hispanic kids at school. Brenda hung out with the low-riders and eventually married a young man whose family was Mexican. Billy joined a Hispanic gang, although Debra says it was more for protection than for anything else. Debra was popular but had her challenges. Some of the girls at school gave her a hard time, so she started carrying a box cutter in her purse. In tenth grade, she got suspended for cutting a student. She explained to me that the girl she'd slashed had been harassing her. "I mean, come on!" she said, brightening up. "What else was I going to do?"

Harry, who was born in 1959, was the youngest of the four kids; he was doted on, babied, and a little spoiled. For a time, he seemed to have some magic that would help him escape the Peak penchant for bad luck. Tall and well built, with the narrow hips and long legs of a cowboy, Harry could have passed as the younger brother of actor Jon Voight. He always told people he wanted to be an actor, even when he was little. His looks and charm made it seem like a possibility. He had other assets. He did well in school when he applied himself. He could write with both hands. He could perform magic tricks. He made people laugh. He was puppy-doggish, immensely likable, eager to please, anxious to entertain, hungry to be noticed. Two or three admiring girls were always trailing behind him like ducklings. One by one, Billy, Brenda, and Debra dropped out of school, but Harry stayed and got his diploma. He was the first one in the family to do so. His brother didn't have much use for him, but the rest of the family savored Harry's potential; he was going to be the family star, the one who got out of town and got big. To be honest, though, his vanity and bragging sometimes annoyed people, including his own family. His sister Brenda once stabbed him with a fork because his showing off got on her nerves. She loved Harry, she told me, but he really thought he was a king.

Not everything was perfect for Harry. He was suspended a few times for homework irregularities. The police roughed him up when he was caught drinking. He liked to get wasted as often as possible. When he was a teenager, he smoked marijuana with a counselor at summer camp, and then the counselor molested him. According to his sisters, the assault devastated him, and afterward, he tried to commit suicide several times. Debra believes that the counselor's assault pushed Harry toward homosexuality. "He didn't want to be gay. He wanted to be straight," she said, flicking the tab on her beer can back and forth until it snapped off. A raven hopped along the edge of the yard, swiveling its head like a windup toy. Debra tossed the tab in the bird's direction, then leaned back in her chair and said, "He really tried to be straight."

For several years after the assault, Harry kept up the appearance of being heterosexual. He tried to act like a player, keeping several interested girls on a string. In his senior year, he finally settled into a steady relationship with one of them, and told everyone they planned to get married. Harry enlisted in the army right after graduation. His girlfriend promised she'd wait for him, but when he got home after his discharge, he discovered that she was seeing someone else. According to Debra, the breakup crushed him.

A few months later, Harry got involved with another girl. Soon after they started seeing each other, she became pregnant with twins. I asked what became of that relationship. "The problem was this girl liked to party," Debra said. "She partied, and lost one of the babies, and kept partying, and then lost the other one." Debra took a deep breath and added, "I think that's what finally turned Harry to being gay. Every time he got serious about a girl, something would happen. He would tell me, 'Deb, it hurts too much.' " She looked over her shoulder and then said, "My parents would kill me for telling you about him being gay. It was so hard on my dad that Harry turned out that way."

Just then, the sliding door to the kitchen opened with a raspy screech, and her father stepped outside. He was a tall, beefy man with a big belly and a friendly, reddish face and silvery hair that stuck out straight, as if it were a quiver of exclamation points. He started yelling something at Debra about his lunch, then caught himself when he noticed me in the chair. I introduced myself and said I was writing about Harry.

"Harry was really something," he replied. He scratched the stubble on his jaw and then began working his fingers through his tangle of hair. "Harry would have gone to the top. He would have."

"He knew a lot of stars, didn't he, Daddy?" Debra said. "He knew people who were on the uppity-ups."

"He knew *eighty percent* of the big stars," her father said, correcting her. He tugged at his hair more, and then added, "He knew Burt Reynolds and what's-her-name that he

90

married. Debra, what's that name?"

"Loni Anderson, Daddy," Debra said. She turned to me. "Harry knew them really well. He knew everything about them. He told me that Burt Reynolds and Loni Anderson would get divorced way before anyone else knew."

"He would have gone to the top," Peak said. Then he scowled and said, "Debra, I'm hungry."

Debra ignored him. "Harry was the biggest bullshitter in the world, wasn't he, Daddy?" She gestured at her father with her empty can. "Wasn't he, Daddy? You know he was. He was always the biggest bullshitter."

Harry broke up with the girlfriend who miscarried their twins, and then he moved to Los Angeles — only fourteen miles but a world away from home. He had no plans except to figure out how to become a star. It was not an easy move for him. In Santa Fe Springs, a handsome guy like Harry was a big deal. In Los Angeles, he was a dime a dozen. The sidewalks in Hollywood sagged under the weight of all the handsome young men who flocked there, who all had someone tell them they were special, and some of them were blonder than Harry, or knew someone important, or were trained as actors, or had some sizzling charisma, whereas Harry was only the best-looking guy in Santa Fe Springs. He shared a house in Hollywood with a few other young men grasping at the tattered edges of show business. One afternoon not long ago, I drove past the house they shared. My guess is that it hasn't changed much since Harry lived there. It is an aging, ageless, slumped little bungalow with a faded lawn and a fence clotted with scraps of street trash — one of a million such bungalows in the city where people with big dreams wait for something wonderful to happen.

Even after he settled in to life in Los Angeles, Harry drove back to Santa Fe Springs whenever he could, so he could party with his high school friends. Maybe he liked to be reminded how it felt to be someone who seemed dazzling. Maybe Los Angeles felt foreign to him. He boasted to his family that he loved being in the city; that he was in the running for some acting jobs; that he made friends with a lot of actors and was getting a taste for Hollywood life. In truth, he was probably just getting by, or maybe not quite getting by. His roommates complained that he was often late with the rent and sometimes skipped it altogether. They forgave him for a while because that's the sort of person Harry was — ingratiating, guileless, beguiling. He was the kind of paradoxical friend who would borrow things and never return them, and yet give you the shirt off his back. Several of his friends used that exact phrase when describing him to me: Harry would literally, actually give you the shirt off his back, but he was so flaky that he drove everyone crazy.

He earned his bit of income doing odd jobs. One of his steadiest employers was a neighbor, Dennis Vines, who hired Harry simply because he never failed to smile and say hello anytime Vines walked by. "He was just endearing," Vines told me recently. "He was a really nice kid. He had that smile — such a wonderful smile. And he had those great teeth, you know?" Vines managed a number of apartments. He thought Harry was "too ditsy" to trust with serious responsibility, but he hired him to do errands and occasionally serve as a chauffeur. When Harry put on a crisp white shirt and black pants and a little driving cap, he looked great at the wheel of Vines's vintage Packard sedan. Harry really enjoyed driving: He loved chatting with people wherever they stopped, especially because the car attracted so much attention.

Vines parted ways with Harry over what he described as "a typical Harry thing." He had asked Harry to hold on to a key ring with keys to all sixty of Vines's properties. Within a few minutes, Harry managed to lose the keys. "I don't know how he did it, but he did it," Vines said when we spoke on the phone. He chuckled and sighed. "That was Harry. He just had a way of messing things up." Though Vines fired him, they remained friendly. "He was really that sweet," Vines said, "or I would never have talked to him again after all the bullshit he pulled."

After losing his job with Vines, Harry started running errands for law firms — one in Los Angeles and one in San Francisco. The lawyers found him blundering but generally reliable. One of them, Robert Sheahen, even counted on Harry as a defense witness in a murder. Sheahen said that Harry, ignoring rules that were explained to him, chatted with jurors on his way to the stand. "That was Harry," Sheahen told me. "He just did things his way." Harry gave his testimony as instructed. Then the district attorney, hoping to discredit the testimony, asked Harry if he was an actor. Sheahen had anticipated the question and had advised Harry to call himself an office assistant, because saying he was an actor would cast doubt on the sincerity of his testimony. Nevertheless, Harry answered that he was an actor. All the credibility he had on the stand crumpled. Harry didn't care; he got to say he was an actor, and he was getting attention, which meant more to him than anything. It was the one thing he seemed to need most in the world.

Even if it was frustrating and humbling and impoverishing, Harry Peak's life in Los Angeles was at least luminous with possibility. It was in the chemical makeup of Los Angeles; possibility was an element, like oxygen. In Santa Fe Springs, there was no sense of potential coursing through the air; what you saw — the lawn, the house, the job — was what you could hope for. In Los Angeles, moments were fortune cookies ready to be cracked open, and in them you might find a movie star, or a successful audition, or a chance encounter with a powerful person who, with a snap of his fingers, would change your life, like a wizard. The feeling that luck might be about to reveal itself kept Harry nourished enough that he couldn't imagine returning to the dullness and dead-ended hope back in Santa Fe Springs. As soon as he imagined himself as a person of note, supersized, lit up by fame, he couldn't picture himself back there. But he didn't have much purchase on the life he was trying to create in L.A. He hovered between what he didn't want anymore and what he wasn't very likely to have.

His days went by in bits and pieces. He did a few hours of work. He got jobs and lost them almost as fast. One time he was hired as a valet at the Sheraton. On his first day, he parked a car in some back corner of the garage and then forgot where it was. The car couldn't be found for hours. He was fired on the spot. Working or not, he spent a lot of time at bars, especially during happy hour, where he could drink a lot for very little money. He went to acting and modeling auditions. To his great dismay, he discovered that he had a bad case of stage fright. The only thing that helped him overcome it was his love of attention, which overrode his fear of being onstage.

He'd told people that at one of those auditions, he met Burt Reynolds, which launched their friendship. I left messages for Burt Reynolds and told him I wanted to ask if he remembered Harry Peak, but he never called me back. I had a feeling that if he had met Harry, it was maybe a handshake on a set or a brief encounter in passing, and he might not really be able to single Harry out from among the many blond, strong-jawed young men who probably spun in and out of his orbit without ever truly crossing his path. Nevertheless, Harry's supposed friendship with Burt Reynolds had the power of legend in his family. His father and his sisters told me that Burt Reynolds once called Harry's mother as a surprise for her birthday, and that she almost hung up on him because she didn't believe it was really him. I wanted to believe what I was learning about Harry, but the more I heard, the more his life seemed like a series of tall tales, conjured scenes full of wishful thinking. I came to believe that it was quite unlikely that Burt Reynolds had ever met Harry Peak at all.

Large blocks of Harry's time during this period are unaccounted for and left no trace. He built no résumé, had no steady employment. He was a tumbleweed, lifted and carried wherever the wind took him, alighting briefly in this job and that and then blowing along, leaving little behind as he rolled on. In 1980, he was hired to be an extra in the remake of *The Postman Always Rings Twice*. On the set, he struck up a friendship with another extra, a photographer named Demitri Hioteles. Within a short time, they became involved, and Harry moved in with him. Hioteles lives in Florida now, and we spoke on the phone recently. "Harry was the sweetest thing on earth," he said. "There was something almost angelic about him." Like everyone else who knew Harry, Hioteles had little patience for his mythmaking. He said that Harry was always coming up with something unbelievable. "He'd come home and say to me, 'Guess where I've been? I was having cocktails with Cher!' " Hioteles said. "And I was like, 'Sure you were, Harry. Sure.' " After three years, the relationship ended because Hioteles grew tired of what he called "Harry's show" — all the lies and stories. What was strange, Hioteles said, was that even though Harry had a such a flair for storytelling, he couldn't bring that flair to acting. He was more comfortable spinning his stories to an audience of one.

One place Harry found some solid ground was an organization in Echo Park that was part mission, part religious group, and part community center. Known as the American Orthodox Church, it functioned as a kind of way station for a ragtag bunch of young men who knocked around Los Angeles, aimless and unmoored. The church was not affiliated with any traditional religious association. Its founder was a man named Father Archie Clark Smith, who also went by the names the Very Reverend Basil Clark, Mr. Basil Clark Smith, and A. C. Smith. The church's cofounder was a chiropodist named Homer Morgan Wilkie, who was also known as the Right Reverend Nicholas Stephen Wilkie. Wilkie and Clark/Smith wore black Russian Orthodox–style cassocks and kept regular hours at the French Quarter, a café on Santa Monica Boulevard, in West Hollywood. The church, as it was, is now long gone. Wilkie and Clark/Smith are also long gone. Like Harry Peak, they had the strange quality of appearing, existing, and then vanishing, leaving no residue of memory or information about who or what they really were. The one lasting impact Reverends Smith and Wilkie had was that they eventually provided Harry Peak with his alibi for the morning of the library fire.

5.

Burning Books (2006)
  By Bosmajian, Haig A.
  098.1 B743

Burning Rubber (2015)
  By Harlem, Lily
  E-book

Burning Chrome (1987)
  By Gibson, William
  SF Ed.a

*Burning Love: Calendar Men
Series, Book 8* (2014)
  By Carr, Cassandra
  E-book

I decided to burn a book, because I wanted
to see and feel what Harry would have seen
and felt that day if he had been at the
library, if he had started the fire. Burning a

book was incredibly hard for me to do. Actually, doing it was a breeze, but preparing to do it was challenging. The problem was that I have never been able to do harm to a book. Even books I don't want, or books that are so worn out and busted that they can't be read any longer, cling to me like thistles. I pile them up with the intention of throwing them away, and then, every time, when the time comes, I can't. I am happy if I can give them away or donate them. But I can't throw a book in the trash, no matter how hard I try. At the last minute, something glues my hands to my sides, and a sensation close to revulsion rises up in me. Many times, I have stood over a trash can, holding a book with a torn cover and a broken binding, and I have hovered there, dangling the book, and finally, I have let the trash can lid snap shut and I have walked away with the goddamn book — a battered, dog-eared, wounded soldier that has been spared to live another day. The only thing that comes close to this feeling is what I experience when I try to throw out a plant, even if it is the baldest, most aphid-ridden, crooked-stemmed plant in the world. The sensation of dropping a living thing into the trash is what makes me queasy. To have that same feeling about a book might seem strange, but this is why I have come to believe that books have souls — why else would I be so reluctant to throw one away? It doesn't matter that I know I'm throwing away a bound, printed block of paper that is easily reproduced. It doesn't feel like that. A book feels like a thing alive in this moment, and also alive on a continuum, from the moment the thoughts about it first percolated in the writer's mind to the moment it sprang off the printing press — a lifeline that continues as someone sits with it and marvels over it, and it continues on, time after time after time. Once words and thoughts are poured into them, books are no longer just paper and ink and glue: They take on a kind of human vitality. The poet Milton called this quality in books "the potency of life." I wasn't sure I had it in me to be a killer.

It is easy to copy anything these days, and most books exist in endless multiples; a single book no longer has the preciousness it had when books came to life through a cumbersome, labored process. So burning one ordinary book should have been easy for me. But it wasn't, not at all. I couldn't even choose a book to burn. First I thought that I could burn a book I didn't like, but that seemed too aggressive, as if I were delighting in a sort of execution. I knew I couldn't burn a book I loved. I suppose I could have burned one of my own books, but the psychology was simply too much for me to sort through, and I own so many copies of my books that they have become something of a generic commodity in my home, more like flour or paper towels than actual books. So while I made the decision to burn a book, I put off choosing a book for weeks, trying to figure out what standard I could use to select the one I would burn. Nothing seemed right. Just as I was about to give up on the idea, my husband presented me with a new copy of *Fahrenheit 451,* a book about the fearsome power of book burning, and I knew this was the one to use.

I chose a windless, warm day and climbed to the top of the hill in my backyard. The San Fernando Valley flung itself before me — all the treetops and houses and buildings blurring together into a wash of stippling and speckling; it was a pale quilt stitched here and there with a flash of red taillights, and above it, in the blue sky, a plane clicked by, dragging its tail of white foam. I had been living in Los Angeles for four years. I'd never thought much about fire before coming here, but now I knew it was prowling everywhere, and that I had to crush any scampering ash and drown any wandering flicker. I'd learned a lot since moving to Los Angeles. I knew the Westside from the Eastside; I knew to avoid traffic on Oscar night; I knew the exquisite beckoning of beauty and acclaim that sings out to anyone here who aches for a life like a highlight reel. I could picture Harry Peak now because I saw him every day in the handsome over-groomed busboys who waited on me, and in the gym-trim extras I sometimes came across when there was filming in my neighborhood — I could recognize their anxious posing, as if each moment bristled with the potential to change their entire lives. I saw him in every person slumped over a laptop in a coffee shop, writing the role of a lifetime, and in the pretty girls wearing too much mascara and nail polish at the grocery store, just in case, just in case. I had come to love Los Angeles; I even loved its preening, grabby, ambitious silliness, its Harryness, because it pulsed with emotion and wishfulness and ripe brokenheartedness, animated in the most naked way.

But now I was at the top of my hill to burn a book, so I turned away from the view of the valley and laid down the copy of *Fahrenheit 451*. I put down a pitcher of water, a box of matches with a rooster on the cover, and an aluminum cookie sheet on which I placed the book. I didn't know if the book would catch immediately or if it would smolder for a while; I didn't know if it would occur in a burst or if I would sit and watch the book go up page by page by page. I had chosen to burn a paperback, even though the books in the library had been hardcovers, because I worried that a hardcover would burn for so long that my neighbors would see the smoke and sound an alarm. People in California jump at even the hint of fire, and to be honest, I was a little afraid of what might happen if the fire got out of control.

I struck the first match and it broke, so I struck a second, which spat out a little tongue of flame. I touched the burning match to the cover of the book, which was decorated with a picture of a matchbook. The flame moved like a bead of water from the tip of the match to the corner of the cover. Then it oozed. It traveled up the cover almost as if it were rolling it up, like a carpet, but as it rolled, the cover disappeared. Then each page inside the book caught fire. The fire first appeared on a page as a decorative orange edge with black fringe. Then, in an instant, the orange edge and the black fringe spread across the whole page, and then the page was gone — a nearly instantaneous combustion — and the entire book was eaten up in a few seconds. It happened so fast that it was as if the book had exploded; the book was there and then in a blink it was gone and meanwhile the day was still warm, the sky still blue, I hadn't moved, the cookie sheet was shiny and empty except for some crumbs of black now strewn on it. There was nothing left, not a trace of anything that resembled a book, a story, a page, a word, an idea. I am told that a big fire is loud, clamoring, windy, groaning. This, though, occurred almost silently, with just the slightest wheezy sound of air, a sort of *whoosh,* as the book ignited. The pages burned so fast they barely crackled; the sound was soft, like a sizzle, or like the crinkly light sound of water spraying out of a shower. As soon as it was over, I felt like I'd just jumped out of an airplane, which is perhaps the natural reaction to doing something I'd resisted so mightily — there was the elation at overriding my own instincts, elation at the fluid beauty of fire, and terrible fright at the seductiveness of it and the realization of how fast a thing full of human stories can be made to disappear.

6.

The Humorous Side of Trucking
(2016)
By Boylan, Buck
814 B7915

Organization, Administration, and Management of the Los Angeles Public Library (1948)
By Los Angeles (Calif.)
027.47949 L879

The Way of Adventure: Transforming Your Life and Work with Spirit and Vision (2000)
By Salz, Jeff
171.3 S186

How to Rehabilitate Abandoned Buildings (1974)
By Brann, Donald R.
Series: Easi-Bild Home Im-

In the course of updating its circulation system in 2009, the Los Angeles Public Library lost some of the information about its cardholders prior to that date, so it's impossible to know whether Harry Peak had a library card, and there is no way to know whether he had ever even been inside Central Library. People pass through the library all the time, unobserved and unremarked upon. Libraries may embody our notion of permanence, but their patrons are always in flux. In truth, a library is as much a portal as it is a place — it is a transit point, a passage. Because Central Library is built around an intersecting pair of corridors, the building is open on every side, and you can cross through it from all directions. The ground floor has the same traffic pattern as Grand Central Station in Manhattan. Both places are animated by a hurrying flow that surges in and out of the doors all day long. You can bob along in that flow, unnoticed. The library is an easy place to be when you have no place you need to go and a desire to be invisible.

It seems simple to define what a library is

— namely, it is a storeroom of books. But the more time I spent at Central, the more I realized that a library is an intricate machine, a contraption of whirring gears. There were days when I came to the library and planted myself near the center of the main corridor and simply watched the whirl and throb of the place. Sometimes people ambled by, with no apparent destination. Some people marched crisply, full of purpose. Many were alone, some were in pairs; occasionally, they traveled in a gaggle. People think that libraries are quiet, but they really aren't. They rumble with voices and footsteps and a whole orchestral range of book-related noises — the snap of covers clapping shut; the breathy whisk of pages fanning open; the distinctive *thunk* of one book being stacked on another; the grumble of book carts in the corridors.

One recent morning, before dawn, I did hear the library in complete silence. I had come to see the shipping department, which opens at five, and then to meet John Szabo, the current city librarian of Los Angeles. Before going down to the shipping department, I stopped in the corridor near the main information desk, just to savor the odd experience of the library heavy with quiet, a slumbering place, interrupted only by the occasional creak and sigh that all old buildings make when they're empty. The shipping department is in the basement, invisible to the rest of the library. It is never quiet. The room is hard-walled and hard-floored; sound ricochets around it like a cue ball. This particular morning, eight men and one woman were at work, standing side by side at a long counter piled high with books.

When I first learned that the library had a shipping department, I didn't know quite what that meant, because I couldn't think of anything a library needed to ship. I came to learn that what gets shipped isn't material going out into the world; it's books traveling from one branch to another. The shipping department at Central moves thirty-two thousand books — the equivalent of an entire branch library — around the city of Los Angeles five days a week. It is as if the city has a bloodstream flowing through it, oxygenated by books. The number of flowing books has been growing ever since the 1990s, when patrons first were able to request books online from any of the city's seventy-two branches and have them delivered to their local branch. "After the Internet came in, shipping just *blew up,*" said George Valdivia, who has been the acting head of the department since 2010. "We used to be able to use vans to deliver the books. Now we have so many books that we need trucks." He gestured across the room toward a truck backed up to the dock, its rear door opened in a huge yawn. The driver, a man with ropy arms named Gonzalo, was counting the plastic bins in the back of the truck. "We got twenty-two!" he yelled to the crew packing the bins, who were all wearing headphones, which were plugged in to their phones. No one responded to Gonzalo's shout. He shifted one of the bins. "Encyclopedias?" he asked George. "So damn heavy."

Gonzalo was about to drive a route that started at the Arroyo Seco branch, on the northeast edge of the city, and continued on to ten other branches, including Chinatown, Little Tokyo, Eagle Rock, Silver Lake, and Echo Park. There are seven delivery routes in the city. Some of the books being shipped are permanently shelved at Central Library and are heading out on loan. Other books are from branches, and because the shipping department uses a hub system, they pass through Central en route to whatever branch requested them and will pass through Central once more on their way home. The books are tagged like luggage. I pawed through a pile that was waiting to be packed. According to the slip of paper tucked inside, Lucia Berlin's short story collection's usual resting place was the Robertson branch, but it was on its way to a patron who had requested it at Arroyo Seco. A DVD called *The Great Indian Railway* had come from the San Pedro branch, was changing planes at Central, and would continue on to Lincoln Heights. Someone at the Westchester branch was waiting for Mo Willems's *Happy Pig Day*, which was traveling via Central from North Hollywood. A patron at the El Sereno branch was waiting for *The Bible Handbook of Difficult Verses*, which had come from Sherman Oaks. *Solids, Liquids, and Gases*, which belonged full-time to Central, was taking a trip to Studio City.

The people in shipping know all the trends. They can tell when a book has been recommended by Oprah, because they will pack dozens of copies that have been requested all over the city. They know that the day after any holiday, the load will be heavy: Apparently, everyone in Los Angeles gets on the computer right after Thanksgiving dinner and makes requests for diet books. For some reason no one can explain, a lot of books from the Arroyo Seco branch end up borrowed by patrons at the Chinatown branch. In the middle of the school year, the SAT study guides are big travelers. Before tax time, all the financial advice books are on the fly.

The one woman in the department, Barbara Davis, dropped Viktor Frankl's *Man's Search for Meaning* and a picture book called *The Bear Ate Your Sandwich* in a bin that was heading to the Northridge branch. "I am *tired,*" she said, unprompted. Barbara is a wide, chesty woman with a close-cropped Afro and an air of deep, bemused exasperation. She took the job in the library's Shipping Department after a stint at the city's Convention Center. "I was packing there, too," she said, "but just tables and chairs. No books." She told me that she was counting the days until retirement. "Hey, I been with the city for thirty-three years, and I'm ready, baby." She tapped the pocket of her blouse and added, "I got my retirement papers right here." I assumed she meant that figuratively, but then she pulled out a wad of paper from the City of Los Angeles noting her upcoming retirement and pension arrangements. She put the papers back in her pocket and asked if I knew how to pack a bin of books. I didn't, so she demonstrated how to wedge them together efficiently. "See, you need to have

113

a strategy," she said. She wiggled a meaty vegetarian cookbook into a sliver of space beside an oversize *The Architecture of John Lautner.* Next, she wedged four large bunny puppets that a children's librarian at Wilshire had requested from the Children's Department at Central into a bin that at first appeared to be completely full. Then she filled a bin with supplies bound for the Wilshire branch, which apparently had a need for several rolls of tape. She did all of this without looking. She said that she didn't mind working at the library, but she didn't count herself as a book lover. "I don't like to read too much," she said, fitting Timothy Ferriss's *The 4-Hour Workweek* into a bin marked for Van Nuys. The bin was now more than full, so she banged on it — a signal to the truck driver that it was ready to load. Gonzalo picked it up and dropped it in the back of the truck. Barbara wiped her hands on her thighs and grabbed an empty bin. Her hands roamed over the pile of books, sizing and squeezing them as if they were melons. She cocked her head at me. "You read and read and read and read," she said, "and then what?"

When John Szabo was in graduate school for library science at the University of

Michigan, he was known as Conan the Librarian, which is hilarious because he is so un-barbarian-like, although back then he was quite fierce about his job running the small library in his residence hall. This was in the early 1990s, the moment when Internet service providers were introduced to the general public, and for the first time in history, the status of libraries as the only and best storehouses of information was challenged. Szabo received his library degree just as people were beginning to wonder whether libraries were viable or even necessary in the newly wired world.

Szabo was born in Orlando in 1968. He grew up in Alabama, mostly near air force bases, where libraries are revered. His father, who was retired from the air force, often left John at the base library on nights when he had his bowling league. Szabo loved books, and he was fascinated by the process of borrowing books — the way they came and went, how they were a medium of exchange and connection within the community. One of his favorite library items was the Gaylord book charger, a big metal box at the checkout desk that stamped due dates on book slips and nipped off a chad to keep the slip properly aligned.

At sixteen, Szabo became a clerk for the

circulation desk at the base library. At twenty-two, he became Conan the Librarian. As soon as he finished graduate school, he applied for a job in Robinson, Illinois — a town of eight thousand people that made its mark in popular culture in 1914, when a local schoolteacher invented the Heath bar. Most of the area's residents either worked at the Heath factory or were farmers, and they were benignly neglectful of the Robinson library. Szabo chose to apply for the job in Robinson because he was impressed by the town's human resources policy, which took unexpectedly progressive positions, considering it was a conservative rural area. One of the first things Szabo did after he settled into the job was introduce himself to local farmers, then persuade them to vote in favor of a tax levy to support the library — a seemingly impossible feat that he achieved through judicious application of his charm and affability. Szabo stayed at the Robinson library over three years and then was hired away to run the library in Palm Harbor, Florida. A few years later, he was recruited to be director of the library system in Clearwater, Florida. He was in Clearwater over six years, and while living in Clearwater, he met his partner, Nick, who is a teacher.

In 2005, Szabo was hired to run the Atlanta library. It was a job many people would have found daunting and some would have deemed impossible. At the time, Atlanta was a sprawling system with a main library and thirty-four branches, a staff of more than five hundred, and a shattered psyche. It was one of the last library systems in the South to integrate — until 1959, it served only white patrons. The adjustment to integration came in fits and starts, and racial issues continued to dog the library for decades. Szabo was hired in the backwash of a particularly divisive incident. In 2000, seven white librarians in the downtown branch were demoted and replaced by African American librarians. This occurred after the chairman of the library board announced that he thought there were too many "old, white women" managing the downtown library and that the board needed "to get rid of them." An African American employee who complained on the white librarians' behalf was also demoted. The librarians sued the board and the library's director for racial discrimination. Library board meetings in Atlanta had always been televised on a public access channel and, most of the time, probably drew an audience in the double digits. During the days of the lawsuit, the meetings were so volatile that people tuned in to watch in droves. After three years of bitter back-and-forth, the librarians won an $18 million settlement, and the following year, the director of the library was fired. Szabo was hired soon after, in 2005.

Szabo is tall and gangly, with a small, square head, a trim goatee, and a seemingly hard-to-reach boiling point. He is a master of the friendly conspiratorial wink and whisper. He gives the impression of being a perfect gentleman, with Southern manners and a military decorum. For Los Angeles to hire him away from Atlanta was considered a coup, because he had developed a reputation in the library world as being one of the few directors who was figuring out the transition from pre-Internet to omnipresent-Internet, and who was successfully rigging the library to sail into the future not as a gigantic, groaning, fusty pile of books but as a sleek ship of information and imagination. Szabo reckoned that the future of libraries was a combination of a people's university, a community hub, and an information base, happily partnered with the Internet rather than in competition with it. In practical terms, Szabo felt the library should begin offering classes and voter registration and literacy programs and story times and speaker series and homeless outreach and business services and computer access and movie rentals and e-book loans and a nice gift shop. Also, books.

In Los Angeles, the library is designated as a city department, just like the police and the city attorney and the dogcatcher. The head of the library is a city manager, hired — and fired — by the mayor. Antonio Villaraigosa, the forty-first mayor of Los Angeles, hired Szabo in 2012. Villaraigosa's term ended just a few months later, while Szabo was still unpacking his belongings. The incoming mayor, Eric Garcetti, began his term by asking every city department head to reapply for his or her job. Some of them did not get their jobs back, but Szabo did, and finished unpacking.

Szabo's office is on the fourth floor of the Goodhue Building, in a room that he has decorated with odds and ends he has come across while rummaging in the library's basement. One side of his office is dominated by ornate brass lamps from the old Children's Reading Room. He found them stowed behind a pile of junked furniture, caked with dust and dirt. On his desk and coffee table, he has a few of the gifts made for people who donated to help restore the library after the fire. One is a fancy metal letter opener modeled on the shape of the building; another is a pair of bookends that are miniatures of the turban-topped sphinxes flanking the staircase near the rotunda.

When I'd left the Shipping Department and made my way up to Szabo's office, he was already in a meeting with the budget analyst, Robert Morales, and the business manager, Madeleine Rackley, in which they were doing some fine-tuning of the library's $172 million annual budget. As a city department, the library is medium-size. It is larger than the zoo, which gets $20 million from the city (a sum that includes $13,000 for reindeer care and $108,000 for a visitor-directed "giraffe feeding experience"), but much smaller than the fire department, which clocks in at $630 million a year.

That day, Szabo was dressed in a button-down shirt with tiny pale blue checks, a blue-and-purple tie, and neatly pressed khakis. He wears round owlish glasses that, combined with his taste for tidy clothes, make him look like a tenure-track English professor. Almost every hour of his day was booked, in part because he was leaving the next morning at dawn to attend a library conference in Toronto about how libraries can innovate. From Toronto he was heading to Ohio for a meeting of Online Computer Library Center, a global cooperative of twenty thousand libraries located in 122 countries around the world. Szabo is the head of the board. After the meeting in Ohio, he was planning to return to Los Angeles, and a short time later, he would be heading to Washington, D.C., to receive the National Medal for Museum and Library Service, which is bestowed on five libraries a year.

Some of Szabo's job has a narrower focus. A few days earlier, a group of local beekeepers asked him for permission to put a colony of hives on the roof of the library. When he told me about the request, I began to wonder who was empowered to give that kind of permission — I wasn't sure whether the library had a roof manager, or an animal colony manager, or someone who served as a combination thereof. It turned out that the authority lies with the city librarian. I asked whether there would soon be library honey. Szabo said the project was likely to rise or fall on the question of whether it would serve the public good, as so many matters in the library do, but in the meantime, he was reading up on urban beekeeping.

The publicness of the public library is an increasingly rare commodity. It becomes harder all the time to think of places that welcome everyone and don't charge any money for that warm embrace. The commitment to inclusion is so powerful that many decisions about the library hinge on whether or not a particular choice would cause a subset of the public to feel uninvited. In the case of the beehives, that subset might include people who are afraid of bees or are allergic to bees. Hives on the roof are a more modest proposition than, say, beehives in the main reading room. But there was the chance that bees living on the roof would wander into the building, or start to hang around the entrances, or be a nuisance in some other way. Szabo seemed to love the idea of making use of the roof, especially for something unexpected, like beehives, but he said the decisive fact would be if there were people who would stay away from the library on account of them.

Consideration of the beehives was tabled for the moment, and Szabo turned to budget details with Morales and Rackley. The library was in the middle of a special amnesty period for book fines.

"How much is this costing us?" Szabo asked Morales.

"It's definitely a loss of revenue," Morales replied. "There are a lot of overdue books." Outside the window, the air was suddenly split by the nasal beep of construction equipment backing up. After about thirty seconds, the beeping stopped sharply, and something heavy and metallic came clattering down. Everyone looked at the window for a moment and then returned to the discussion. The book-fine amnesty seemed to be settled, and Szabo ran his finger up and down his notepad. Once he found his place, he looked up and said he was planning to ask the city council to fund a monthly homeless outreach program at the library.

"Our core mission is not to end homelessness," Rackley cautioned. "Our core mission is to be a library."

"But the homeless are already here," Szabo said. "We want to provide a setting to coordinate entry into all of the city's different homeless services." A test run of the program, called The Source, was scheduled for later that week. Szabo wrote something on his pad and then continued to the next topics: an update on the new digital maker space; a flu shot program; and the news that Terminal 7 at LAX Airport had agreed to install a library kiosk, which would enable travelers to check out audio and e-books on the spot. Discussion of the kiosk reminded Szabo that a bike-share company had asked to place one of its stands on the sidewalk outside the library.

"I love bicycles," Szabo said. "It'd be great to have it here."

"Can we move the stand, adjust its location, once it's plopped down?" Rackley asked, looking worried. "If we don't like where it is?"

Szabo said he would find out, glanced at his watch, excused himself, and then stood up to leave to head to his next appointment, which was at the Washington Irving Branch Library.

We rode the staff elevator downstairs and crossed through the shipping department. Szabo greeted many of the crew by name, and they waved at him without removing their headphones. We walked into the main part of the garage and hopped in Szabo's car. When we emerged from the dim garage, the sun hit us with a wallop, like a blast from a water cannon. We headed to a neighborhood between the Santa Monica Freeway and Crenshaw Boulevard. The neighborhood is officially called Mid-City, but it is often referred to as Crenshaw. The area is wide and bright, a grid of small streets crisscrossed with boulevards and the welt of the I-10 freeway running along its southern edge. Szabo turned off the main road onto a sunny residential street and then parked near a chain-link fence. A lean, dark-haired woman was waiting by the fence with a clipboard and an expectant expression. "You made it!" she said, leaning toward the car. She introduced herself as Eloisa Sarao, the library's assistant business manager. A rogue gust of wind rolled down the street and fiddled with the sheets on her clipboard. She slapped them down and said, "Let's go in!"

The chain-link fence encircled a brick and stucco building that looked like it had once been beautiful but now was ruined by the ragged, ashen look of abandonment. Its grand lintel, carved with the words LOS ANGELES PUBLIC LIBRARY WASHINGTON IRVING BRANCH, sat like a stone crown. The library had been built in the neoclassical temple style popular in library design in 1926. The neighborhood around it had been working class, but slipped in the last few decades; unemployment and crime in Crenshaw are now higher than city averages. The houses are square and simple, with slivers of lawns and security bars on their living room windows. Even in its distress, the library sits among them with a regal presence. In 1987, the building was added to the National Register of Historic Places. Like many of the libraries of its period, it didn't meet earthquake standards and had inadequate parking and a dearth of space inside. Its location, right on a residential street, was hard to find. Nonetheless, the community loved it.

In 1990, the city announced that it was closing the Washington Irving branch and building a new library thirteen blocks away, on the site of a former car wash. The neighbors turned out in force to protest, but the city council prevailed. The new library was built. Ever since, the old one, which had served the neighborhood for sixty-five years, has stood empty, settling into dereliction like an old dog settling onto a shabby couch. The sun has punished it. The fence has become almost a feature of the natural landscape; it leans like a tree in the wind and has rusted into a smudgy, earthen shade of silvery red. The tough, grasping roots of bindweed and goosegrass and mare's tail have cracked the ground around the fence and cut a crazed pattern in the pavement around the building. The boarded-up windows look like punched-out eyes in a blank face.

As we stood taking in the sadness of the scene, crickets trilled merrily in the weeds. Marigold-yellow No Trespassing tape fluttered and swayed like a festival banner. Signs announcing various individuals' desire to buy ugly houses and to clean gutters were zip-tied to the fence. A faded paperback of *Strawberry Shortcake's Cooking Fun* was stuck at the bottom of the fence beside a batch of brown leaves and some plastic wrappers, like flotsam beached at low tide. The street, Arlington Avenue, was enveloped in a midday hush. A block away, traffic raged. A plump man walked past us, leading a blue-eyed dog on a piece of twine. After a moment, Sarao opened the padlock and pushed the fence open, then unlocked the library's front door. It opened reluctantly, with a hard, harsh cough. The main room was grand, with high ceilings spanned by glossy wooden trusses. "My goodness," Szabo said, picking his way across the floor. The litter was ankle-deep. It included beer cans, a fairly nice-looking size-M leather belt, a bottle of Oil of Olay body wash, a number of flattened potato chip bags, and a lot of unidentifiable clumps of assorted trash. A copy of a book called *The Way of Adventure: Transforming Your Life and Work with Spirit and Vision* sat on the front desk, as if someone had been standing there with it, waiting to check out, at the very moment the library closed and became frozen in time.

I have never been in a building as forlorn as this old library, with its bruised beauty, its loneliness. Abandoned buildings have a quaking, aching emptiness deeper than the emptiness of a building that has never been filled up. This building was full of what it was missing. It was as if the people who passed through had left a small indent in the air: Their absence was present, it lingered. The kid who learned to read here; the student who wrote a term paper here; the bookworm who wandered happily through these shelves: all gone, gone, gone. A few books were still on the shelves — books that had mysteriously been overlooked when the place was cleared out, like survivors of a neutron bomb. They made the ones that were missing have a slippery, hinted-at presence, as if I were seeing ghosts.

We looked for a light to turn on, but most of the switches clacked futilely. It was a sunny day outside, but in the library, it was dusk. The windows were so dirty that only streaky light poured in. The mournfulness felt like a hand pressing on my chest. I have seen plenty of vacant buildings, but this felt more than vacant. This building made the permanence of libraries feel forsaken. This was a shrine to being forgotten; to memories sprinkled like salt; ideas vaporized as if they never had been formed; stories evaporated as if they had no substance and no weight keeping them bound to the earth and to each of us, and most of all, to the yet-unfolded future.

We roamed around the reading room for a while, shouldering the gloom, and then I mentioned to Szabo that the library might make a very nice house, especially for someone who liked reading. He said it was an interesting idea but that the city was considering something more along the lines of a community center. This thinking has been going on since 1990 and has yet to congeal into a plan. "Such a cool building," Szabo said, shaking his head. Sarao nodded and said, "It would be great to get it back into use." We peered out the windows and paced around the main room, opening a few cabinets and doors. I sensed that some small, fierce animals might view the empty library as a pleasant place to nest, which meant that each time I opened a cabinet or door, I suffered from an unpleasant dose of suspense.

Szabo had come to Washington Irving to check on its condition and try to appease neighbors who were dismayed by its dilapidation. Once, the street had been elevated by the library's handsomeness. Now it was the ugliest neighbor on the block and getting uglier all the time. There was no money to do anything significant, so Szabo was seeing what he could afford to do for the neighbors' sake. As he was discussing this with Sarao, it occurred to me that a large part of a city librarian's job is to be a property manager. Szabo is responsible for seventy-three large structures that are spread across the 503 square miles of the city of Los Angeles. To even visit each one of the branches is a major proposition. Szabo's days seesaw between big thoughts on the future of global information systems and minutiae such as requisitioning a city gardener to trim the weeds around the Washington Irving library. "We should sweep up in here," he said to Sarao, pushing some rubbish around with his foot. "But let's focus outside and clean up for the neighbors." He sighed. "We should definitely clear everything growing around the fence. It will look a lot better."

Back in Szabo's car, we drove to City Hall,

where he had a meeting scheduled with the city's homelessness policy director, Alisa Orduña. Fifty years ago, it would have been very unlikely that the city librarian would have had a meeting with a homelessness policy director. In fact, fifty years ago, the city wouldn't have had a homelessness policy director. Now it is an essential post. In the late 1960s, the media brought attention to the terrible conditions in psychiatric hospitals. Along with the development of antipsychotic drugs and President Reagan's rollback on mental health funding, state psychiatric hospitals subsequently discharged a large number of patients. Many of these patients didn't have a home to return to or were too disabled to manage a home on their own. Over the next few decades, money for social service programs and low-income housing withered. Then the Great Recession and the thunderclap of foreclosures around the country contributed mightily to the growing population of people living on the streets or in shelters. By 2009, more than 1.5 million people in the United States met the federal definition of homeless — anyone without a "fixed, regular, and adequate nighttime residence." Los Angeles has more homeless people than almost any other city except New York: At last count, in 2017, there were almost sixty thousand homeless people in Los Angeles.

One of the few places homeless people are welcomed, given access to computers and the Internet, and permitted to dally all day (unless they act out) is a public library. Libraries have become a de facto community center for the homeless across the globe. There is not a library in the world that hasn't grappled with the issue of how — and how much — to provide for the homeless. Many librarians have told me that they consider this the defining question facing libraries right now, and that they despair of finding a balance between welcoming homeless people and somehow accommodating other patrons who occasionally are scared of them or find them smelly or messy or alienating. Central Library is an amble away from several large shelters and highway overpasses lined with homeless encampments. In the morning, before the library opens, many of the people waiting to enter the building are carrying their worldly goods on their backs. Szabo acknowledges the fact that the library has attained a sort of guardianship of many of Los Angeles's street people. When he ran the library system in Atlanta, he sent bookmobiles to the motels where many homeless people lived, to offer books and story hours for the children. He included a public health nurse on the bookmobile so the nurse could check on residents' well-being once the bookmobile had drawn them out.

Alisa Orduña met us in the cool, shiny lobby of City Hall and led us upstairs to her office. She is a broad-shouldered, forthright woman with a luminous smile and a spill of freckles across her nose. Despite dealing all day long with the intractable issue of disenfranchised and mentally ill people, she seems jolly and energetic, nearly buoyant. She and Szabo are in regular contact. Today's meeting was occasioned by a new city ordinance limiting the size of items allowed on city sidewalks, which was a roundabout way of discouraging people from setting up camps with tents and shopping carts and suitcases. No one was quite sure how the results would ripple through the city when the law went into effect, but it would certainly have an impact on the library. "So, it's a go for tomorrow," Orduña said to Szabo about the ordinance. "My guess is that it will create tension."

Szabo tapped his chin for a moment and then said, "We do have policies on the size of backpacks people can bring into the library. Do we need to be more lenient, to help ease that? In case people come in carrying a lot of their stuff from the camps?" They talked about whether there was a way the library could provide a checkroom with storage space for large items, since people would now be required to clean up their campsites during the day and probably would have nowhere to stash their belongings.

"That would be great. Plus, it would be a chance to do some intake," Orduña said. "We would love that data."

"I'd love the data, too," Szabo said. They talked for a while about whether there was space somewhere in the library that was sitting idle. Szabo tried to be enthusiastic but warned Orduña that the building was already too full. Then Szabo said he'd requested funds in his next budget for the homeless outreach program, The Source, that he had mentioned earlier in the day. Orduña perked up and asked whether the library could accommodate social workers to meet with homeless clients. Szabo winced and said he didn't think so but took notes so he could research the question further. Orduña sighed and said, "John, you know how it is. What we're doing is to try to sustain hope while folks are waiting for housing. Just having hope is important."

Szabo said that he could have bookmobiles dispatched to areas where homeless families were living, as he had done in Atlanta, if they could figure out how to get supplies and funding for bookmobiles without having to go through the ordinary municipal channels. "I've heard nightmares," Szabo said as Orduña nodded. "Two years to get anything, even a vacuum cleaner, that kind of thing."

"My God!" Orduña gasped. "For a vacuum cleaner?"

Szabo's next appointment was across town in Little Tokyo. The neighborhood has its own branch library, a low, long concrete building that opened in 2005. The front of the building is utilitarian; the back is connected to Redbird, one of the fanciest restaurants in downtown Los Angeles. The head of the branch had asked Szabo to stop by so they could discuss a parking agreement with the neighboring building and the plans for the unused land between the back of the library and Redbird. Little Tokyo Branch Library is only a stone's throw from Central, but it feels entirely different. It is definitely a neighborhood library — compact, specific, homey. Its collections reflect the neighborhood. Central Library has a good-size manga section, but Little Tokyo has a huge manga section. Families in the neighborhood have lots of little kids, so the branch has a large children's section, with books in English as well as Japanese.

Just inside the front door, a wiry man with gray grizzle dotting his cheeks and chin sat at a plastic card table. He explained to us that he was a volunteer doing outreach for AmeriCorps veterans' programs. His card table had dozens of pamphlets fanned out like rosettes, and he handed us several.

"Busy day?" Szabo asked him.

The man shook his head and said, "Nah, not much business." He adjusted one of the rosettes of pamphlets and grinned. "I guess everyone's outside working on their tans."

Szabo went off to find the branch's head librarian, so I wandered alone through the reading room. It was purring with that soothing library noise — not a din, not a racket, just a constant, warm, shapeless sound — space inhabited peacefully and purposefully by many strangers. I walked through the grove of bookshelves toward the children's section. Two old men and an elderly woman were browsing there, pulling books off the shelves and then conferring in Japanese about each one. They might have been grandparents choosing books for their grandchildren, but the librarian on duty told me they were getting the books for themselves. She said that many people in the neighborhood used picture books to practice their English.

Szabo emerged after a few minutes. He seemed excited and said that it looked like the parking issue was resolved; the library had agreed to let the owners of the Redbird building develop the empty lot. The plan included raised garden beds, a fountain, olive trees, and a tank for raising trout. In the meantime, the branch manager had successfully requested that the Little Tokyo library get power-washed.

It was closing in on five P.M., but Szabo had one more meeting back in his office, with a young woman named Kren Malone, who would soon be taking over as the director of Central Library services. The current director, Eva Mitnick, was becoming the director of engagement and learning, a wide-ranging position Szabo had created, which would include overseeing the bilingual and multilingual librarians, services for new Americans, and all library programs for veterans.

The director of Central is a job distinct from Szabo's. Szabo runs the entire citywide library system and has his office in Central

Library, along with the rest of the library administration. The director of Central runs the main library itself, and reports to Szabo, just as the head of the Little Tokyo branch runs that particular branch and reports to Szabo. The difference is the size and the complexity of Central Library's collections — rare books, research materials, special collections, along with the usual library books.

Malone, a tall, unruffled African American woman with long curvy hair and a shy smile, had worked at the library for the last seventeen years. When we arrived, she was waiting in Szabo's office, reading a spread-sheet of book orders. Szabo greeted her and began by telling her about the bike-share kiosk that was going to be installed. They chatted about it while Szabo took off his jacket, straightened his tie, and sat down. The conversation then glided from Central Library to Boyle Heights, a neighborhood east of downtown. A battery recycling plant in the neighborhood had contaminated soil with toxic levels of lead, necessitating the largest lead cleanup in California history. Exide Technologies, which operated the plant, had just agreed to fund blood tests for the twenty-one thousand households in the neighborhood. The tests would be conducted at the Boyle Heights Branch Library. In times of trouble, libraries are sanctuaries. They become town squares and community centers — even blood-draw locations. In Los Angeles, there have been plenty of disasters requiring libraries to fill that role. In 2016, for instance, a gas storage facility in the Porter Ranch neighborhood sprang a leak, and methane whooshed out, giving residents headaches, nosebleeds, stomachaches, and breathing problems. Eventually, the entire area had to be evacuated. With the help of industrial-strength air purifiers, the library managed to stay open. It became a clearinghouse for information about the crisis, as well as a place where residents could gather while exiled from home. The head of the branch noticed how anxious patrons seemed, so she set up yoga and meditation classes to help people relieve stress. Staff librarians learned how to fill out the expense forms from Southern California Gas so they could assist people applying to get reimbursed for housing and medical costs. *American Libraries Magazine* applauded the library's response, noting, "Amid a devastating gas leak, Porter Ranch library remains a constant."

Szabo and Malone traded updates on various projects. The new library cards, designed by artist Shepard Fairey, would be done soon. Circulation numbers were good. Additional security cameras for the building had been ordered and would arrive in a week or two. Malone took notes and nodded along with each sentence. She asked Szabo when he would be back from the trip he'd be starting at dawn the next day. "A week," he said, and then smiled and added, "you won't have time to miss me!"

Just as Malone prepared to leave, Szabo mentioned that he would be back in time for an upcoming celebration at the library. In 2014, Szabo had established Career Online High School — COHS — which is the first accredited library-based high school program in the United States. Through the library's website, adults who had not gotten their high school diploma could take any of the nine hundred COHS online classes for free, and graduate with a diploma rather than a high school equivalency certificate. Szabo frequently preaches the gospel of the library as the people's university, and with COHS, he had managed to make good on that notion. It was an idea so obvious and so well suited to a library setting that right after Szabo launched it, fifty other libraries around the country, inspired by the Los Angeles program, began their own adult high school courses. Launching COHS had been one of the most satisfying aspects of his time in Los Angeles, Szabo said. Just a few weeks after he returned from his trips to Toronto and Ohio, he would be officiating at the first graduation ceremony of COHS, where twenty-two adults would receive their high school diplomas, courtesy of the Los Angeles Public Library.

7.

Fire Captain Don Sturkey inspects the damage

The Art of Condolence: What to
Write, What to Say, What to Do
at a Time of Loss (1991)
  By Zunin, Leonard M.
  177.9 Z95

No Time for Tears: Coping with Grief in a Busy World (2015)
  By Heath, Judy
  157.3 H437

How Everyday Products Make People Sick: Toxins at Home and in the Workplace (2007)
  By Blanc, Paul D.
  615.9 B638

Rock Names: From Abba to ZZ Top: How Rock Bands Got Their Names (1995)
  Dolgins, Adam
  781.9903 D664

As soon as the news of the fire at Central Library spread, condolence notes arrived from libraries in Belgium, Japan, England, Germany, from all around the world. The director of France's Bibliothèque nationale wrote, "When the time comes and if you consider it possible, [we would like to] receive all information . . . about the causes of this sinister occurrence." Notes also came from libraries across the United States — from New York, San Diego, Detroit, Kansas City, the Library of Congress, from universities and colleges. "The staff at the Harvard Museum of Comparative Zoology has been deeply distressed by the news of your recent tragedy." "We at the Los Angeles County Medical Center share your shock and distress over the tragic fire." "We at the Oklahoma City Library are so sorry to hear of your library's calamity. Keep your socks up!" The sentiments expressed most often in these notes were grief, shock, distress, and devastation.

The Central Library staff came to work, but they weren't sure what "work" meant in a library that was now closed to the public and empty of books. Some of the staff was dispatched to the warehouse in East Los Angeles where many of the undamaged books were being stored. Others were sent into the burned building, where they swept the floors and tried to organize anything left behind. The mood was bleak. The fire felt like a personal violation. Glen Creason felt a "crippling blackness" after the fire. He told me it was the worst day of his life; the second worst was the day his father died. Sylva Monooghian became so depressed that she wore only white clothes for the next several months, hoping that would help her feel pure again. A staff member posted an anonymous note saying, "We should have held prayer sessions . . to prevent the firebug from striking. [Now] there's the taste of death . . . and the soulless, empty fear and despair overwhelms you." According to the note, most of the staff had developed "the library cough" and "the library shuffle, a sort of no-destination movement of the feet, forward-back-forward."

The library cough came from the sooty air. The library shuffle was the sleepwalk of anxiety. Even though the city's safety department assured them otherwise, the staff feared that the fire had torn open walls and released asbestos. They worried that the library would never reopen or would never rebuild its collection. They worried that the arsonist would try again. Even worse, they worried that the arsonist was someone on the staff. Many people at the library considered their coworkers family. Now the family was riven with suspicion. One clerk in the History Department sent a memo to the police accusing another clerk of being the arsonist. "She has developed a reputation for being belligerent and angry with coworkers," he wrote, noting that the clerk had access to the area where the fire started. Investigators didn't dismiss the possibility that someone on the staff started the fire, and they questioned many staff members, including anyone who called in sick the day of the fire. Any staff member who could be described as "disgruntled" was questioned, too. Not long ago, I spent the afternoon with a retired librarian named Mel Rosenberg, who happened to have been out of town the day of the fire. "Oh, they checked up on me," Rosenberg said. "They wanted to make sure I was where I said I was." He began laughing loudly and recalled that when he was hired, Wyman Jones had warned him that he better not be too liberal. "I said, oh my God, Wyman, do you think there are any conservative librarians?" Rosenberg was laughing so hard that I thought he might cry. Then he started thinking about the fire again and grew somber. "All the magazines in my department, the Art Department, were gone. All of them. It was terrible. You have no idea."

The arson investigators continued interviewing staff, with special attention to anyone who stood out for any reason. A memo was circulated to administrators, suggesting there should be a "plan of action" if the arsonist turned out to be an employee. The plan included a news blackout, a rehearsal for answering "difficult questions," and a suggestion that the staff should be informed by either "telephone network" or "a hand-carried written memo."

Twenty-four of Central's 250 librarians soon asked for transfers to other branches. A survey of the remaining staff asked what the most stressful aspect of the fire was. The answers were dire. They included: "Feeling of powerlessness, helplessness brought about by confusion . . . feeling of isolation of having to work in an almost empty shell of a building that was once a vital place"; "Being afraid that, even though nobody was killed in the fire, somebody is going to get killed or badly hurt because of so many safety problems"; and "Feeling like a refugee. Holes ripped in an organic entity." Local newspapers reported on the staff's malaise. POST-FIRE DESPAIR RAISING TENSIONS AMONG LIBRARIANS, one story was headlined. The librarians complained of eye infections, breathing difficulties, skin irritation, and post-traumatic stress disorder. The head of the Audiovisual Department told the *Los Angeles Daily News*, "The first few days after the fire, I'd come home and light a match, and the whole library came back into my head." One memo between administrators warned, "The staff here can't stand the conditions. They are sweeping floors and scrubbing sinks . . . There should be guards during working hours at least since the arsonist is still at large." One senior librarian, interviewed by the Librarians' Guild, said, "Well, working conditions are abysmal. Morale varies . . . There has been an amazing amount of public support. Many librarians don't know how the public supports them in any concrete way." On the other hand, some librarians felt so isolated in their gloom that they became estranged from their spouses. Glen Creason told me that many marriages, included his, imploded in the months after the fire.

The library's administration became so concerned about the librarians' state of mind that they brought in a psychologist, Dr. Stanley Ksionzky, to conduct group therapy sessions. Dr. Ksionzky encouraged the librarians to engage in "fantasy visualization" of how nice the library would be when it reopened. For those who worried that their patrons felt abandoned, Dr. Ksionzky encouraged them to imagine the patrons using other branches and doing well. The librarians themselves tried to find something to laugh about in the wreckage. Those who were relocated to a gloomy city building on Rio Vista Avenue wrote a song to the tune of "Oklahoma!" that began, "Rio Vista / Where the car thieves pass the time of day / And if you survive the eight-to-five / You'll go home with a dollar twenty-five / And so we are taking this stand / For the dust we are breathing is grand . . ." Someone suggested they should form a library band because the song was such a hit with the staff. A note was posted on the staff bulletin board reading, "Whereas the only available succor has been dangled as a carrot in the form of group therapy, the following groups are signed up to avail themselves of the existing means of healing and mending." It was followed by a list of proposed band names, incorporating names of some of the librarians, including "Betty Gay and the Depressions," "Dan Dupill and the Bitters," and "Bill Byrne and the Arsonists."

8.

Tales from the Time Loop: The Most Comprehensive Exposé of the Global Conspiracy Ever Written and All You Need to Know to Be Truly Free (2003)
  By Icke, David
  909 I17-3

Drunk, Divorced & Covered in Cat Hair: The True-Life Misadventures of a 30-Something Who Learned to Knit After He Split (2007)
  By Perry, Laurie
  392.3428 P463

Hackers and Hacking: A Reference Handbook (2013)
  By Holt, Thomas J.
  364.38 H7578

Every month, more than seven hundred new books arrive at the library. They are then offloaded, unboxed, stamped, stickered, linked to the electronic catalog system, snugged in a Mylar cover, bar-coded, and, finally, let loose on the shelves. It takes almost a week to process a new book. One afternoon when I was in the Collection Services Department, where this processing takes place, the books that had just arrived included *100 Interiors Around the World; Hoover's War on Gays: Exposing the FBI's "Sex Deviates" Program;* and *Don't Be a Jerk: And Other Practical Advice from Dogen, Japan's Greatest Zen Master.* There was also a stack of Spanish, Russian, Armenian, and Swedish books that were making their way to the International Languages Department.

Peggy Murphy, who manages Collection Services, started her library career as a teenager in Mount Vernon, New York, at a time when the head librarian summoned clerks using the kind of metal clicker now most often used to train dogs. Each clerk was summoned by his or her unique click pattern. Murphy's was two short clicks. The books that the head librarian in Mount Vernon deemed "dangerous" — that is, sexual — were shelved in a locked metal cage in the basement of the library. Baudelaire, Balzac, and Masters and Johnson were there, behind bars. Somehow, Murphy figured out where the key to the cage was stored, and during her breaks, she sneaked in and read. By the time she graduated from high school, she had managed to read every single one of the caged books. "It broadened my worldview," she likes to say.

A popular book that gets checked out often begins to fall apart in a year, so many of the books that arrive in the Catalog Department are replacement copies of books the library already owns. A book like, say, *The Da Vinci Code,* which is checked out dozens of times each month, is lucky to last a full year. Some books are replaced before they fall apart. For instance, babyname books are traded out regularly. "Pregnant women don't want to handle a grubby book, so we keep those nice and fresh," Murphy said.

Other books have a tendency to be loaned

out and never returned. The library has bought countless copies of Carlos Castaneda's books because so many of them journey out and never come back. Another author, David Icke, who writes about his global conspiracy theories and about a race of reptilian aliens he believes will eventually dominate Earth, are ranked — anecdotally, at least — as the books that disappear most frequently. Icke has such acquisitive readers that for a while the library simply stopped ordering replacement copies of his books because it was costing too much to keep up. The day Elvis Presley died, someone checked out all of the library's Elvis records and never returned them. The files about the Manson Family and about the Black Dahlia murder, which included clippings and ephemera, disappeared decades ago; they are essentially irreplaceable. In 1981, investigators discovered a woman selling books out of a suite in a Beverly Hills hotel. She was earning approximately forty thousand dollars a year with her used-book business. All of the books had been stolen from the Los Angeles Public Library. In 1982, ten thousand books that had gone missing from the library were found in the Los Angeles home of a library clerk named Glenn Swartz, who said he thought he had a hoarding problem. (He resigned from his job.) People have been caught trying to sneak books out in baby strollers, which sometimes have babies in them and sometimes don't.

For years, movie studios were major book-pinching culprits. Rather than simply checking out books they needed for their research — and thus having to abide by the due date — studios sometimes dispatched two assistants to the library to steal them. The scheme involved one of the assistants taking a position outside a window and the other pitching the desired book out the window to his or her counterpart. This happened so often that the library had an employee whose main job was to visit the studios on a regular basis to get the books back. To help foil the through-the-window scheme, the librarians also wired shut all the windows that were most often used. (In spite of this obvious case of cross-purposes, the library has always had a close relationship with the studios. A 1950s library brochure called *THEY WANTED THE FACTS . . . and Found Them in the Library* noted, "Motion picture studios try to avoid boners by extensive [library] . . . research. Twentieth Century Fox combed the library's files . . . for contemporary views on a famous murder case!")

Near Peggy Murphy's office sits an old book-stitching machine — a bulky metal contraption about the size and shape of a snowplow. The machine is so old that ready-made parts are no longer available for it. The City of Los Angeles used to have an in-house municipal bindery department. Over time, the bindery was reduced from a large department to a small department and eventually to a single bookbinder, who sewed up broken books from the library as well as from other city departments. When you think about it, cities own thousands of books and bound material — law journals for district attorneys; directories; reference material; city ordinances; and more. The last of the city's official bookbinders retired in 2014. No one was hired to replace her, and "bookbinder salary" is no longer a line item in the city budget. These days, library books that are rare or expensive are sent to private restorers if they need emergency surgery. Ordinary books that start to fall apart are simply thrown out, and new copies are bought in their place.

The old book-stitching machine sits about ten yards from a cluster of seven-foot-tall computer towers through which flow a hundred megabytes of information per second. The Los Angeles Public Library has been online since 1994, which was much earlier than many other systems. This was an unanticipated upside of the fire. Rudimentary electronic book catalogs became available in the seventies, but the more sophisticated online systems similar to what are available today were developed around 1990. Initially, many libraries resisted upgrading to these improved systems because they had already invested in the first iteration of the electronic catalogs and couldn't afford to upgrade yet again. But Los Angeles had lost so many books in the fire that its old-fashioned card catalog was no longer even remotely accurate, and it had never bought into the early electronic catalogs because the fire had made a book inventory impossible. The surviving collection had to be inventoried again, along with the hundreds of thousands of books that were purchased to replace the burned ones. Rather than rebuilding the original catalog, the library decided to start fresh with an electronic one. It was one of the first major libraries in the country to do so.

According to Matthew Mattson, who is in charge of it, the library's website was visited more than eleven million times in 2015, and the catalog was browsed more than ten million times. Among the visitors are quite a few hackers. Mattson told me that he observes someone trying to hack into the library's website almost every day. Most of the intruders appear to be based in China or Russia. Hacking into a library's website seems pointless, since you can access it legitimately anytime, so I asked Mattson why anyone would bother. "They're practicing," he said. As he explained it, people hack into the library to rehearse hacking into bigger, more secure, and more valuable targets.

The most popular picture in the library's photography collection is of a five-year-old elephant named Bimbo Jr. riding a surfboard. The picture ran in the *Los Angeles Herald* in 1962. According to the caption, Bimbo Jr. had "the rare distinction of being the youngest elephant to perform this remarkable feat," a peculiar sort of caption that implies that other elephants surf, too, and Bimbo's specialness was only his tender age. The second most popular photo, measured by how often it is visited online or ordered as a print, is one from the 1950s featuring girls in tight bloomers shooting arrows at a stack of beach balls. The runner-up is a picture of a Volkswagen bus filled with a large number of cats, parked on Venice's Muscle Beach; the date and photographer are unknown. Most of the 3.4 million photos in the library's collection came into its possession as physical prints. Every day, a few more are scanned and put online, where they can be searched by keywords and descriptions. Some pictures in the collection are the work of famous photographers. Ansel Adams came to Los Angeles in 1939 and documented the early years of the aerospace industry, and he donated those negatives to the library. African American photographer Roland Curtis documented Los Angeles's black community in the 1960s and '70s and donated his archives as well. Most of the 3.4 million pictures are everyday photographs. The *Los Angeles Herald Examiner,* published from 1903 until 1989, donated its collection of two million images to the library in 1991. The *Valley Times,* a suburban paper published from the 1940s until the 1970s, donated its library of forty-five thousand images when it closed down.

It will take four years to scan all of the *Valley Times* photographs. One of the people working on all that scanning is a library assistant named Lisa Ondoy. When I dropped by the department one afternoon, Ondoy was working on indexing a picture of three kids who looked about fourteen or fifteen years old and were holding a gigantic watermelon. The scan of the picture was up on her computer screen, and Ondoy examined it for a few minutes, craning her neck so she could see every detail. She typed "teenagers" and "San Fernando Valley" as tags, leaned back in her chair, and thought for a moment. "I'll probably tag it with 'watermelons,' too," she said. "There must have been a heat wave here in 1960, because there are lots of stories about what people in the valley were doing to beat the heat."

Ondoy had been working on creating search tools — the descriptive tags — for the *Valley Times* archives for two years. She had already completed the tags for 18,500 pictures. She said if she worked carefully, she could finish three or four pictures an hour. The job seems exacting and somewhat tedious, but Ondoy loves it. "I'm a total geek about it," she said. "I love when I find things in the pictures that I thought had disappeared. Forgotten things. Maybe this is corny, but I almost feel like I'm saving them." She said she loved how the *Valley Times* photos documented ordinary life. "We get a lot of birthday cake pictures and a lot of golden anniversary pictures," she said, and she beamed, adding, "I really love those."

She typed in a few more tags for the watermelon picture, filed it, and called up the next photograph in her queue, which showed a huge, wiry Airedale dog getting a shampoo. Ondoy said the *Valley Times* archives included a lot of dog pictures, and those included a lot of dogs having baths. As she was telling me this, she typed in the tags "dogs," "grooming," "baths," and "San Fernando Valley." She zoomed in on the picture and studied it. She pointed out that a pile of towels was just visible in the corner of the frame, so she added "towels." She also added "lawns," because the dog's bathtub was sitting on a large patch of grass, and according to Ondoy, people often search for photographs of lawns, so she likes to tag those generously. Another frequent search term is "swimming pools," so any picture that features even a pixel of pool is tagged just in case. We spent some time discussing whether the plastic tub the Airedale was sitting in would qualify as a pool, but Ondoy decided against it. She filed the Airedale photograph and moved on.

The next photograph was a portrait of a priest who was smiling broadly. He had his arms around a neatly dressed man and woman who were also smiling but not quite as much. The picture had run in the *Valley Times* in 1961 with the caption "Father Collins Signs Couple for Counseling." Lisa scrolled down to read the story, which discussed the rate of divorce in Los Angeles — it was the highest in the United States at the time — and the Catholic Church's efforts to remedy it. Ondoy tagged the picture of the smiling Father Collins ("Catholic Church"; "priest"; "divorce") and pulled up one more picture to work on before she left for her break. It was another dog. She zoomed in to examine the picture. This dog was not having a bath. It was very dry and had long wavy fur. The photo caption read, "Big Soft Friend."

Across the room, Xochitl Oliva, the senior librarian in charge of digitization and special collections at Central, opened the first of several boxes that had just been delivered to the department. They were donated to the library by a student anti-war group, active from 1967 to 1971, known as the L.A. Resistance. The material in the box was ephemera produced for the group's activities, including posters, pictures, newsletters, and leaflets. Most of the material had spent the last thirty years stored in a Northern

California tree house belonging to one of the members. Recently, the group members had decided to empty their closets and, evidently, their tree houses, and wanted to find a permanent home for their archives. The library had come to mind. The donation was enthusiastically accepted. "This is amazing stuff," Oliva said, rifling through the box. "It's real history."

I left the Digitization Department and took one of my frequent walks around the building. I was just trying to soak in the place, to notice it. Sometimes it's harder to notice a place you think you know well; your eyes glide over it, seeing it but not seeing it at all. It's almost as if familiarity gives you a kind of temporary blindness. I had to force myself to look harder and try to see beyond the concept of library that was so latent in my brain.

Right before learning about the library fire, I had decided I was done with writing books. Working on them felt like a slow-motion wrestling match, and I wasn't in the mood to grapple with such a big commitment again. But here I was. I knew part of what hooked me had been the shock of familiarity I felt when I took my son to our local library — the way it telegraphed my childhood, my relationship to my parents, my love of books. It brought me close, in my musings, to my mother, and to our sojourns to the library. It was wonderful and it was bittersweet, because just as I was rediscovering those memories, my mother was losing all of hers. When I first told her that I was writing a book about libraries, she was delighted, and she said she was proud that she had a part in making me find them wondrous. But soon the dark fingers of dementia got her in their grip, and they pried loose random bits of her memory every day. The next time I reminded her about the project and told her how much I had been thinking about our trips to Bertram Woods, she smiled with encouragement but with no apparent recognition of what I meant. Each time I visited, she receded a little more — she became vague, absent, isolated in her thoughts or maybe in some pillowy blankness that filled in where the memories had been chipped away — and I knew that now I was carrying the remembrance for both of us.

My mother imbued me with a love of libraries. The reason why I finally embraced this book project — wanted, and then needed, to write it — was my realization that I was losing her. I found myself wondering whether a shared memory can exist if one of the people sharing it no longer remembers it. Is the circuit broken, the memory darkened? My mother was the one person besides me who knew what those gauzy afternoons had been like. I knew I was writing this because I was trying hard to preserve those afternoons. I convinced myself that committing them to a page meant the memory was saved, somehow, from the corrosive effect of time.

The idea of being forgotten is terrifying. I fear not just that I, personally, will be forgotten, but that we are all doomed to being forgotten — that the sum of life is ultimately nothing; that we experience joy and disappointment and aches and delights and loss, make our little mark on the world, and then we vanish, and the mark is erased, and it is as if we never existed. If you gaze into that bleakness even for a moment, the sum of life becomes null and void, because if nothing lasts, nothing matters. It means that everything we experience unfolds without a pattern, and life is just a wild, random, baffling occurrence, a scattering of notes with no melody. But if something you learn or observe or imagine can be set down and saved, and if you can see your life reflected in previous lives, and can imagine it reflected in subsequent ones, you can begin to discover order and harmony. You know that you are a part of a larger story that has shape and purpose — a tangible, familiar past and a constantly refreshed future. We are all whispering in a tin can on a string, but we are heard, so we whisper the message into the next tin can and the next string. Writing a book, just like building a library, is an act of sheer defiance. It is a declaration that you believe in the persistence of memory.

In Senegal, the polite expression for saying someone died is to say his or her library has burned. When I first heard the phrase, I didn't understand it, but over time I came to realize it was perfect. Our minds and souls contain volumes inscribed by our experiences and emotions; each individual's consciousness is a collection of memories we've cataloged and stored inside us, a private library of a life lived. It is something that no one else can entirely share, one that burns down and disappears when we die. But if you can take something from that internal collection and share it — with one person or with the larger world, on the page or in a story recited — it takes on a life of its own.

9.

La biblioteca perdida (2013)
By Dean, A. M.
S

*Vom Kaiserhof zur Reichskanzlei:
Eine Historische Darstellung in
Tagebuchblattern (Vom 1. Januar
1932 bis Zum 1. Mai 1933)* (1934)
By Goebbels, Joseph
G 943.085 G593-2

*The Protection of Cultural
Property in the Event of Armed
Conflict: Commentary on the
Convention for the Protection
of Cultural Property in the
Event of Armed Conflict and Its
Protocol, Signed 14 May, 1954 in
The Hague, and on Other Instru-
ments* (1996)
By Toman, Jiri

*The Holocaust and the Book:
Destruction and Preservation*
(2001)
Edited by Rose, Jonathan.
Series: Studies in Print Culture
and the History of the Book
940.5315296 H7545-4

People have been burning libraries for
nearly as long as they've been building
libraries. As William Blades wrote in 1880
in one of the first books about burning
books, libraries are easy victims of "chance
conflagrations, fanatic incendiarism, judicial
bonfires, and even household stoves." The
first recorded instance of book burning was
in 213 BC, when Chinese emperor Qin Shi
Huang decided to incinerate any history
books that contradicted his version of the
past. In addition, he buried more than four
hundred scholars alive.

The most celebrated lost library of the
ancient world was Egypt's Library of Alexandria. Though it figures large in anecdotal
history, very little is actually known about
the library. There is no record of what the
building looked like or even its exact location. Supposedly, the library contained a

half million documents and manuscripts and had a staff of one hundred resident librarians. The Library of Alexandria is said to have burned several times. The first occasion was when Julius Caesar attacked the Port of Alexandria in 48 BCE. Caesar hadn't targeted the library, but the fire he started in the port spread and eventually engulfed it. The library was rebuilt and restocked, but it was burned twice more in subsequent assaults on the city. Each time it was restored.

The last and final burning, which erased it from history forever, occurred in AD 640. By that time, the library was awe-inspiring and a little scary. People had begun to believe it was a living thing — an enormous, infinite communal brain containing all the existing knowledge in the entire world, with the potential for the sort of independent intelligence we now fear in supercomputers. When Caliph Omar, who led the Muslim invasion of Egypt, came upon the library, he told his generals that its contents either contradicted the Koran, in which case they needed to be destroyed, or they supported the Koran, in which case they were redundant. Either way, the library was doomed. It burned for six months until there was almost nothing left to burn, and the few remaining books were used as fuel to heat water at local bathhouses.

Everything about the Library of Alexandria was enigmatic. To this day, no one is sure whether the stories about it are true. Even its dramatic end by fire has been questioned; some historians believe that earthquakes and a shrunken budget brought on its demise. It is a touchstone of all library history, but its beginning, middle, and end remain a mystery.

In the saga of humankind, most things are done for money — arson especially — but there is no money to be made by burning libraries. Instead, libraries are usually burned because they contain ideas that someone finds problematic. In the thirteenth and fourteenth centuries, the pope ordered Jewish books to be collected and "cremated" (the choice of terms at the time) because he believed they spread anti-Catholic thought. The Spanish Inquisition introduced the idea of book-burning festivals, which were community gatherings around bonfires made of "heretical" books, including any written in Hebrew, especially the Torah.

The Spanish continued their book burning abroad. In the mid-1500s, Hernán Cortés and his soldiers burned scores of Aztec manuscripts on the grounds that they contained black magic. After Cortés's victory, a priest named Diego de Landa was assigned to inflict Catholicism on the Mayan people. De Landa was fascinated by Mayan culture, yet he oversaw the torture and murder of scores of Mayans, and he burned every Mayan book and image he found. Only a few codices are known to have survived De Landa's purge, and those are among the only remaining documents of the Mayan civilization.

You could fill a book with the list of lost libraries of the world, and in fact, there have been many books written about them, including one with the haunting title *Libricide,* written by a professor of library science. Early in history, when there were fewer books, and printing copies was expensive and time-consuming, the loss of a library could be terminal. UNESCO released studies in 1949 and in 1996 listing all the libraries that have been demolished throughout modern history. The number of books destroyed, by UNESCO's count, is so enormous — in the billions — that I sometimes find it hard to believe there are any books left in the world.

War is the greatest slayer of libraries. Some

of the loss is incidental. Because libraries are usually in the center of cities, they are often damaged when cities are attacked. Other times, though, libraries are specific targets. World War II destroyed more books and libraries than any event in human history. The Nazis alone destroyed an estimated hundred million books during their twelve years in power. Book burning was, as author George Orwell remarked, "the most characteristic [Nazi] activity." The assault on books in Germany began even before the war. As soon as Hitler became chancellor, he banned all publications that he designated as subversive. Books by Jewish and leftist authors were automatically included in the ban. On May 10, 1933, thousands of the banned books were collected in Berlin's Opera Square for an event called *Feuersprüche,* or "Fire Incantations." The *Feuersprüche* was a pet project of Joseph Goebbels, the Nazi Party's propaganda chief, who understood how fundamental books were to Jewish culture, theology, and identity. Burning Jewish books, in his opinion, was an ideal form of bloodless torture, demonstrating the limitlessness of German control. Members of the German student union carried out the book burning with enthusiasm. At Opera Square, the students formed a human chain, passed the books from hand to hand, and then cast them into a pile. Estimates of the number of books in the bonfire pile range from twenty-five thousand to ninety thousand. As each book was thrown in, a student announced the reason this particular book was being "sentenced to death." The reasons were stated like criminal charges. The books of Sigmund Freud, for instance, were charged with spiritual corruption and "the exaggeration and unhealthy complication of sexuality." After reading the charge, the student threw the book into the pile while declaring, "I commit to the flames the works of Sigmund Freud!" Other charges included "Judeo-democratic tendencies"; "mutilation of the German language"; and "literary betrayal of the soldiers of the Great War." Once the pile was complete, it was drenched with gasoline and set on fire.

The *Feuersprüche* had a party atmosphere, with dancing, singing, and live music. At midnight, Goebbels appeared and gave a raving discourse known as the Fire Speech. That same night, similar events were held in Munich, Dresden, Frankfurt, and Breslau, and more than thirty other *Feuersprüches* took place in university towns around Germany over the next year.

In Bonn, as the books were being consumed, the mayor reportedly said that the ashes looked as if "the Jewish soul [had flown] into the sky."

The spectacle of destroying books was particularly excruciating for Jews, who have long been known as "people of the book." Judaism considers books sacred, and its most sacred text, the Torah, is doted upon, dressed in a cloth mantle, and decorated with jewels, a silver breastplate, and a crown. When religious books wear out, they are buried and receive a funeral service. Jews believe books are more than just printed documents; they believe books have a kind of humanity and a soul. Rabbinical authors often stop using their given names and choose to be called by the title of their books. The irony of the *Feuersprüche* was that they treated books as seriously as Jews did. To feel the need to destroy them acknowledged the potency and value of books, and recognized the steadfast Jewish attachment to them.

The grinding destruction of the war crushed the libraries of Europe. Some were merely unlucky and got caught in fire bombings and aerial attacks meant for more strategic targets. But the German army singled out books for destruction. Special book-burning squads known as "Brenn-Kommandos" were sent out to burn libraries and synagogues. The squads were effective. Enumerating the losses of libraries in the war, both incidental and purposeful, is dizzying. Twenty major libraries containing two million books were destroyed in Italy. France lost millions more, including 300,000 in Strasbourg, 42,000 in Beauvais, 23,000 in Chartres, and 110,000 in Douai. The Library of the National Assembly in Paris burned down, taking with it countless historic arts and science books. In Metz, officials hid the library's most valuable books in an unmarked warehouse for safekeeping. A German soldier found the warehouse and threw an incendiary device into it. Most of the books, including rare eleventh- and thirteenth-century manuscripts, were destroyed. During the Blitz, twenty million books in Great Britain burned or were wrecked by the water used to extinguish the fires. The Central Lending Library in Liverpool was completely ruined. (The rest of the city's libraries stayed open throughout the Blitz, maintaining regular hours and levying the usual overdue fines.)

After the 1938 Munich Conference, every book in the Czech language that dealt with geography, biography, or history was confiscated and either burned or mashed into pulp. In Vilnius, Lithuania, the library in the Jewish ghetto was set on fire. A few months later, the residents of the ghetto were shipped to concentration camps and gassed, illustrating the truth in German poet Heinrich Heine's warning: "There where one burns books, one in the end burns men." In Budapest, all small libraries and at least part of every major one was destroyed. Belgium's huge Library of the University of Louvain suffered more than almost any library in Europe. In World War I, the German army had burned it down. After the Armistice, a consortium of European nations rebuilt the library, and it reopened to great celebration. In 1940, the library was hit by German artillery fire, and all of the books in its stacks were lost, including Old Masters prints and almost one thousand books published before 1500. In Poland, eighty percent of all books in the country were destroyed. In Kiev, German soldiers paved the streets with reference books from the city's library to provide footing for their armored vehicles in the mud. The troops then set the city's libraries on fire, burning four million books. As they made their way across Russia, the troops burned an estimated ninety-six million more.

The Allies' bombing of city centers in Japan and Germany inevitably hit libraries. Theodore Welch, who studies libraries in Japan, has written that by the time the American army arrived in 1945, three quarters of all the books in the country's libraries had been burned or damaged. The losses in Germany were astonishing. Most of the library books in cities including Bremen, Aachen, Stuttgart, Leipzig, Dresden, Munich, Hanover, Münster, and Hamburg were incinerated. Three quarters of a million were destroyed in Darmstadt; more than a million in Frankfurt; two million in Berlin. By the end of the war, more than one third of all the books in Germany were gone.

The devastation of libraries and other cultural property during the war frightened the world's governments into taking measures to ensure it would never happen again. In 1954, an international treaty known as The Hague Convention for the Protection of Cultural Property in the Event of Armed Conflict was adopted. Currently, 127 countries are signatories. Nevertheless, the protection of cultural property, including books, manuscripts, art, monuments, and important archaeological sites, has been negligible. Destruction occurred even immediately after the treaty was signed. It is almost as if the flamboyance of the Nazi *Feuersprüche* confirmed that burning books was an easy way to land a vicious blow on a community, and the idea was adopted by other oppressive regimes. When he was in his mid-twenties, Mao Tse-tung was an assistant librarian at Peking University. He often said that spending time in the library was how he discovered Karl Marx and had his political awakening. But just as some doctors become murderers, Mao was a librarian who became a book burner. Once in power, he ordered the destruction of any books he deemed "reactionary, obscene, and absurd." During the Cultural Revolution, he ordered a purge of books that espoused old ideas and customs, and he sent the Red Guard to "cleanse" the libraries of Tibet. In some libraries, every book was burned except for those by Marx, Lenin, and Mao himself.

More recently, the Khmer Rouge threw the books of the Cambodian National Library on the streets and burned them; only twenty percent survived. The Iraqi army burned most of the libraries in Kuwait after the 1990 invasion. Almost two hundred libraries were burned during the Bosnian

War, and ninety percent of the contents of the National Library of Sarajevo was destroyed. The poet Phil Cousineau wrote that "the ashes from the million and a half books burning" blackened the snow that fell on Sarajevo. Under Taliban rule, fifteen of the eighteen libraries in Kabul, Afghanistan, were closed, and most of their books were burned. During the Iraq war, only thirty percent of the books in the Iraqi National Library were spared. Some of them had been removed from the building before fighting reached Baghdad: Saddam Hussein had stolen many for his private collection, and Iraqis who suspected that the library would not survive the war had hidden books in their homes. As Islamist jihadis retreated from Timbuktu in 2013, they destroyed many of the Timbuktu Library's irreplaceable manuscripts, including some from as early as the thirteenth century.

There have been a number of book burnings in the United States, mostly as statements of outrage over the content of the books. In the 1940s, for instance, a West Virginia schoolteacher named Mabel Riddle, with the support of the Catholic Church, began a campaign to collect and burn comic books because of their enthusiastic portrayal of crime and sex. The bonfire, which consumed several thousand comics, was so warmly received that the idea spread to towns across the country, and many local parishes sponsored their own comic-book fires. In a few instances, nuns lit the first match.

Burning books is an inefficient way to conduct a war, since books and libraries have no military value, but it is a devastating act. Destroying a library is a kind of terrorism. People think of libraries as the safest and most open places in society. Setting them on fire is like announcing that nothing, and nowhere, is safe. The deepest effect of burning books is emotional. When libraries burn, the books are sometimes described as being "wounded" or as "casualties," just as human beings would be.

Books are a sort of cultural DNA, the code for who, as a society, we are, and what we know. All the wonders and failures, all the champions and villains, all the legends and ideas and revelations of a culture last forever in its books. Destroying those books is a way of saying that the culture itself no longer exists; its history has disappeared; the continuity between its past and its future is ruptured. Taking books away from a culture is to take away its shared memory.

It's like taking away the ability to remember your dreams. Destroying a culture's books is sentencing it to something worse than death: It is sentencing it to seem as if it never lived.

A few months after World War II ended and the libraries of Europe were still smoldering, a writer named Ray Bradbury began working on a story he called "The Fireman," set in a fictional society that has outlawed books. If a book is discovered secreted away in someone's home, firemen are summoned to burn it. Just like the Brenn-Kommandos, these firemen start fires rather than put them out. Bradbury was thirty years old when he started "The Fireman." He grew up in Los Angeles and had been writing fantasy and science fiction since he was a teenager. He was soon selling stories to sci-fi magazines like *Imagination, Amazing Stories,* and *Super Science Stories.* He graduated from high school in 1938, the dead center of the Depression. His family couldn't afford to send him to college. He had always loved the library, so as an alternative to college, he spent almost every day for the next thirteen years at the Los Angeles Public Library, reading his way through each department. He often referred to himself as "library-educated," and he believed he'd learned more at the library than he would have at a university. "I began when I was fourteen and graduated at twenty-seven," he said later. "I was in every damn room in the whole building. In some rooms, I read maybe one hundred books . . . . All the poetry in the world. All the plays. All the murder mysteries. All the essays." It began as a necessity for Bradbury, but soon libraries — especially Central Library — became his passion. "The library was my nesting place," he wrote, "my birthing place; it was my growing place."

Bradbury worked on "The Fireman" for a few months, grew frustrated with it, and put it aside. Four years later, the right-wing agitator Senator Joseph McCarthy gave a speech claiming that the State Department was riddled with Communists and "loyalty risks," triggering a spasm of paranoia across the United States. Bradbury, who once described McCarthy as "that strange senator," was horrified. He decided to try to finish "The Fireman," which had eerie premonitions of the current state of politics.

Bradbury and his wife had four young daughters. When he tried to work at home, he spent more time playing with his children than writing. He couldn't afford an office, but he knew of a room in the basement of UCLA's Powell Library, where typewriters could be rented for ten cents an hour. It occurred to him that there would be a fine symmetry if he wrote a book about book burning at a library. Over the course of nine days in the typewriter room at UCLA, Bradbury finished "The Fireman," expanding it into a short novel. He spent $9.80 on the typewriter rental.

The story of "The Fireman" is haunting. The protagonist is a young fireman named Montag, who lives with his wife, Mildred. Their life seems orderly, but it is also featureless and constrained. Mildred shuffles through life like a sleepwalker, narcotized by an unceasing stream of televised entertainment and drugs. Montag appears to be an obedient fireman, but he has a dangerous secret: He has become curious about books and has begun squirreling away a few that he was assigned to burn. In his job, he has torched thousands of books obediently, but once he begins reading, he appreciates the weight of what he has destroyed. "For the first time," he thinks, "I realized that a man was behind each one of the books." One day, Mildred discovers him reading and reports him to his colleagues in the fire department, and they descend, burning down his house and his books. The firemen then try to kill him, but Montag manages to escape. He flees the city, and eventually, he stumbles on a camp of outcasts. They are book lovers, living on the lam, who are trying to preserve literature by memorizing books. They constantly recite to help them memorize; the encampment pulses with the sound of voices chanting Shakespeare and Proust all day long. As one member of the group tells Montag, they are "bums on the outside, libraries inside." They are saving books by returning them to their origins — to the tradition of oral storytelling, which gave stories their durability before paper and ink could.

Unexpectedly, Bradbury's description of books on fire isn't horrible; in fact, they seem marvelous, almost magical. He describes them as "black butterflies" or roasted birds, "their wings ablaze with red and yellow feathers." In the book, fire isn't repulsive; it's seductive — a gorgeous, mysterious power that can transmute material objects. Fire is "the thing man wanted to invent but never did." The elegance of these descriptions makes the idea of incinerating books even more disturbing: It's like a ballet depicting a million little murders.

When he finished writing the book, Bradbury tried to come up with a better title than "The Fireman." He couldn't think of a title he liked, so one day, on an impulse, he called the chief of the Los Angeles Fire Department and asked him the temperature at which paper burned. The chief's answer became Bradbury's title: *Fahrenheit 451.* When Central Library burned in 1986, everything in the Fiction section from A through L was destroyed, including all of the books by Ray Bradbury.

Libraries burn during peacetime, too. There are about two hundred library fires a year in the United States, and countless more in libraries around the world. Many are caused by accidents such as short circuits, over-heated fans, bad coffeepots, lightning strikes. Flames that leaped from a fireplace to a floorboard destroyed Harvard Library in 1764. A sparking floor fan resulted in the loss of all the books in Temple University's law library in 1972. In 1988, one of the largest libraries in the world — the National Academy of Sciences Library in Leningrad, which had a collection begun in 1714 — was consumed by a huge fire that destroyed or damaged four hundred thousand books; millions more that were soaked with water were ruined. The fire was attributed to bad wiring. While the library was burning, firefighters didn't go into the building; they just parked two dozen fire engines nearby and sprayed water on it for close to twenty-four hours. When the fire was finally extinguished, a bulldozer arrived to clear the piles of damaged books, but protesters turned it away. They then gathered the salvageable wet books and took them home, hung them on clotheslines, and attempted to repair them. The day after the fire, the director of the library, Vladimir Filov, told reporters that only five thousand dollars' worth of books had been damaged. The following day, Filov was hospitalized with what was reported to be "heart problems." He then disappeared from public view.

Many library fires are the result of casual vandalism. Over the years, lit matches tossed in book return slots caused many fires. Perhaps a few people mistook the book return for a trash receptacle, but most people probably did it because they were compelled to do something stupid. These kinds of fires became so common that most libraries now have book drops separated from the main building, so if a fire breaks out in the drop, it will have nowhere to go.

For a long time, it was believed that the leading cause of library fires was careless smoking. Then libraries banned smoking. The number of fires should have declined, but in fact, they increased. Investigators now believe that the majority of library fires are deliberately set. Arson is a popular crime. In 1986, the year Central Library burned, 5,400 arsons were reported in Los Angeles. In most cases, arson is for profit — typically, someone will burn his or her own building in order to collect insurance money. Some fires are set to avenge a broken romance or a failed business deal. Some fires in government buildings are political statements. People sometimes set fires with plans to put them out so they will appear valiant. Firefighters call these "vanity fires" or "hero fires." Fires are sometimes set to cover up other crimes. That is, a person might murder someone and then burn the building that contains the body so it becomes more difficult to investigate the murder or even know that it was a murder. (This is a movie plot cliché, but it happens to occur in real life.) Some fires are set by people who suffer from pyromania, an impulse control disorder that causes them to find gratification in seeing things burn.

Los Angeles has had its share of spectacular fires. It is a hot, dry, crackling city, a firebox. You have the sensation here of flame simmering just below the surface, brooding, lapping at underbrush; in the dry brush and parched grass you feel the presence of fire unborn, waiting to explode. The buildings burn and the hills burn. The fires in Los Angeles have names. The Thomas Fire. The La Tuna Fire. The Proud Bird Fire. The Station Fire. In the 1980s, a rash of fires broke out in and around Los Angeles, a hot ring necklacing the city. They were triggered by a simple incendiary device made of a lit cigarette, three matches, and a rubber band, wrapped in a piece of notebook paper. The majority of the arsons were in the city of Glendale, which abuts Los Angeles, and over the course of a few years, sixty-seven houses were destroyed there. Several fires were set near conventions of arson investigators; a few were set in hardware stores; many were on vacant lots. One at Warner Bros. Studios destroyed the set of *The Waltons*. By the mid-1980s, the fires caused by this little device had done millions of dollars in damage.

Around this time, a Glendale fire captain and arson expert named John Leonard Orr wrote a novel. He described *Points of Origin* to a literary agent as a fact-based work that followed a series of actual arsons. "As in the real case," he wrote, "the arsonist in my novel is a firefighter." The agent agreed to represent the book. When publishers asked about the novel's uncanny parallels to the ongoing arsons in Los Angeles, the agent shrugged them off, saying, "We live in L.A.! Everyone's got a script or book they're trying to sell." Shortly before the novel was shopped around to publishers, a Glendale hardware store called Ole's Home Center burned down, killing four people. A similar scene was described in *Points of Origin.* Orr's book was published in paperback by a company called Infinity Publishing. Even though he was a fire captain, something about Orr's demeanor bothered the rest of the Glendale arson team, and they placed a tracking device in his car. It revealed that he had visited many of the arson sites just before the fires broke out. Later, his fingerprint was found at one scene. He was always considered a decent guy but also a bit of an oddball. As suspicion about him grew, detectives discovered Orr had once applied to the Los Angeles Police Department but was rejected because the police psychologist assessed him as being "schizoid." Eventually, Orr was charged with more than twenty counts of arson and four counts of murder. He was convicted of most of the counts. He faced the death penalty but was sentenced to life in prison without possibility of parole. He is thought to have set more than two thousand fires in and around Los Angeles. After he was incarcerated, the number of brush fires in the Glendale area dropped by ninety percent.

The fire at Central Library wasn't the only time a library in Los Angeles burned. In 1982, the Hollywood Branch Library was destroyed by an arson fire that remains unsolved. It is believed that someone had started a small fire near the building that then spread out of control. The library was so badly damaged that it had to be torn down, and only twenty thousand of its books could be saved. Central Library itself burned two times after the main fire in April 1986. That September, a fire started in the middle of the music and arts collection, where a number of books and manuscripts were still on the shelves. It was relatively small compared to April's seven-hour fire-storm, and crews extinguished it in a quick thirty-six minutes. But investigators were baffled. The building had been closed to all but salvage crews and a skeleton staff of librarians. The room had only one access point, and a guard had inspected it fifteen minutes before the fire began. A man lingering outside the building during the fire was arrested, but it turned out he had been hanging around in hopes of selling marijuana. The library staff, already shaken by the main fire, was unnerved by the second one. A month later, another fire broke out, this time in the library's basement. This one, at least, had an obvious source: A worker on the salvage crew accidentally dropped heated material in a chute to the basement, where it landed in a trash pile and began to burn.

10.

Flipping Properties: Generate Instant Cash Profits in Real Estate (2006)
By Bronchick, William
333.6 B869

Devious Maids: The Complete First Season (2014)
DVD

The 21-Day Yoga Body: A Metabolic Makeover & Life-Styling Manual to Get You Fit, Fierce, and Fabulous in Just 3 Weeks (2013)
By Nardini, Sadie
613.71 N224

Street Fighter: The Graphic Novel, Based on the Video Game (1994)

For a while, Arin Kasparian was making sandwiches at Subway. He didn't think of it as a permanent career, but he was settling into the Subway life so comfortably that his mother began to worry. She wanted him to do something more worthwhile than making meatball marinara foot-longs, so she urged him to apply for a job at the library. At first Kasparian wasn't interested — for one thing, he got free food at Subway — but his sister persuaded him to apply just to make their mother happy. "I had to choose between getting free sandwiches or being with books," Kasparian said. "And making Ma happy." Kasparian is in his mid-twenties, with mussy black hair and a chirpy, playful manner. When we spoke, he was at the circulation desk in the main lobby of Central Library, just starting his shift. "Applying for the library turned out to be the best thing I've ever done," he said. His real ambition had always been to direct movies, but then "reality hit," as he puts it, and he took the full measure of how difficult it could be to achieve that goal. Now he plans to go to library school and become a children's and young adult librarian. He said he wakes up in the morning feeling happy. "I feel like . . . I'm all right!" he said. "Everything's good!"

In 1997, library school administrators began to notice that applications were inching up; that the average age of applicants was inching down; and that many library science students were coming from backgrounds in arts, or social justice, or technology. Many, or at least more than in the past, were male. A number of them had tattoos. Many said they were drawn to the profession because it combined information management with public good. Librarians also make a decent living. In the Los Angeles system, the entry level salary is more than sixty thousand dollars, and a division librarian, overseeing many branches, can earn close to two hundred thousand. The new, younger interest in the profession has changed it already. There is a comic-book series about a librarian; an action figure of beloved Seattle librarian Nancy Pearl; dozens of librarian blogs, including one called *The World's Strongest Librarian;* and a sense that being a librarian is an opportunity to be a social activist championing free speech and immigrant rights and homelessness concerns while working within the Dewey decimal system. As far as I could tell, Kasparian was the end result of a change that might have dated from 1995, when Parker Posey played a library clerk in the independent film *Party Girl*.

Kasparian called out, "Next!" and a teenage girl with grass green hair stepped forward and checked out a graphic novel. After her, a good-looking older man in a taupe business suit checked out two travel guides to Taipei. Kasparian kept his eyes glued on the patrons' faces while he waited on them, processing their books more by feel than by sight. When the businessman left, Kasparian whispered to me, "I never know if I should look or not look at what they're checking out." He grinned. "Sometimes I do look, and you just can't *believe* such a book exists." Just then, a woman a few spots back in the line waved to him. He told me she was a library patron — "I know her, but I don't really *know* her. I mean, I know her from here, so I know her in that certain way . . ." He trailed off, not sure he was describing the relationship accurately. When the woman got up to the desk, Kasparian greeted her brightly and said he hadn't seen her in a while. The woman smiled and said, "You're right, I haven't been here in a while. I had twins."

Behind her was a sad-faced woman with

her hair in a messy bun. She inhaled, exhaled, and then said, "I'm looking for a yoga book."

A gray-haired man in a baggy brown coat approached the desk holding a list of twenty movie titles in alphabetical order, starting with *Anaconda* and *Gigli*. "Can I get these?" he asked Kasparian, who nodded and said, "You certainly can!"

A young man with hair in braids that reached his waist came up next, saying, "Where would I find an AA book?"

Two middle-aged men, wearing matching polo shirts, checked out three guides to Disney World.

A small woman with a head of brown ringlets came to the desk and dropped a towering pile of Magic Tree House books on the desk. "For my eight-year-old daughter," she said to Kasparian without being asked. "She just can't get enough of these."

A young man with a shaved head, returning fifteen books. "Some of these are overdue," he said. Kasparian looked at his computer and said the fines came to $10.40. "Okay," the young man said with deliberation, "I'll pay ten dollars."

At the desk beside Kasparian, Nelson Torres was at the end of his shift. He told me he always knew he wanted to work with the public because he considers himself friendly and easygoing. He said he never had been much of a reader, but he started working at the library when he was in high school and has stayed ever since. While he was talking, a man approached the desk and asked if the library had a DVD of a television show called *Devious Maids*.

"That's a good show," Torres said, nodding. As he was looking up where *Devious Maids* was shelved, a woman stopped and patted his desk. "How's your mother, Nelson?" she said. "Great," he said to her, and then turned back to the man and gave directions to *Devious Maids*.

Another library assistant, Garrett Langan, walked over from behind the desk and put his hand on Torres's shoulder. "You're done, Nelson," Langan said, laughing. "The guards will put your chains back on now."

Selena Terrazas, the principal librarian whose fiefdom includes the Computer Center, the reference desk, the Children's and Teen Department, and the circulation desk, strolled by and cast an appraising eye on the scene. She is a warm, droll woman with blue hair and fashionable glasses. She looked at her fitness tracker and said, "I put on ten thousand steps a day running around this building!" and then disappeared into

196

the workroom behind the desk.

When I turned back to Kasparian, he was helping a young man from England apply for a library card. A woman with wild hair and a dirty pink backpack ambled by, looking woozy. Kasparian said that when he first started working at the library, "the sight of the homeless was kind of scary," but now he recognizes many of them, so it isn't as scary. He said knowing them actually made him feel good, and in his words, "they sort of give me energy." I asked him to elaborate, and he said, "It makes me feel . . . important." He sounded a little bashful, and then added, "Like I'm doing something that really helps."

11.

Downtown with Huell Howser [videorecording]/#110, Church of the Open Door (2007)
  DVD 979.41 L88Do-6

ARCO at 125 Years: Celebrating the Past, Anticipating the Future (1992)
  By Cook, Lodwrick M.
  338.78 A8815Co

Missouri: A Guide to the "Show Me" State (1941)
  By Writers' Program of The Works Projects Administration in the State of Missouri
  977.8 W956

How to Write Successful Fundraising Letters (1996)

To have been city librarian of Los Angeles at the time of the fire would have been trying. The staff was distraught. The main library was closed, with no schedule for reopening. Insurance helped cover damage to the building — the cracked concrete, the layers of soot and grime, the holes drilled into the roof by the fire department. Actually, Central Library, with its thick skin, had weathered the fire quite well. What the insurance didn't cover was the building's contents. The estimated cost of replacing the four hundred thousand lost books was over $14 million — $6 million for books, $6 million for periodicals, and over $2 million for the patent collection and other science and technology documents. The cost of storing and repairing the seven hundred thousand damaged books could only be guessed at. The money to restock the library simply didn't exist.

The city librarian, Wyman Jones, considered himself well acquainted with struggle. He was born in Missouri in 1929. His father had been a high school principal, but his extended family were dirt farmers. "It was really bad for us, the Depression," he told me recently. I had called him in Portland, Oregon, where he moved after retiring from the library. When I first explained that I was writing a book about the library, he said he wouldn't talk to me because he was planning to write his own book on the subject. He said he was going to call his book "Downwind of a Belly Dancer." After insisting in forceful terms that he had no intention of granting me an interview, he kept me on the phone over an hour. This was the pattern every time we spoke over the next several months:

He would tell me why he wasn't going to talk to me, and then he wouldn't let me off the phone. Sometimes I made up fake excuses to hang up after an hour or so, when my hand had gotten tired from taking notes or I had to cook dinner. Talking to him was like engaging in a fistfight with someone gazing at himself in a mirror while punching you. "Before you write your book, you should really learn something about libraries," he said more than once. "What do you know about it? You're not a librarian." During our first conversation, he returned several times to the subject of the Depression, then repeated that it had been very hard for his family. "I'm not trying to

CALIFORNIA
LIBRARIAN

January 1971

Wyman Jones

convince you, Susan," he said. "I'm *telling* you."

Jones ran library systems in Texas before he came to Los Angeles. He had the reputation there as a builder of branches, and when he arrived in California in 1970, he intended to tear down Central Library and construct something newer, bigger, and at a different address. He had no attachment to the landmark Bertram Goodhue Building.

Whenever we talked about the building, he dismissed it as the work of a "prima donna architect" who didn't know "a damn thing about libraries." He thought Goodhue was overrated in general. "The architectural world doesn't think much of this building," he said. I told him that I had actually read a lot of praise for it, and that many architects considered it something of a masterpiece. "Well, there may be a certain amount of public sentimentality because people used to go there to read or something like that," he said, practically snorting. "I don't like anyone kidding me by telling me it's a wonderful piece of architecture."

When a coalition of architects, preservationists, and urban planners prevailed and the city finally decided to renovate and expand Central rather than tear it down, Jones conceded the point and grudgingly oversaw the plans. He treated the fire as just one more thing in a long list of annoyances visited upon him in his twenty years as city librarian. "Look, I went through three earthquakes and three riots while I was there," he said one afternoon when we were on the phone. "That, plus three heart attacks." He said he found the librarians often maddening and always too liberal. ("Their union is ridiculous. Twenty years I ran that place, and they never gave me credit for a single thing.") Worse were city administrators, whom he regarded with particular disgust. "City council? I thought of them as a difficult girlfriend," he said. "You got to do a magic trick, you got to play the piano for them, you got to keep them happy, that's all. I just had too many years of working with second-rate politicians and incompetents. And you know what? I worked so hard and so long, and still I never took a single bribe." He told me that he was so well-known in Los Angeles during his tenure at the library that he couldn't go anywhere without being recognized. I was surprised to hear this, because I don't think most people recognize the head of libraries in their city, especially out of context, but Jones insisted that if he had dinner out at a restaurant, he would be buttonholed countless times. "I was at the library twenty years. Twenty years! I couldn't go anywhere without someone wanting something from me. Do you know what that's like? Can you see why I wouldn't retire in a city like that?" he asked me. "Can you understand why I moved?" When I didn't respond immediately, he snapped, "Hey, give me an answer! Don't try to please me. Tell me why I had to move."

Even if the city had a spare $14 million sitting around, restocking a major library like Central would have been a chore. Jones said that many of the books were out of print, and the ones that were available had to be ordered from seven thousand different vendors. "It takes enormous expertise to know where to get these damn things in the first place," Jones said sharply. "It takes a lot of time and a hell of a lot of money. Do you think it would be easy? Do you? Well, believe me, it wasn't."

Lodwrick Cook, the head of ARCO, was the cochairman of the "Save the Books" campaign, which was formed to raise funds to replace the library's lost books. Cook could see the library from his offices on Fifth Street, and as soon as the fire was tamped down, he offered Wyman Jones and the library's administrative staff space in the ARCO offices. ARCO's head of public relations, Carlton Norris, warned the librarians that "oil people on occasion . . . use terse, coarse, and direct language" that they might find disconcerting, but Jones nonetheless accepted the offer.

The librarians were used to scrimping on a municipal budget, so they were awed by the luxury of ARCO's offices. According to

Carlton Norris, the collating copy machine was the greatest source of wonder. The ARCO staff was, in turn, awed by the librarians. Norris said many of them had grown up in oil towns so small they didn't have libraries. They viewed the librarians as elegant, learned, refined.

Lodwrick Cook kicked off Save the Books with a five-hundred-thousand-dollar gift from ARCO and began rallying support. He wrote personal letters to half of Hollywood. "Dear George," he wrote to director George Lucas, "a terrible tragedy summons you and me . . . God knows you are besieged almost hourly with someone plucking at your lapel, asking for money . . . but the Library is singularly the seedbed and the feeding ground for the creative community in this town." He wrote to Jack Valenti, head of the Motion Picture Association of America, who agreed to serve on the committee once he heard that Lew Wasserman, who owned Universal Studios, had signed on. Together, Valenti and Cook sent letters to every studio head and major producer in the city, asking for contributions. The goal was to raise $10 million to save the city's books.

The solicitations went out immediately. The money came fast. Some of the donations were large. The J. Paul Getty Trust, for instance, gave $2 million; the Times Mirror Foundation, which then owned the *Los Angeles Times,* gave $500,000. Sidney Sheldon, the author of best-selling potboilers such as *The Other Side of Midnight,* gave $25,000. Dr. Seuss gave $10,000. Some donations were just a few dollars. Many of the small donations were accompanied by notes explaining why the donor wanted to support the library. The reasons were myriad. "Why would an old couple in San Francisco give to the Los Angeles Library to save the books?" one note read. "Well, [my] father collapsed and died in the LA Public Library on July 17, 1952. Heart Attack or stroke. I never found out which. Good luck with your campaign." There were donations of books, including a complete hardbound set by Louis L'Amour from his widow; a large collection from the family of *Tarzan* author Edgar Rice Burroughs; fourteen hundred cookbooks from the estate of a collector. Charlton Heston threw a fundraiser cocktail party for Save the Books. Outdoor advertising companies donated almost sixty billboards around the city to help spread the word.

Mayor Tom Bradley urged his constituents to give whatever they could. Library fundraising spread across the city. Schoolkids held bottle and aluminum can drives. Neighborhoods had Save the Books yard sales. There was a shared sense of purpose in the city that many people found inspiring. It was another version of that volunteer brigade on the day of the fire: Strangers working side by side, book by book, to save what the fire had missed. In a city that could seem at times fractured and fractious, concern for the library offered a rare experience of being glued together. Still, every now and then, objections were raised. "Dear Mayor Bradley," one dissenter wrote,

I find it obscene that people are eager to spend vast sums of money to save BOOKS when dozens of beautiful, healthy, intelligent, loving dogs and cats are put to sleep by the city EVERY DAY, because the city is TOO DAMN CHEAP to keep animals up for adoption . . . As usual, their needs continue to be forgotten, while a momentarily fashionable cause is subscribed to by a bunch of PRETENSION INTELLECTUALS. PS: And let's not forget the dolphins that are dying in Santa Monica Bay. *'Save the Books'* indeed!

The committee brainstormed other fundraising schemes to complement the donations. Jones suggested holding the world's biggest bingo game (the proposal was voted down). Someone else suggested a Los Angeles Lakers inter-squad charity game with celebrity coaches, such as Joan Van Ark from *Knots Landing* (approved and scheduled, with Coach Van Ark on duty). A shop with Save the Books merchandise (mugs, bookmarks, T-shirts) opened in the lobby of the ARCO building. A big-ticket fundraising gala featuring Prince Andrew and Sarah Ferguson was organized with military precision, including providing library supporters with conversation topics for the special guests. Lodwrick Cook's wife was given a briefing sheet warning that Sarah Ferguson "is not interested in fashion or hairstyles" and that Prince Andrew "is not into sports, but Sarah is."

Twenty thousand schoolkids and two thousand adults entered the Save the Books essay contest, which offered round-trip tickets to Europe among its prizes. The essay subject was "What the Library Means to Me." Ray Bradbury was one of the judges. The winning essays were deep, disquieting, and darkly emotional. Most of them read like confessions of an almost brutal sense of loneliness, eased only by a place like the library, where lonely people can feel slightly less lonely together. "For years, I was a castle in the library, sharing a countryside of silence, in silence, with others similarly locked in their own solitude . . ." one began. "I began to understand the planet I live on and learned to hang on to my hope . . . and somehow the sadness of everyday life around me became bearable . . ."

A winning entry was a poem written by a librarian named Jill Crane, who had worked on the cleanup after the fire. It began:

We held charred and watersoaked
chunks of books in our hands.
history, imagination, knowledge
crumbling in our fingers.
we packed what was left.

Just across from the library's south entrance and a block from the ARCO building sat a hulking turn-of-the-century structure on Hope Street with a four-thousand-seat auditorium and a facade spanned by nine large archways. For decades, the building had been the tallest in Los Angeles. It was built originally as the headquarters of an evangelical Christian congregation called the Church of the Open Door. The building's neon signs, which spelled out JESUS

SAVES, could be seen from almost anywhere in town, and hymns blasted from the carillon twice a day could be heard almost as widely.

As its downtown membership dwindled, the Church of the Open Door decided to relocate to the suburbs. The building was sold in 1986 to Gene Scott, the pastor of a Pentacostal congregation known as the Westcott Christian Center. Scott was a Stanford Ph.D. from rural Idaho who described himself as "the most agnostic believer and the most believing agnostic." After youthful rebellion, followed by slightly less youthful introspection — all of which is detailed in his essay "A Philosopher Looks at Christ" — Scott began preaching in 1968. He attracted an ardent following. Beginning in 1975, his services were televised on the Faith Broadcasting Network. Within a few years, his show was broadcast around the clock and could be seen in 180 countries. His followers viewed his sermons as prescriptive. The staff at Central Library noticed that whenever Scott preached about a particular book, there was an enormous uptick in requests for it. Scott occasionally discussed what he believed was the mystical power of the Great Pyramids. Whenever he did, there was a run on Peter Tompkins's

Secrets of the Great Pyramid at the library.

Scott didn't comport himself like an ordinary church elder. He had lush silver hair and a bushy beard and wore tiny round reading glasses on the end of his nose. He was fond of wearing headgear such as pith helmets and sombreros during his sermons, and he had a habit of scribbling in Greek, Hebrew, and Aramaic on chalkboards set around him. When he wasn't at the chalkboard, he tended to stare straight into the camera. Some people found his gaze unnerving, but others found it magnetic. In general, his tone was blunt. He often directed questions straight into the camera — questions like, for example, "Do you find me boring?" While preaching, he often swore. Occasionally, during homilies, he smoked cigars. On other occasions, he had nice-looking young women dance on-stage while he preached. Later in his career, he was filmed for his television show preaching from the backseat of his Cadillac convertible, accompanied by some of those same young women dressed in bikinis. Scott was divorced and lived on an estate in Pasadena. He was something of a polymath. He played guitar, owned one of the largest private collections of Bibles in the world, and was a playwright. One of his plays, *Jumpin' at the*

Oval Office, was the story of an imagined jam session between Fats Waller and President Franklin Delano Roosevelt. He was a deft fund-raiser. He liked to exhort his listeners to donate to his church with declarations like "If you don't send money, you should vomit on yourself with your head up in the air." His technique seemed to be effective. On a preacher's salary, he bought a private jet and a few horse ranches. When questioned about the appropriateness of his church raising so much money, Scott answered, "As far as I know, my ministry is not a member of the Evangelical Council for Financial Accountability."

Someone at the library suggested that it would be great for Save the Books to have a fund-raising telethon like the one Jerry Lewis did for muscular dystrophy. Gene Scott, who was on the Save the Books committee, announced that he wanted to host the telethon in the church's vast auditorium and act as the master of ceremonies. Some members of the committee found Gene Scott a bit outrageous, but they acknowledged that having him host would be a boon because of his enormous audience and persuasive personality. His participation was endorsed by Wyman Jones, who offered to demonstrate both of his extracurricular talents — jazz piano and magic — on the show.

The telethon was held in January 1987 and ran live for twenty-four hours straight, then was rerun for the following twenty-four hours. Volunteers manned a bank of two hundred phones for call-in pledges. The fund-raising goal was $2 million. Celebrities were wrangled to appear on the show, reading from their favorite books. There were dozens of celebrity readers, including Red Buttons, former governor Pat Brown, Angie Dickinson, Lakers coach Pat Riley, Ernest Borgnine, Eddie Albert, and Henry Kissinger. Dinah Shore read from *The Prince of Tides.* Charlton Heston read the last chapter of *Moby-Dick.* Zsa Zsa Gabor showed up but forgot to bring a book.

Some of the other celebrity guests performed. Lodwrick Cook, known as a staid corporate executive, danced alone onstage to the song "Just a Gigolo." A reporter covering the event described his presentation as "seductive." Cook's wife later told the *Los Angeles Times,* "My mother called me and told me [Lod] was dancing . . . and I said, 'Oh, my God.' " Cook's performance was so stimulating that, within minutes, it generated a hundred thousand dollars in pledges. Wyman Jones excelled, especially on piano. Throughout the telethon, Gene Scott's band, which was named the Un-Band, played Beatles covers. Scott smoked his way through a case of cigars, announced each reader and performer with a flourish, and in general seemed delighted by the spectacle, by the gush of pledges, by the unusual assortment of powerful and famous people arrayed on his stage. In the end, the telethon exceeded its $2 million goal. It might have been one of the strangest nights in the history of Los Angeles, which is a city that has had its share of strange nights.

12.

*Special Report of the History
and Present Condition of the
Sheep Industry of the United
States* (1892)
Published by Authority of the
Secretary of Agriculture
636.305 U51

Let's Go Gold Mining (1964)
By Hall, J. P.
332.4973 H177

*Slavery in the West: The Untold
Story of the Slavery of Native
Americans in the West* (2011)
By Nixon, Guy
970.3 M685Ni

Les Caresses . . . (1921)
By Richepin, Jean
F.841 R528-4

Among the first books acquired by the Los Angeles library were *Hints to Horse-keepers; On the Sheep Industry; How to Make Money;* and the simply titled *Honey Bees.* The earliest public library in the city was established in 1844, when a social club called Amigos del País opened a reading room in their dance hall. At that time, there weren't very many books in Southern California, and the larger collections were in the Spanish missions and unavailable to the public. When Amigos del País fell into debt, the reading room closed. Interest in having a library in town persevered, and in 1872, an association formed to establish a library in the city. To raise money, the association sponsored a "Dickens Party," which partygoers attended dressed as their favorite Charles Dickens character. The party lasted for a full week. *Hints to Horse-keepers* and *On the Sheep Industry* were purchased with proceeds of the party.

The first thing the library needed was a building. A member of the library association named John Downey agreed to donate space in a building he owned, the Downey Block, in the center of the city. The block had small offices and an outdoor arena where weekly slave-labor auctions were held. The slavery was permitted under an

1850 California law that allowed white people to buy Native American children as "apprentices," and to "bid" on Native Americans who were declared "vagrant," and oblige them to work off the cost of the bid. (The law, known as Act for the Government and Protection of Indians, was not repealed entirely until 1937.)

The library opened in January 1873. Membership was five dollars a year. At the time, five dollars represented several days' pay for an average worker, so only affluent people were able to join. Library rules were schoolmarmish and scoldy. Men were required to remove their hats upon entering the library, and patrons were discouraged from reading too many novels, lest they turn into what the association labeled "fiction fiends." Books considered to be "of dubious moral effect, or trashy, ill-written ones, or flabby ones" were excluded from the collection. Women were not allowed to use the main facilities, but a "Ladies Room" with a selection of magazines was added soon after the library opened. Children were not allowed in the library at all.

The space in the Downey Block consisted of a reading room furnished with long tables and straight-backed chairs. There was a small checkroom where patrons stored their hats and umbrellas; on occasion, people stored chickens, ducks, and turkeys. Even though the new library was welcomed, many people worried that sharing books and being in close quarters could spread disease. The space was "cramped and inadequate ... a menace to life," according to the *Los Angeles Herald.* At the time, influenza, smallpox, and typhus were rampant in cities. One city official told the *Los Angeles Times* that anyone who checked out a book knowing someone in his or her family had a contagious disease was committing "nothing short of a crime."

The first city librarian of Los Angeles was a dour asthmatic named John Littlefield. He hated the crowded space more than anyone, and he tore out of the reading room whenever he could to hide in his office and smoke a medicinal compound of jimsonweed to soothe his lungs. According to one of the library's early annual reports, Littlefield's smoking was unpopular with library patrons. "As [Littlefield] coughed and wheezed and gurgled and smoked," the report states, "the abominable fumes of the burning [jimsonweed] permeated the whole establishment and nearly choked everybody in it." Littlefield, in general, seemed burdened, regretful, and tormented. Any time

Mary Foy

he was called out of his office, he muttered, "Well, if I must, I suppose I must," which was followed by a loud groan. Somehow he managed to last six years in the post. His successor was an alcoholic painter named Patrick Connolly who barely made it through the year.

Mary Foy was only eighteen years old when she was hired to replace Connolly. While it is surprising that such a young person would have been considered for the position, the bigger surprise was that this young person was a woman, since in 1880 the library was still an organization run by, and catering to, men. Women were not yet allowed to have their own library cards and were permitted only in the Ladies' Room. No library in the country had a female head librarian, and only a quarter of all American library employees were women. The feminization of librarianship was still a decade away.

Foy turned out to be a stern and efficient administrator, even though she was so young that her father had to walk her home from work every day. The library didn't have a catalog, but Foy was so familiar with the material that she could find anything on the shelves in just a matter of minutes. She pursued overdue fines with a vengeance, depositing them in a leather purse she wore slung across her chest like a bandolier. The adult male patrons respected her. Among her regular responsibilities was refereeing their chess and checker games, which were played all day long in the reading room. She was also constantly settling bets between patrons who were arguing points of trivia.

Mary Foy probably would have continued as city librarian for years, but when the mayor who had appointed her left office in

1884, the library board voted to remove her. The reason cited was that Foy's father was doing well enough financially that he could now afford to take care of her; it was presumed that she no longer needed a job. In addition, a popular rancher named L. D. Gavitt had just passed away, and his daughter Jessie was desperate for work, so the board decided to appoint her to the position. Foy left under protest and published a sharp criticism of the library board in the newspaper as she left. She went on to become a teacher and a suffragette.

Gavitt and then her successor, Lydia Prescott, ran the library quietly and without incident. In 1889, a newspaper reporter from Ohio named Tessa Kelso was appointed to the job. Kelso was broad and busty, wore her hair short, and went out in public bareheaded — a shock at a time when most women had long hair tied up in chignons or topknots and never appeared on the street without a hat. Kelso was unmarried and smoked cigarettes. People referred to her as "unconventional." She was so brilliant and forceful that she persuaded the board to hire her even though she had no relevant job experience except that she once covered a library convention for her newspaper.

Kelso thought the library was stodgy and needed to modernize. She abolished the membership fee. In no time, the number of cardholders rose from a little more than one hundred people to twenty thousand. She moved most of the books onto open shelves and allowed children over twelve years old to use the library if they had an average of ninety on their school exams. She set up "delivery stations," an early version of branch libraries, in outlying areas where immigrants were settling. She moved the library from its crowded rooms in the Downey Block to a much larger space in the new City Hall building. With the additional space, she hoped the library could expand and begin loaning more than books; she pictured a storeroom of tennis racquets, footballs, "indoor games, magic lanterns, and the whole paraphernalia of healthy, wholesome amusement that is . . . out of the reach of the average boy and girl." She believed a library could be more than a repository of books; she felt it should be "the entertainment and educational center of the city." This ambition never came to pass during her tenure, but it anticipated by almost a hundred years the modern notion of what a library can be.

Although Kelso wasn't trained as a librarian, she wanted a highly trained staff. She hired as her deputy a woman named Adelaide Hasse, who was the champion female bicycle racer in Los Angeles as well as a trained librarian, and they established a library school — one of the first library programs on the West Coast. The school became famous for its rigor. A number of its students reacted to the academic pressure with fainting spells and nervous breakdowns. In 1898, a student at the school named Corinne Wise died suddenly. Some people attributed her death to extreme anxiety over her exams. Kelso dismissed this as nonsense and even suspended two students for gossiping about Wise's death.

When Kelso arrived, the library's collection was just twelve thousand books. She acquired new books, and during her tenure, the collection grew to three hundred thousand. In 1893, Kelso signed a purchase order for a large number of novels, including one by the French author Jean Richepin. A protégé of Baudelaire, Richepin was known for the fulsome erotic tone of his work. After he published *La Chanson des gueux* in 1876, Richepin was charged and tried in French courts on the grounds of gross indecency. By the time Kelso ordered

Le Cadet, Richepin had attained a measure of acclaim in Europe, but his work was still considered shocking in the United States.

The library's book committee signed off on the purchase of *Le Cadet,* but it's unclear whether anyone on the committee knew what the book contained. For one thing, none of them spoke French, and the book might have been one of many on a list that was only quickly perused. *Le Cadet* arrived at the library with no fanfare. It was processed and shelved like any other book and might well have stayed unnoticed for decades. But through some serendipity, the book was noticed by a *Los Angeles Examiner* reporter who was familiar with Richepin's racy reputation. The reporter's resulting story about the book caused a commotion. It triggered a score of critical editorials in local papers, calling Kelso's judgment into question. The head of the First Methodist Church of Los Angeles, Reverend J. W. Campbell, believed Kelso was flirting with the devil, so he began a public prayer vigil for her soul. "Oh Lord, vouchsafe thy saving grace to the librarian of the Los Angeles City Library," Campbell preached, "and cleanse her of all sin, and make her a woman worthy of her office."

Kelso left *Le Cadet* on the shelf and then

took what the *Los Angeles Times* called "a sensational and decidedly novel action" — namely, she sued Reverend Campbell for slander. She argued that his condemnation had interfered with her ability to do her job and that she hadn't known that *Le Cadet* was controversial. What was more, she pointed out that the book committee, not she, approved all acquisitions. In her suit, she noted that she wasn't a Methodist, so it was particularly slanderous for a Methodist minister to condemn her. She asked for $5,000 in damages — the equivalent of almost $140,000 today.

The case twisted and turned the issue of free speech for months. Kelso maintained that the acquisition of the book was an expression of her free speech. Reverend Campbell argued that his right to pray for someone's soul was an expression of *his* free speech. As the lawsuit advanced, Reverend Campbell's right to free speech seemed to gain the moral upper hand, though the court decided in Kelso's favor on the grounds that Campbell had indeed intended to disparage her. The church settled for an undisclosed amount, but the victory cost Kelso far more: Public opinion and the library board were never on her side again.

Shortly after the Campbell case, Kelso

sued the city, saying she had never been reimbursed for expenses she had incurred when traveling to a library convention. She was awarded the money, but the enthusiasm for litigation finally did her in, and as soon as that suit was settled, the library board urged her to leave. She resisted, saying she had been good for the library, but the board persisted and prevailed. All library matters were followed by the entire city, so Kelso's forced resignation played out very publicly. The front page of the *Los Angeles Times* declared, "IT'S ALL OVER! Surcease of Agony on the Librarian Question. A special meeting of the board . . . was called yesterday afternoon for the purpose of removing Miss Kelso's scalp with all due ceremony."

After Kelso, the library chugged along under the quiet stewardship of directors Clara Bell Fowler and then Harriet Child Wadleigh. It grew and grew and then outgrew the quarters in City Hall that had at first seemed so capacious. The library was a bit of a madhouse. Patrons elbowed each other at the reading tables. Books spilled out of shelves and off countertops and were stacked on stairs and in the attic. Some moldered in the basement. At the urging of Harriet Wadleigh, the library board launched an appeal to fund a new freestanding library, but nothing came of it. "WANT NEW LIBRARY," a story in the *Los Angeles Herald* reported. "No Funds in Sight Is the Reply."

The library expanded like the city expanded. Los Angeles was flourishing and spreading. In 1887 alone, two thousand Realtors sold property in the city. Southern Pacific Railroad and the Santa Fe Railway were in the middle of a price war, and at one point, a train ticket from Chicago to Los Angeles cost just one dollar, an almost irresistible temptation to head west. The railway compressed the immense, yawning distance across the country into a few days and some spare change. Hundreds of thousands of people rushed to California. Over the next quarter century, it proved to be one of the largest internal migrations in United States history.

In 1898, Harriet Wadleigh's husband struck a vein of gold in their backyard orange grove, and in 1900, the couple decided to go on permanent vacation. The timing was auspicious, as Wadleigh had been tangling with the library board. Her replacement, Mary Letitia Jones, was the first city librarian of Los Angeles to have graduated from a library school. Before coming to Los

Angeles, Jones ran libraries in Nebraska and Illinois, where she had been commended for her pleasantness and professionalism. Jones was thin-lipped and tall and wore a blond chignon that added six inches to her height. She was serious, efficient, and innovative in her own quiet way. She began her term by dropping the age limit for children in the library by two years, allowing ten-year-olds to come in. She recruited African American librarians for branches in neighborhoods with large black populations and encouraged them to build a collection of books about "the Negro experience." The library thrived. It was circulating about four hundred thousand books annually when Jones took over. By 1904, that number had almost doubled.

The general public didn't really agree on the value of public libraries until the end of the nineteenth century. Before that, libraries were viewed as scholarly and elite, rather than an indispensable and democratic public resource. Many public libraries still had membership fees. The change of attitude began with the philanthropy of Scottish businessman Andrew Carnegie, who launched a library-building project in 1890. Carnegie was born in Scotland and then emigrated to the United States. His father was a weaver, and the family teetered between poverty and modest comfort throughout his childhood. As a young boy, he had little money to spare; for instance, he couldn't afford the two-dollar membership fee for the local library. Eventually, he made a fortune in steel and railroads, and at one time he was the richest man in the world. When he reached middle age, he decided to commit the last third of his life to giving away his money. The disappointment of not being able to afford the local library had stuck with him, and he chose libraries as one of the main beneficiaries of his philanthropy. He offered large grants to build libraries in communities that would commit to supporting them with tax revenues. Towns and cities began lobbying to get Carnegie funding, and the process of applying had the effect of rallying interest and support for public libraries. Carnegie ended up building nearly 1,700 libraries in 1,400 communities. He funded six small libraries in Los Angeles, which were added to the main system as branches.

By the time she had reached her fifth year on the job, Mary Jones had reason to assume her job was secure. The board's 1904 annual report noted her fine work. In June 1905, Jones attended the monthly board

Mary Jones

meeting. After the business at hand was completed, the head of the board, a lawyer named Isidore Dockweiler, turned to Jones and asked her to resign. As Jones sat dumbfounded, Dockweiler explained that the board believed it would be in everyone's best interest to have a man run the library. He already had a man in mind — a journalist, poet, editor, historian, and adventurer named Charles Fletcher Lummis.

Even by the standards of the time, Jones's

firing was baffling. Women had run the library in Los Angeles since 1880, dominating the institution before most libraries around the country had women in charge. Unlike Kelso, Jones was uncontroversial. The one rumor that followed her was that Dockweiler, who was a candidate for lieutenant governor and the father of thirteen children, had propositioned her, and that she had turned him down.

The earliest figures in the American library movement were men, most of them from wealthy New England families, who took on librarianship as a form of missionary work, conveying wisdom to the ignorant masses. There were some female librarians, but they were an unempowered minority usually in subordinate roles. When the American Library Association formed in 1876, the founding members were ninety men and thirteen women. Eleven years later, the first library school was established by Melvil Dewey, the creator of the Dewey decimal system. The professionalizing of the field attracted more women, and they were accepted at a time when there were few careers available to women. In addition, many libraries were funded by women's clubs, which made them even more receptive to female employees. But what really brought women into the field was the monumental growth of libraries at the end of the 1800s, primed by Carnegie's example. Communities around the country began building libraries at a clip. The boom meant that there was an immediate need for more librarians. At the time, one of the few job paths open to women was teaching, and librarianship was a natural lateral move. Because the need for librarians was so great, the usual male resistance to opening ranks was overridden by the urgency for more staff. Moreover, as an 1876 article titled "How to Make Town Libraries Successful" suggested, even highly educated women could be offered lower pay than male librarians and still be willing to take the job.

Charles Lummis had arrived in Los Angeles in 1885, when the *Los Angeles Times* offered him a position on its staff. At the time, Lummis was a newspaper reporter in Ohio. He accepted the offer and packed his belongings. Then he decided that he would walk from Ohio to California. The first outfit Lummis wore on his trip was a pair of knickers, a flannel shirt, tomato-red knee socks, low-cut street shoes, and a canvas coat with twenty-three pockets, which he filled with odds and ends picked up along the way, including gold nuggets, deer antlers, tobacco, pretty rocks, and rattlesnake skins. Midway through his walk to California, he swapped his knickers for a pair of buckskin leggings. After arriving in Los Angeles, Lummis continued to dress in a manner that was not typical for a Caucasian male of the 1880s. His favorite outfit was a three-button suit coat and trousers made of bright green wide-wale corduroy, which he wore with a red-and-black-patterned cummerbund. His second favorite outfit was a cropped bolero made of suede and a pair of bell-bottom pants that were so tight no one could figure out how he stuffed himself into them. He almost always accessorized with a wide-brimmed Stetson sombrero and a pair of moccasins. He wore these outfits for the rest of his life, including the five years he served as the city librarian of Los Angeles.

Overall, Lummis's appearance was arresting. He had a long, oval face, a fierce gaze, a beak of a nose, and a rosebud of a mouth. He was small and sinewy, with a prizefighter's tight, taut muscles. He was born in Lynn, Massachusetts, in 1859. His father, a widower, was a stern, unyielding Methodist minister who wanted to raise stern, unyielding children. Lummis rebelled the moment he could ease out of his father's grasp. He went to Harvard for college and socialized with Teddy Roosevelt. Lummis barely squeaked by academically, but he had a reputation as an excellent wrestler, boxer, and poker player. He was also famous for being the man with the longest hair on campus. Many students found the length of Lummis's hair offensive. When he was a sophomore, members of the senior class posted a warning in the student newspaper saying that if Lummis didn't cut his hair, they would get scissors and do it for him.

Lummis didn't have an appetite for a conventional education, but he read and wrote voraciously, especially poetry. In the summer of his junior year, he decided to publish his poems. He thought a book with paper pages would be too ordinary, so he came up with the idea of having the poems printed on birch bark. He got a supply of bark and shaved it into nearly translucent, paperlike sheets. He sewed the binding of each book himself. The book is beautiful, peculiar, light as dust, and tiny — about the size of a large pillbox. Many of the poems are Lummis's ruminations on the natural splendor of New England, but the most popular was an ode to tobacco, one of Lummis's great passions. Called "My Cigarette," it begins:

My Cigarette! Can I forget
How Kate and I, in sunny weather,
Sat in the shade the elm-tree made,
And rolled the fragrant weed together . . .

Lummis had talent for poetry, but his greater talent was for self-promotion. He sent copies of *Birch Bark Poems* to newspapers and magazines. He managed to get the book into the hands of Walt Whitman and Henry Longfellow, who both praised it. Lummis's odd little book ended up selling thousands of copies, an astonishing number for poetry written by a college kid.

After publishing *Birch Bark Poems,* Lummis lost all interest in college. He dropped out of Harvard and told friends he was going to become a newspaperman. Then, in an about-face, he married his girlfriend, a medical student named Dorothea Rhodes, and moved to her family's farm in Ohio. According to Mark Thompson's excellent book *American Character: The Curious Life of Charles Fletcher Lummis and the Rediscovery of the Southwest,* Lummis managed the Rhodes's farm while looking for opportunities to write. Within a year, he was offered a column in the local paper. His column became so popular that it came to the attention of Harrison Gray Otis, the publisher

of the newly launched *Los Angeles Times,*
who persuaded Lummis to move to Los
Angeles and write for his paper.

Lummis liked to say that he walked to
California because he sought "joy and
information." He was ashamed to know so
little about America, and he believed that
crossing it on foot was the remedy. Also, a
long walk suited him; he was restless, curious, and keen for physical challenge. He
was happy to flee the East Coast bourgeoi-
sie. The West seemed raw and original,
somewhere he could invent himself in the
moment — the kind of place where no one
would chase you with scissors if you grew
your hair long. Lummis saw the walk to Los
Angeles, which he called "my tramp," as an
essential journey. It was the first of many he
would undertake in his life.

His tramp was also a performance — a
shrewd bit of packaging, like printing his
poems on birch bark. He knew that if he arrived in California on foot, rather than in a
more typical fashion, he would get attention. Before leaving Ohio, he convinced a
local newspaper to publish his travel diary,
which he would write in the form of a
weekly letter. His first column was titled,
extravagantly, "LUMMIS' LEGS: How

They Measure the Distance Between Cincinnati and Los Angeles. Sixty-three Miles Already Traversed and Only Three Thousand One Hundred and Thirty-Seven Yet to Walk." The columns were funny and chatty and exclamatory. He described the simple challenge of walking thirty miles a day, and what he saw and experienced while he was walking — what he shot while hunting or caught while fishing, whom he met, his many aches and pains, his excitement at meeting his first real cowboys. As he crossed the middle of the country, he described his new fascination with the Southwest and with Native American culture.

The trip was arduous. He was robbed by hoboes in Missouri and struggled through the snow on mountain passes in New Mexico. In Arizona, he fell off a rock outcropping and broke his arm, which he had to set himself using branches and strips of torn cloth. (He later said he was saved from outright calamity because he taught himself to roll cigarettes with one hand.) There were periods when he had very little to eat or drink. For most of the trip, he was completely alone. In Colorado, he adopted an abandoned greyhound puppy that he named Shadow. He loved having Shadow's company, but after a few weeks, the dog developed rabies, and Lummis was forced to shoot him.

Despite the challenges, it was the best time of his life. He was on his own, living by his wits, surrounded by frontier, feeling or seeing something new every mile. He felt alive. He was convinced that the walk was good for his soul. It was definitely good for publicity. His column was carried in a score of newspapers across the country. Other papers covered his trip as a news event. Crowds gathered to watch him pass by. Sometimes when he walked into towns, several hundred people cheered him. By the time he got to California, he was a celebrity.

13.

Charles Lummis

Some Strange Corners of Our Country: The Wonderland of the Southwest (1906)
   By Lummis, Charles Fletcher
   987 L958-3

20,000 Leagues Under the Sea
[sound resource] (2003)
  By Verne, Jules
  E-Audiobook

Century of Struggle: The Women's Rights Movement in the United States (1968)
  By Flexner, Eleanor
  324.373 F619

Encyclopedia of All Nations (1861)
  By Murray, Hugh
  910.3 M982

Lummis didn't seem particularly excited when he arrived in Los Angeles. He described it as "a dull little place of some 12,000 persons . . . [and] perhaps six buildings of three stories or better." Los Angeles of 1885 wasn't much compared to Boston, where Lummis had spent most of his life. It was barely a city. Even in California, Los Angeles was considered much less sophisticated and significant than San Francisco. The city disappointed him, but Lummis was excited about his job at the *Los Angeles Times.* The attention he'd drawn during his tramp followed him there, and circulation jumped the minute his byline appeared.

But almost immediately, his restlessness resurfaced. He did not actually like having a job. He missed the drama of his tramp. To mollify him, the *Times*'s publisher encouraged Lummis to cover stories outside the city. The Apache Wars were ongoing in the Southwest, so Lummis began traveling there to write about them. His interest in the region and its people was abiding. He decided to learn Spanish and began speaking in a patchwork of English and Spanish whenever he could.

On one of those trips, Lummis suffered an attack of paralysis. He recovered enough to be able to ride, shoot a rifle, and roll cigarettes, but he got worse when he returned to Los Angeles, and he could barely drag himself to work. Finally, he told the *Times* that he needed a leave of absence so he could recuperate. He moved to the village of San Mateo, New Mexico. He assumed his job would be waiting for him whenever he was ready for it. But the *Times* had grown impatient with Lummis's wanderlust and unreliability, as had Lummis's wife. The publisher fired him; Dorothea divorced him. Lummis had always spent whatever he'd earned on books and artifacts and travel. He'd never saved any money, and without a job, he struggled along. Once his health improved, he began freelancing as a writer and photographer. He wrote fearlessly about corruption in San Mateo. He had to leave town after one of his stories appeared because he was told that the crime bosses there planned to have him killed. (A hit man tracked him down and shot him in the leg a few months after he left San Mateo.)

As soon as he and Dorothea divorced, he married a woman named Eve Douglas, whom he had met in New Mexico, and then traveled to Peru and Guatemala with the ethnographer Adolph Bandelier, who was studying indigenous people. He and Eve returned to Los Angeles in 1893. He was barely solvent. He worked furiously, taking any job he could find. Against his better instincts, he accepted a position as editor of a regional magazine called *Land of Sunshine,* sponsored by the Chamber of Commerce. Lummis ended up changing the magazine from a boosterish glossy into a serious publication. He renamed it *Out West* and persuaded writers such as Jack London and John Muir to contribute stories. He also began writing his own column. He called it "In the Lion's Den" and wrote it in the voice of an opinionated English-speaking mountain lion.

In addition to *Out West*, he wrote books and poetry and translated important Spanish documents into English. He treasured the scrappy ranch feel of old California, which was quickly disappearing as the region's population grew. Devoting himself to preserving that history, he founded the Southwest Museum and the Landmarks Club of Southern California, which was dedicated to preserving the old Spanish missions. He also spent a lot of his time lobbying for Native American rights, to the annoyance of the federal government.

Lummis scratched together enough money to buy a parcel of land in East Los Angeles, on the edge of Arroyo Seco, and began building a house there. It took him ten years to complete the whimsical stone structure, which he constructed with a frame of abandoned telephone poles and railroad ties. He called the house El Alisal. It was the Lummis family home, but it was also the site of constant gatherings of artists and writers. Lummis nicknamed his parties "noises." Some of the noises were Spanish-themed, with troubadours and traditional food. Others were mock trials in which Lummis accused one of the guests of not knowing how to have fun. The defendant was then interrogated by the other guests, found not guilty, and released to join the festivities. Most of the parties at El Alisal included a lot of alcohol.

Lummis's life wasn't on a course that would lead naturally to becoming a librarian. Most likely, he never imagined having the job until it was offered to him. He was an avid reader, and he did occasionally meet with the library board to encourage collecting books about California and the Southwest. Several members of the library board were regular attendees of the noises at El Alisal. But Lummis did not have any experience or training in the management of a library. When his appointment as city librarian of Los Angeles was announced in 1905, the *Los Angeles Times* editorial board argued he was unfit for the job because he had "never set foot in a library school, wore eccentric corduroy suits and was known to drink and swear on occasion."

At that point, Lummis's personal life was in tatters. He had conducted dozens of extramarital affairs. His partners were rumored to include Arcadia Bandini de Stearns Baker, one of the wealthiest women in California; Kate Wiggin, author of the novel *Rebecca of Sunnybrook Farm;* several of his secretaries; evangelist Aimee Semple

Exterior of El Alisal

The El Alisal living room

McPherson; and the teenage daughter of Harrison Gray Otis, publisher of the *Los Angeles Times,* who first summoned him to Los Angeles. Lummis had also just learned that he had an illegitimate daughter as the result of a brief romance during college. After they met, the girl moved to Los Angeles to live with him.

Not surprisingly, Lummis was the focus of endless gossip. He was reckless, dramatic, quixotic, romantic, and perhaps a bit of a tall-tale teller. He drank a lot. He suffered from a series of mysterious illnesses that might have been psychosomatic. His flair for being noticed, which was once unerring and graceful, now struck some people as effortful and egotistical. Isidore Dockweiler was a good friend of Lummis's and a regular guest at El Alisal. When he suggested that Lummis should take over the library, it must have seemed to Lummis like a chance for calm in his stormy life.

Mary Jones did not agree that she should be removed from the library, and she particularly objected to the idea that she should yield her position simply because she was not a man. She ignored the library board's request and came to work the next day. She told her staff that they should proceed as if it were an ordinary day, and that she didn't wish to discuss the matter any further. That evening, the library board met with Lummis to work out the details of his new job. The salary he was offered was twice what Jones was being paid. The board invited Jones to join the meeting, with the hope that she would come bearing her letter of resignation. She did attend, but without either the letter or any intention of resigning. Instead, she read a statement saying she had no plans to leave her job "when such resignation is requested solely on the ground that the best interests of the department demand that its affairs no longer be administered by a woman."

Dockweiler responded that Jones didn't need to resign because she was being fired. Lummis was sitting in the back of the room. After a moment of fraught silence, he stood up and said that he had accepted the job because he had been told that Jones was leaving willingly. He added that he looked forward to "upbuilding the character of the library, which already has such a fine reputation." Lummis, who was passionate about the rights of minorities, didn't seem fazed by the circumstances of his hiring.

The next day, the Friday Morning Club, which was the city's most distinguished women's organization, held a meeting at which Mary Jones spoke. She told the audience that she still considered herself the city librarian, and that she had the keys to her office and to the library's safe and she intended to keep them. The women of the Friday Morning Club cheered. Jones then went to work. Lummis stewed at home and wrote a column for *Out West* sulkily justifying his decision to take the job, noting, "no other public business . . . in California is administered by a woman, nor is expected to be."

The next day, one thousand women signed a petition saying that the Great Library War of Los Angeles would end only if Jones was reconfirmed as head librarian and the commissioners behind the attempted ouster were kicked off the board. Neither the board nor the mayor, Owen McAleer, to whom the board reported, responded. A few days later, led by the Friday Morning Club, the women of Los Angeles marched in support of Mary Jones. The streets were filled. The crowds did not deter Lummis, who came to City Hall wearing his green corduroy suit and Stetson sombrero, and was sworn in as city librarian. He then left town to go trout fishing with his son. Jones continued to report to her office at the library, probably jangling her keys.

News of the battle got around, and librarians around the country rallied in support of Mary Jones. Some traveled to Los Angeles to take part in the protests. Many visited Jones in her office; a number of them brought her flowers. Mayor McAleer hated the attention the controversy was bringing to the city and wanted to resolve the situation as quickly as possible, so he called for a general meeting. Thousands of women, including feminist activists Susan B. Anthony and Reverend Anna H. Shaw, attended. The resulting discussion was raucous and inconclusive. The members of the library board refused to speak when they were addressed. Mayor McAleer then announced that he was firing all of the members of the library board. They, however, refused to be fired. The stalemate continued for weeks. For the time being, the Los Angeles Public Library was run by a fired head librarian who refused to leave, and a fired board of commissioners who refused to yield.

The Great Library War could have continued indefinitely, since Mary Jones made it clear that she had no plans to surrender, but Mayor McAleer became so exasperated that he asked the city attorney to see if there was a legal remedy. This was sixty years before federal law prohibited job discrimination based on gender. A few days later, the city attorney announced his decision, saying that the city librarian served at will, and therefore the board had the legal right to fire her for any reason at all, including the fact that she was a woman. Jones and her supporters were outraged and continued to protest, but it became clear that the city attorney's ruling would not be shaken loose. At last, Jones turned in her keys and left Los Angeles for good, accepting a job as the head of the library at Bryn Mawr, a women's college in Pennsylvania. Her defeat was summed up in the *Los Angeles Times* with the headline SEQUEL TO LONG QUARREL OVER WHETHER MAN OR WOMAN SHALL BE IN CHARGE — ISIDORE DOCKWEILER AND "MUSHY" MILLER AT LAST GET MISS JONES' SCALP.

As soon as Jones had vacated her office, the city's annual report introduced the new city librarian. Lummis was "probably the best-known book-man in California . . . an author of national reputation . . . whose name is in all recent encyclopedias; a man of ripe experience as an editor, explorer, author, critic of literature and history, historian, lexicographer, organizer and director of several important utilities; a scholar and yet a practical leader." The announcement acknowledged that Lummis "was not the product of library training school" but that his "education in books and men, his common-sense, determination and poise, and his well-known faculty for 'getting things done,' were believed to be far more important."

Lummis returned from his fishing trip for his first official day on the job. He sent a memo to his staff regarding the storm that had accompanied his hiring. "Through no fault of ours, you and I are in a situation not altogether without its embarrassment," he wrote. "Who was, could, or should be librarian is no longer our business. I am librarian — and shall be for plenty long enough for you and me to acquire the fixed habit of pulling together . . . I am going to give this library the best there is in me." Lummis still wore his hair in the same long, flowing style that had gotten him in hot water at Harvard. He decided to mark this new beginning at the library with a haircut, which the local papers covered as if it were a major news event.

One thing you could count on with Charles Lummis was that he never did things in an ordinary way. He didn't get to Los Angeles in an ordinary way. He didn't conduct his personal life in an ordinary way. He did not become an ordinary librarian. He referred to his management style as "An Experiment in Democracy." He viewed running the library as another of his grand projects, and he became obsessed with perfecting it. He fixated on details as well as the broader strokes: He worked on an ambitious plan to make the library one of the best in the world, and at the same time, he made recommendations on what his staff should eat for lunch. (He declared, "No more pickles and candy lunches for the library girls. They need three square meals eaten regularly.")

He felt personally responsible for the intellectual health of the library's patrons. The popularity of pseudoscience books, which he considered "not worth the match to burn them up," worried him. Instead of removing the books from the collection, he established what he called the "Literary Pure Food Act" to warn readers about them. He hired a blacksmith to make a branding iron in the shape of a skull and crossbones — the poison warning symbol — and used it to brand the frontispiece of the offending books. He also created warning cards to insert in the questionable books. He wanted the cards to say, "This book is of the worst class that we can possibly keep in the library. We are sorry that you have not any better sense than to read it," but he was persuaded to use a more restrained tone. The cards, shaped like bookmarks, said, "For Later and More Scientific Treatment of This Subject, Consult _____," followed by a blank space for librarians to list better books on the topic. Lummis noted in his diary that he considered the poison-label brand one of his finest innovations at the library. He also used a branding iron to solve another problem. Many of the library's most valuable reference books were being stolen off the shelves, so he branded them "Property of the Los Angeles Library." Patrons complained that Lummis was defacing library property, but he was unrepentant. "We brand cows, don't we?" he wrote in one of his annual reports. "Are our reference books less valuable?"

He loved the library, but he felt out of place among other head librarians he met at national conventions. He thought they were "pompous asses," so he created a group he hoped would provide refuge for himself and his fellow librarian iconoclasts. He called it "The Bibliosmiles," and it was also known as "Librarians Who Are Nevertheless Human." One of the founding members was Tessa Kelso, who shared Lummis's contempt for the status quo. The group's slogan was "Cheer up, American Library Association!" Its official beverage was apricot brandy. Each member had a Bibliosmiles nickname. Lummis's nickname was "Grim Reality."

From the beginning, there were complaints that Lummis disappeared from the library for days at a time. He did go fishing frequently, and he spent time attending to his other projects — his books, the Southwest Museum, his continued attention to Native American issues — but much of the time he was gone from the library, he was working at El Alisal, where he sometimes spent fourteen or fifteen hours a day attending to library business. It suited him to work from home. Though he was an unconventional executive, he was passionate about the job, and much of what he did for the library made it the institution it is today. At the time he took over, the library was a good loaning library; he pushed for it to become a serious research center for scholars. He established a photography collection, a California history collection, and a Spanish history collection. He thought an autograph collection would be a great asset, so he designed special "autograph collection" stationery and wrote to all the notable people of the day — everyone from his old friend Teddy Roosevelt to William Jennings Bryan to Frederick Remington — asking for a signature and some kind of addition to the page such as a comment or a doodle. Nearly everyone he approached sent him an autograph and, in many cases, elaborate drawings. By the time he left the library in 1910, Lummis had collected 760 autographs, many with sketches and notation, from the most significant artists, writers, politicians, and scientists in the world.

When Lummis took over, the library's shelving system was somewhat illogical. The Philosophy Department, for example, included books on palmistry, cockfighting, adultery, bicycle racing, and servant girls. Lummis reorganized the subject departments; his goal was to devise a system that would enable anyone to find anything on the shelves in under ten minutes. His ambition was to make the library completely accessible — "a workshop for scholars including every painter's apprentice or working boy or streetcar man who wishes to learn, just as much as it includes the Greek professors or the art dilettante." His attitude of inclusiveness was unusual for the time. He campaigned to bring in patrons who hadn't considered using the library before. To attract them, he posted notices in schools and stores and factories, saying

Do you CARE to READ? Do you CARE to LEARN? The Los Angeles Public Library is meant FOR YOU.

The notices urged people not to be afraid of the library.

[The library] has not only the books but the people to help you find and use them. Ask in the Reference Room for what you want. If you don't find it (and cheerful service with it) drop me a postal card . . . The more you learn, the larger salary you will command. Sincerely yours, CHAS. F. LUMMIS, Librarian.

He sent a letter to railway companies, asking them to urge their employees to join the library, because "books are the last things that any human being can afford to do without."

Lummis's efforts to attract more people was so successful that the library soon needed to find larger quarters. Most of Los Angeles's residents had voted in favor of a library-building proposal in 1904, but the city had made no effort to move forward with a plan. In 1906, Lummis signed a lease for the top floor of the Homer Laughlin Building, across the street from Angels Flight, a funicular that carried the wealthy residents of Bunker Hill down the sheer side of the hill to the central business district. The Homer Laughlin space was almost twice as large as what the library had in City Hall and could accommodate the 123,000 books that were now in the collection. To Lummis's delight, there was also room for a smoking area and a rooftop garden. "It [will not be] a toy garden with terracotta teacup flowers, but a real garden," he wrote, "probably the only one of its sort [in any library] in the world."

But after just two years in the Homer Laughlin Building, the library again needed more space. It had grown exponentially: Its collection was now the sixteenth largest of any public library in the United States. It was growing at a time when Los Angeles was growing, too. In 1900, Los Angeles was the thirty-sixth largest city in the country; by 1905, it was the seventeenth largest. In 1908, Lummis signed a lease for the third floor in a building downtown that was three times bigger than the space in Homer Laughlin. The building's chief tenant was a department store, so library patrons had to ride the elevator up through the store, with stops along the way to load and unload shoppers. The rent was exorbitant, and the terms of the lease were terrible. If anyone raised a question about renting the space, Lummis clearly ignored it. He loved the fact that it was a great location in a fine building, and the roof had a beautiful view.

One thing Lummis couldn't abide was the thought that any of his patrons might wander around the library feeling lost. His solution was to train the staff to be aggressively useful. "Don't wait for anyone to wake you up," he instructed them. "Look for a chance to be helpful!" To that end, Lummis established the library's Department of Reading, Study, and Research. The department had two full-time clerks who were assigned to "pounce" — this was Lummis's choice of verbs — on anyone who came into the library with "an unfamiliar air and apparently not knowing where to go." To head the new department, Lummis hired an old friend, Dr. C. J. K. Jones. Dr. Jones was a former Unitarian pastor, a member of the library board, and the owner of more than two hundred books on the cultivation of oranges, lemons, and grapefruits — in fact, Dr. Jones owned the finest private library on citrus farming in the entire state, according to a 1918 profile of him in *California Citragraph Magazine*. Citing Jones's "eminent qualifications" to lead the department, without specifying what those qualifications were, Lummis allotted Jones a large salary and the title "The Human Encyclopedia." Jones was to be "a walking information desk" who would rove around the library and provide answers to any questions the patrons might have.

Dr. Jones was a large man with a pinched arc of a mouth and a trim white beard and an air of weaning self-importance. He had a habit of tapping his forehead after being asked a question, as if he had to jar the answer loose from a storage bin in his brain. There is no record of how patrons of the library felt about him, but the library staff hated him. They resented his vanity and his salary, which was nearly double the salary of senior librarians. Jones suspected that he was not well liked. He complained to Lummis that he sometimes found lemons and hammers on his desk, which he interpreted as an insult. Word of the friction between the staff and the Human Encyclopedia made its way into the news. IS THE L.A. PUBLIC LIBRARY THE HOUSE OF A THOUSAND SCANDALS? screamed one *Los Angeles Times* story, speculating that the highly paid Dr. Jones spent most of his time in the library's roof garden, watering the geraniums.

259

Dr. C. J. K. Jones, "The Human Encyclopedia"

Not long after the *Times* questioned Dr. Jones's effectiveness as a library resource, it came to light that he had been hired without having taken the civil service test required of all library employees. When the city administration told him that he had to take the test or risk losing his job, Jones was indignant, arguing that his intellectual stature spoke for itself. The city insisted, so Jones finally submitted to the test. He flunked. Among the questions he got wrong were: "Name three children's anthologies and describe them"; "Give a brief account of present copyright law"; and "What is meant by 'Arthurian legends'?" According to the person who graded the test, Dr. Jones also "failed to give satisfactory replies to questions pertaining to fairy lore." Apparently, when he was asked to list three fairy tales, Jones included Jules Verne's *20,000 Leagues Under the Sea*. His modest performance on the test made front-page news. The *Los Angeles Herald* headline was HIGH-PRICED RESEARCH DIRECTOR FAILS TO PASS EXAMINATION.

Jones's failure on the test and his unpopularity with the library staff reflected poorly on Lummis. But he defended Jones and explained that his knowledge was so broad that it couldn't be adequately measured by any test. It's hard to understand why Lummis was so determined to protect Jones; he seemed blind to the man's inflated self-esteem and narcissism. On his second try, Jones did pass the test, so he was able to keep his job as Human Encyclopedia, but his reputation never recovered, and the local press seemed to delight in mocking him. The *Times* summed up the incident by writing, "The human race . . . . has reason to rejoice in this, the dawn of the twentieth century, that has produced . . . and washed out upon the shores of time, Dr. C. J. K. Jones . . ."

Lummis was smart about many things. He had a knack for getting attention and a genius for getting things done that many people would have thought were impossible. He was brave. He was enterprising. He drew people to him with the sheer force of his own convictions; he was magnetic. He thrived on drama and challenge and a certain amount of chaos. When he started his job at the library, his personal life was in turmoil, and the scene at El Alisal was a circus. El Alisal was a small, rough house; Lummis and his wife and their children and his illegitimate daughter lived there, along with a family of troubadours and an endless stream of partygoers who came and went on no particular schedule. In 1907, one of the troubadours murdered one of Lummis's housekeepers. Still, the parties continued, as many as two or three a week, one blurring into the other, with some guests who never bothered to leave. One day in 1909, Lummis's wife, Eve, came across the diaries in which he detailed close to fifty extramarital affairs. Outraged, Eve left El Alisal and moved to San Francisco with two of their children, Turbesé and Keith. Their son Quimu stayed with Lummis. Lummis adored his children. He clung to them, especially after his oldest son, Amado, died of pneumonia at the age of six. He loved being around babies so much that he often invited pregnant women to be long-term houseguests at El Alisal, so they would stay for a while once their babies were born. When Turbesé and Keith moved to San Francisco with Eve, Lummis was devastated. Eve's divorce filing and the details of his infidelities consumed the local media. It was the most press Lummis had ever gotten in Los Angeles, which is notable, since his life had drawn media attention since the day he arrived.

As brilliant as he was, Lummis had no instinct for self-preservation. As when he was working at the *Los Angeles Times* — when losing his job had come as such a surprise to him — he never considered that his behavior or the controversy that buzzed around him might compromise his position at the library. He lived on bullheadedness, self-involvement, and a daredevil's willful obliviousness. He was proud of the new space in the Hamburger Department Store Building but failed to appreciate that signing an unfavorable lease would be held against him. The board recognized that he had improved the library's collection and that he had attracted vast numbers of new patrons. But his transgressions were equally recognized. He was away from the library almost eighty days in 1907, for instance, and he charged his cigars to his library expense account. Hiring Dr. Jones without the necessary testing made him appear careless. In the end, his loyalty to Dr. Jones didn't even pay him dividends as a friend. It was Jones who first broadcast that Lummis was frequently absent from the library: He mentioned it when he gave testimony in a lawsuit brought by a clerk who claimed the library was being mismanaged.

Lummis's annual written reports to the library board were not the usual tallying and tedium; they were anecdotal and discursive, full of pronouncements on the state of libraries and the city and life, and often included long, elaborate descriptions of other city libraries he visited around the United States. He took great pleasure in writing the reports. He divided them into sections with titles like "The Battle of the Shelves" and "Beans When the Bag Is Open" and "What Are We Here For?" The reports sometimes ran longer than 120 pages. To head librarians around the country, Lummis's reports became legendary, and they often requested copies so they could read and then pass them around to their staff. Because of the reports, Lummis was perhaps the best-known librarian in the United States.

But after five years of reading Lummis's reports, the Los Angeles library commissioners no longer found them charming, and they reprimanded him for his verbosity and flamboyance. Lummis ignored their criticism, attributing it to petty politicking. The library board was indeed political. One of its newest members was a woman named Shelly Tollhurst, who had been an active supporter of Mary Jones in the Great Library War. Lummis treated the board as a necessary annoyance. "The library is a magnificent institution which nothing can hinder . . . except peanut politics," Lummis complained to the mayor, citing "the inability of certain good people to understand the responsibilities and the functions of a great public library."

Lummis changed the Los Angeles Public Library forever. He made it more democratic and yet more sophisticated; more substantial, more accessible, more celebrated. At the same time, he offended people and spent too much money and became much too famous for his personal travails. Finally, his friends on the library board forsook him, and at the end of 1910, he was pressured to leave. Even the Human Encyclopedia, whom he had defended to his detriment, abandoned him: As soon as Lummis announced his resignation, Dr. C. J. K. Jones applied for his job.

The dismissal from the library stung Lummis. "You will remember I was not a Sweet Girl Graduate of a Library School," he wrote later to Isidore Dockweiler. "I was a Scholar and Frontiersman and a Two-fisted He-Person and that I went to the roots of that Sissy Library and made it, within two years, an Institution of Character, a He-Library, of which we were all proud." To his friends, Lummis pretended that leaving the library was a happy turn of events. He said he was tired of the job, that it had "absorbed all there was of me," and that it had "wasted" six years which he could have devoted to writing his own books. "I feel pretty good," he wrote in his diary after his firing. "After a little while I will be able to build the house and get out-door exercise . . . and finish up my books and write new ones and write articles and . . . restore the missions which need it pretty bad . . . I have also a suspicion that I will get up and catch a trout this spring the first time in many years . . . It will seem fine when I don't have to bother about anything in the library and do as I please." He embarked on a program of self-improvement. He quit drinking, smoking, and swearing. He tried to bring some semblance of order to his life, which was the usual mess; he had no money, a divorce to finalize, and several books he had promised to write; and he somehow managed to have two lovers living with him at El Alisal.

The end of his time at the library was the beginning of the end of his life. He never again displayed the bluster and confidence that had propelled him three thousand miles on foot across America, and to the jungles of Central America, and to the tribal towns of the Southwest — all those journeys of energy and curiosity that had made his life so singular and inspired. In 1911, he did travel on an archaeological trip to Guatemala, but while he was there, he contracted a fever that left him totally blind. He managed to continue writing by relying on a rotating crew of secretaries, some of whom were also his rotating lovers. He even continued taking photographs. He accomplished this by having his son Quimu describe the scene and guide his camera. Some of his friends doubted he was really blind. After so many years of hearing Lummis's dramatic stories, they never quite believed him anymore. In fact, in 1912, he announced that his sight had miraculously returned, which convinced many of his friends that it had been a charade all along.

The big swashbuckling life Lummis had fashioned for himself began to contract. He was forced out of the Southwest Museum, which he had founded. His writing, which used to come so easily to him, stalled. The books he hoped to work on didn't materialize. He started writing a column for the *Los Angeles Times*, but after just a short run, the paper dropped it. In 1915, Lummis got some good news. The king of Spain was knighting him in appreciation of all he had done to honor the Spanish contributions to American culture. In a sense, it was a vindication of his life's work, and Lummis wore the emblem of the knighthood around his neck for the rest of his days. Unfortunately, it did little to steady his life. He was nearly bankrupt. He begged Isidore Dockweiler to help him find a civil service job; he said he was willing to take anything in any department and that he rather liked the

idea of doing physical labor. He told Dockweiler he was sure his writing would bring
him income soon, but in the meantime, he
needed to eat. Dockweiler never responded.

Somehow Lummis scraped by. He still
threw the occasional party at El Alisal. He
married one more time. He took one more
trip to the dry adobe villages of the Southwest that he loved so much. He wrote in his
diary of the trip, of the dreamlike landscapes
there, of the red mountains and wild valleys, the rumbling herds of antelope, the
clouds scudding along the flat horizon.
These were the landscapes he had first
encountered in 1884 as a young man walking across the country, when these landscapes were as untouched as the moon, and
his melancholy made it seem that he knew
they would never be as pure again. But for
that moment, on that last trip, it was as if
New Mexico were still ancient and un-
spoiled, and he was a young man again,
fearless, no longer tired, not lonely, still full
of ambitions that most people would have
thought impossible or insane, and still
convinced he would see them all to comple-
tion. When he returned to Los Angeles, a
lump he had thought was an infected insect
bite was diagnosed as cancer. As he was dying, he wrote two more books — a collec-

tion of poems called *A Bronco Pegasus,* and a collection of essays called *Flowers of Our Lost Romance.* He lived long enough to see the first copies of *A Bronco Pegasus* delivered to El Alisal, and to learn that *Flowers of Our Lost Romance* had been accepted for publication. Perhaps he imagined he would have one more spin through the world, but late in the evening of November 25, 1928, Charles Fletcher Lummis died. Currently, the Los Angeles Public Library has his library reports; his journals; his coverage of the Apache Wars; his *Birch Bark Poems;* his books about the Spanish missions, Pueblo Indians, Moqui Indians, and the history of Mexico; and the book *Letters from the Southwest, September 20, 1884, to March 14, 1885,* the collection of the columns he wrote while on his glorious tramp across the country.

14.

Wasa-Wasa: A Tale of Trails and Treasure in the Far North (1951)
  By Macfie, Harry
  971.05 M144

Map Librarianship: An Introduction (1987)
  By Larsgaard, Mary Lynette
  025.176 L334

Buried in Treasures: Help for Compulsive Acquiring, Saving, and Hoarding (2014)
  Series: Treatments That Work
  By Tolin, David F.
  616.8522 T649

Genealogy, and Enjoying It (1982)
  By Coleman, Ruby Roberts
  929.01 C692-1

History is on the lowest floor of the library and occupies the largest space of any department, stretching from the bottom of the escalator across the width of the building's new wing. Glen Creason, one of the department's senior librarians, entered library school in 1979 on a whim, thinking it would be a good place to meet attractive women. That year, the head of the RAND Corporation announced that libraries would soon be obsolete. Creason is now the longest-tenured librarian at Central Library. He has a scramble of blondish-white hair with unruly bangs, a scrubby beard, and a body like an exclamation point. He likes pretending to be stern and cynical, perhaps to hide the fact that he is a softie and deeply sentimental. He has waxed nostalgic about such things as the days when the library had a switchboard, operated by an elegant lady named Pearl; when material was moved from department to department via pneumatic tubes; the days when one addressed librarians as "Mrs." or "Miss" or, on that rare occasion, "Mr."; the days when a librarian named Tom Owens walked five miles to and from work every day; when Creason would have lunch with a clerk named Ted Itagaki, who "could swallow an entire hamburger in three bites." He has waxed less nostalgic about the days after the fire, when he was overcome by despair. That was when he was working in the library's temporary location on Spring Street and hypodermic needles would fall off the shelves as he was putting books away. Over the years, he has become a sort of library himself: He is the repository of endless stories about the library's most interesting patrons. One that he described to me, for instance, was a former math teacher from Wisconsin who had a nervous breakdown and ended up in Los Angeles; he spent almost every day in the History Department, reading or cutting his hair over the wastebasket, and sometimes making announcements to the librarians like "I walked from Racine to Sheboygan in the dead of winter. Froze my penis and my nipples," before returning to his hair cutting or his books. Or the octogenarian twins — Creason and his colleagues referred to them as Heckle and Jeckle — who came to the library daily, spending their time reading Herodotus and Thucydides and telling Creason the very same joke every day for seven years. Or the patron who claimed he was the sultan of Brunei (he wasn't) and insisted that he had suffered a brain hemorrhage at the exact minute when John F. Kennedy was assassinated. Over the months

I spent with him, Creason told me stories about Rubber Man and Antler Man and Stopwatch Man and Stampy and General Hershey Bar and his sidekick, Colonel Dismay, and someone Creason had nicknamed the Prospector, who wore gold-digging clothes and always requested *Buried Treasure* magazine. Creason's stories about patrons are bemused and mostly fond. The first time he and I met, he described, with no cynicism, an attractively dressed woman who came to the desk one day and told him she had been in the Atlantic Ocean since 1912, then had turned into a seal and swum to the port of Los Angeles.

Creason's tenure at Central Library has spanned the fire; the AIDS crisis, which killed eleven librarians; the reopening of the building; the library's adjustment to omnipresent Internet; his divorce, which he blames partly on his depression after the fire; and the addition of his daughter Katya to the library staff. They are one of many parent-child duos on staff in the L.A. system. Creason has helped historians Will and Ariel Durant find books. He also waited on a patron named Richard Ramirez, who was looking for books on torture and astrology. (It turned out that Ramirez was the serial killer known as the Night Stalker and was sentenced to death for thirteen murders in Los Angeles. "He was definitely really creepy," Creason says.) Bobby Fischer, the chess master, used to come to the History Department regularly, carrying a heavy brown suitcase, but he generally kept to himself. Sometimes Creason makes noises about retiring, but it's hard to picture him anywhere other than behind a library desk — with the exception of a Dodgers game. He seems like a librarian through and through when he says things like "When the library reopened, we were so happy to see our books again!"

One Saturday morning, Creason called and said he had someone he wanted me to meet. It was drowsy in the department when I arrived. A few people were seated at the desks, thumbing through books. One woman at a table in a far corner of the room was putting polish on her toenails. I walked around the department's information desk and past a cart marked DISCARD. The casualties included a biography of Billy Carter; *The Vital Records of Franklin, Maine;* and a stained and tattered copy of a book of folk tales titled *Wasa-Wasa,* translated from the original Swedish. The History Department is a bit of a portmanteau; it encompasses all of the library's history materials, as well as the very popular Genealogy Department, and the library's map collection, one of the five largest in the United States. The map collection has grown exponentially since it was established at the founding of the library. The only significant subtraction has been the closing of the Army Map Room, which existed during World War II as a repository of official army service maps and charts.

Creason is the senior librarian in charge of the Map Department. When I tracked him down that morning, he was standing with three other people near the flat files where the most valuable maps are stored. One of them — a bouncy, bowlegged man with a brushy white mustache who introduced himself as Brian Hatcher — was a map collector with a specialty in maps printed by the Automobile Club of Southern California. That day, Hatcher had three bins full of assorted maps to donate to the library. He said he wasn't happy about doing it, but his wife had demanded that he start culling his collection or she'd do it for him.

Next to Hatcher stood a young man wearing thick glasses, hearing aids, and a sweet, distracted look on his face. "This is C.J., the person I wanted you to meet," Creason said, motioning to the young man. "He's here to work on the maps." The other man in the group was C.J.'s father, John Moon. John told me that C.J. was deaf and autistic, and that he was fascinated by maps and had an extraordinary knowledge of them. C.J.'s focus on maps started early. When he was five years old, his Christmas wish list consisted of just one thing: a *Thomas Guide,* which is one of those spiral-bound block-by-block atlases of metropolitan areas, favored by taxi drivers and real estate agents. C.J. didn't want just any *Thomas Guide* — he wanted a 1974 edition of the San Bernardino *Thomas Guide.* By the time he was eleven years old, C.J. was probably one of the world's experts on *Thomas Guides.* While his father was telling me this, C.J. was studying the shelves of maps. He suddenly turned to me and asked my home address. After I told him, he stood for a moment with his eyes closed, then announced what page my house was on in the Los Angeles *Thomas Guide.* Creason found the guide on the shelf, and we turned to the page, just to check. My street was right in the center of the page.

C.J. and Hatcher had met on a map-collector website and decided to get together today; it was the first time they'd met in real life. The Map Department was a natural rendezvous. C.J. is a regular at the library. He and his father travel the hour from their home to Central at least once a month. "This is C.J.'s paradise," John said, circling his arm over his head. "This is his world."

For the last year, C.J. has been helping Creason index a group of maps and atlases called the Feathers Collection. John Feathers was a shy hospital dietician with a cleft palate and a dislike of mingling. In his fifties, he found happiness at last with an older man named Walter Keller. He moved into Keller's house, a cottage in an isolated corner of a Los Angeles neighborhood called Mount Washington, next door to the headquarters of the Self-Realization Fellowship. What Feathers did in his spare time was collect maps. He gathered tract maps and pictorial maps and topographic studies; city plans and touring guides and road maps published by State Farm and Rand McNally and Hagstrom; sportsmen's atlases; strip maps; geologic surveys. He gathered an almost complete set of *Thomas Guides*, including the first four ever published, as well as an almost complete set of the *Thomas* competitor, the *Renie Atlas*. He had common maps and also many rare ones

Glen Creason with one of the library's many maps

— special atlases from 1891 and from 1903; a map of Europe published in 1592. The cottage was tiny — not even a thousand square feet — but Feathers had managed to wedge approximately one hundred thousand maps into it, along with his collections of hotel soap and restaurant matches.

In 2012, Feathers died at the age of fifty-six. Keller had predeceased him. Ownership of the cottage passed to relatives of Keller's, who decided to sell it as a teardown, and hired a broker named Matthew Greenberg to put it on the market. Keller and Feathers had led quiet lives in their tiny cottage. When Greenberg went to see it for the first time, he expected to find the usual backwash of lives flown by — perhaps a spare and sad-making landscape of shoes and jackets, a neglected planter, a pinned photo, a broken dish. But the Keller cottage was bursting. Every inch was jammed with Feathers's maps, which were piled on the floor and in file boxes, stacked inside the kitchen cabinets, even stacked in the oven. A stereo system had had its guts pulled out to make space for a heap of *Thomas Guides*. Greenberg wasn't sure what to make of it and had no idea whether the maps were trash or valuable, but he couldn't bring himself to call for a Dumpster. Instead, he called the library and was connected to Glen Creason. "You should come see this," Greenberg told him. "I have a houseful of maps."

That night, Creason was so excited that he couldn't sleep. When morning finally rolled in, he headed to the cottage with ten librarian friends and some empty boxes. Over the course of the day, they packed more than two hundred cartons of material. At that instant, the size of the library's map collection doubled. The sheer bulk of the Feathers Collection is staggering. It occupies the equivalent of two football fields of shelving. The complication of this walloping find is that it arrived in a jumble, without any sort of order at all — a cardinal sin in a library, where the commitment to findability is absolute. Indexing maps is tedious and time-consuming work — exacting, eye-straining — with no margin for error. Each map has to be indexed by the name of the company that printed it, the name of the map, the year it was printed, the place it depicts, and any distinguishing features that need to be noted in order to categorize it. As of the day we met, C.J. had indexed two thousand maps. He likes to do seven hours of indexing work with no lunch break when he comes to the library, but his father insists that he at least eat a sandwich. He was getting impatient to get started, so Creason walked with him through a locked door to the stacks, where the unindexed maps were kept. While we waited for them to return, his father told me, almost offhandedly, that the Moon family had a special history with the library.

"In what way?" I asked.

"You know the fire here in 1986?" John said. "C.J.'s grandfather was one of the firemen who helped put out the fire. There's a plaque by the front door for the firefighters. You can find his name on it. Captain Howard Slaven."

As I stood there gobsmacked by this serendipity, Creason came back from the stacks holding a map C.J. had just found between pages of a street atlas. Creason, who is a serious map aficionado and has a soft spot for pictorial maps, spread the map on the table and leaned over it, taking it in. He said "Wow" under his breath several times. Finally, he straightened up, tapped the map, and said, "This is one of those moments . . . one of those rare moments . . ." He shook his head. "I have *never* seen this before. I have never laid my eyes on this before." It was a map of the 1932 Summer Olympics, which were held in Los Angeles just as the Great Depression bore down. These were the Olympics that first introduced the great athlete Babe Didrikson Zaharias to the world. The map was creamy yellow and had fine-lined roads and red rectangles marking many Olympic venues in the city, including the Rose Bowl, Griffith Park, and Marine Stadium. It was evidently meant to help tourists at the Olympics find their way around the giant sprawl of Los Angeles; along the top of the map was the encouraging yet commanding phrase AVOID CONFUSION. The map had the frozen-moment quality of a snapshot. It might have stayed stuck between pages in a street atlas forever, had C.J. not come across it. Now it was found, rescued. It would be indexed and cataloged as a part of the Los Angeles Public Library's Feathers Map Collection, one more piece of the bigger puzzle the library is always seeking to assemble — the looping, unending story of who we are.

15.

the old L.A. Public Library burned
down
that library downtown
and with it went
a large part of my
youth.
. . . .
that wondrous place
the L.A. Public Library

Charles Bukowski, "The Burning
of the Dream" *Septuagenarian
Stew* (1990)
  By Bukowski, Charles
  818 B932-1

As soon as the fire was extinguished, the
fire department began investigating. All
three of the department's arson teams were
assigned to the case, and federal Alcohol,
Tobacco, and Firearms agents joined them.

Several investigators went undercover at the library in case the arsonist returned. The rest canvassed the neighborhood, answered the tip line, followed leads, scoured for evidence.

The city publicized the search with billboards and radio spots. All hundred thousand municipal employees found notes in their pay envelopes asking for information and offering a thirty-thousand-dollar reward. More than four hundred people called or mailed in tips. Many of the tips were not useful. One repeated tip was the suggestion that Libyan agents might have set the fire because the relationship between Libya and the United States was so troubled. Other tips were more specific:

Sirs, the ARSONIST who burned your library is . . . Mr. Theadore V — of the X Porno Cinema . . . he is the #1 MAFIA DON in Massachusetts . . . he is also a Drug Kingpin and was pushing his drugs while in LA!

Dear Sirs, in regards to the arson at the library, consider [name redacted]. 1. This person has a mental problem . . . Ask a psychiatrist concerning this matter; he

285

would diagnose that person as instantly insane.

Dear Sir, This man, Richard W —, may have set FIRE to your library. He thinks he is GOD-Realized. He was born an Aries. Admitted to rape with a motorcycle gang and may have murdered others. Last year I told him to go to HELL and stay away from me. He keeps harassing me to BE his devotee, because he's very prejudiced. Because I'm Oriental. He told me I was a witch and had 3 months to live. If he . . . checks out books it would BE anything on GOD Realization, Buddhism, Zen Religion, or witchcraft. Perhaps he didn't want to return any books. So he burnt the library because he was unable to check anything out.

The investigators learned that a well-known psychic in Los Angeles, Gary Bowman, had commented on the case. Bowman was seventy-five thousand years old and lived in a South American jungle with a herd of magical miniature horses while also managing to be a resident of Los Angeles. His spirit guide was John the Apostle. Somewhat jarringly, when John the Apostle spoke through Bowman, he had a strong

286

Australian accent. Audiences embraced Bowman; his radio show, *Out of the Ordinary Radio,* had a wide audience. He was channeling John the Apostle when he commented on the library fire.

Questioner: Is it possible to name or identify the persons involved [with the library fire]?

Bowman (John the Apostle): We are not interested in doing this.

Questioner: Will there be further attempts to burn the library?

Bowman/John: Yes, within six months. There will be further attempts to burn the library — the old facility — within six months.

Audience (gasping): Why?!

Bowman/John: Because *[the perpetrators]* are stupid. Their motives are actually that they are angry . . . So they will take that which is of value to others and seek to deprive them of it because they feel that they are deprived. Do you understand that? And so it is that they lash out at . . . they will attempt it again in six months.

Arson is vexingly hard to investigate. Even the biggest fire can be started with a single match — a slender bit of evidence at best, which is likely to be consumed by what it has started. A fire can smolder slowly. The arsonist has plenty of time to walk away before anything seems amiss. The beginning of a fire can be nothing much — a twinkle of flame, a tendril of smoke. By the time it fully blooms, the arsonist can be far away. It is hard to imagine a more perfect crime than one in which the weapon disappears and the act itself can unfold almost unnoticeably. Of all major criminal offenses, arson is the least successfully prosecuted. The rate of conviction is less than one percent. An arsonist has a ninety-nine percent likelihood of getting away with the crime.

What made the library fire especially hard to investigate was that it occurred in a public space. Unless you borrow a book, your time in a library is unrecorded and anonymous. The fire at Central Library began an hour after opening. There were already two hundred patrons in the building, and there is no way to know how many other people came in and out before that. The library is open to everyone, which meant that everyone was a possible suspect. There was no means for investigators to narrow their search.

The arson squad hoped the library staff

might have noticed someone acting out of turn that morning, which would at least give them somewhere to begin. A senior librarian mentioned that she had seen a young fair-haired stranger walk into the staff workroom that morning and pour himself a cup of coffee. The workroom was easy to access, but it is clearly not part of the department's public space. The librarian had shooed him away. In another department, a young man — possibly the same young man — had been seen entering a restricted area. When the librarian on duty reprimanded him, the man had said he was a new employee and was taking a look at the stacks. The librarian sheepishly welcomed him to the staff and went back to work. Around the same time, a young man was seen in the History stacks, which are closed to everyone except staff. When the department librarian noticed him, she asked if he was an employee, and he answered that he was looking for a newspaper. He lingered for ten minutes and then abruptly turned and left. At the Hope Street entrance — which employees use before the library opens to the public — a young man who didn't have an employee badge tried to walk in the door. The security guard on duty stopped him and explained that the library wasn't open to the public yet. The man replied that he was looking for a telephone, and started to head inside. The guard grabbed his arm and repeated that he couldn't come in. The young man angrily wrenched his arm out of the guard's grasp, and then turned on his heel and left.

Such trespasses at the library were unusual but not remarkable. The young man eventually complied with every request to leave, so no one made any further note of it, or got his name, or called for additional security. Each incident lasted only an instant and didn't make much of an impression. All the staff could recall was that the young man was of average size and weight and that he had blond hair brushed back off his forehead in soft wings. It was a description very similar to the one given by the elderly woman who had been knocked over by a man rushing to leave the library after the fire alarm sounded. Based on these descriptions, a sketch artist began working on a drawing. The result was a portrait of a man in his twenties with prominent wide-set eyes; a thick nose; a walrus mustache; and hair that looked like a shorter version of Farrah Fawcett's on *Charlie's Angels.*

Where was Harry Peak after April 29, 1986?

As far as I can tell, he kept up his usual ambling ways, picking up odd jobs here and there, hanging out with friends, auditioning for roles, dreaming the dream. He ran errands for a lawyer named Leonard Martinet, who was based in San Francisco. Harry and Demitri Hioteles were no longer a couple by this time, but they remained friends. Hioteles operated a limousine service and sometimes hired Harry as a driver. As with anything that involved Harry, this patronage came at a cost. Once, Harry offered to change the oil on one of the limos. He drained the engine, and then, before putting in the new oil, he wandered off for a cigarette. Perhaps he then had another cigarette, or maybe he took a walk; in any case, he was gone for hours. In the meantime, another one of the drivers took the limo without realizing it had no oil. Within a few miles, the engine blew up. Hioteles told me this story with a deep sigh. "That was just Harry being Harry," he said, "doing stupid things like that."

On the day of the fire, Hioteles had been at the valet desk at the Sheraton, chatting with a friend. The phone rang. It was Harry, sounding giddy. He insisted that Hioteles guess where he'd spent the morning. Hioteles waited for him to unfurl one of his stories of how he had gone drinking with someone like Jack Nicholson or Nick Nolte. Instead, Harry exclaimed that he had been at the library fire. He chattered about how intense it had been, and how it had gotten so hot that a handsome fireman had to carry him out of the building. The story sounded almost believable, but it didn't make sense. Hioteles couldn't picture Harry at a library; he couldn't recall ever seeing Harry read a book. Harry loved to insert himself into any public spectacle, so Hioteles let him spin the story for a while and then put it out of his mind, the way he did with so many of Harry's tales.

Hearing the story out loud must have sparked something in Harry. Perhaps he found some pleasure in being listened to, some thrill in being a character in a dark drama. That night, he went back to Santa Fe Springs and got stoned and drunk with friends from high school. He told them about the fire; this time his story was a little grander. He said he'd been at the fire, and a handsome fireman had carried him out, and then added, offhandedly, that he had started the fire. It was boozy talk, easily dismissed, and his friends doubted him, but Harry insisted it was true. When he got back to Los Angeles, Harry told his roommates yet another version of the story. He said he had been at the library doing research for Martinet's law firm, and after the fire had started, he'd helped an elderly lady escape through a window. Then a handsome fireman had carried him out of the building.

He kept repeating the story, adjusting it a touch each time, as if he were a tailor working on a jacket, taking in a bit of fabric here, letting out a seam there, then stepping back to consider what fit best. He told Dennis Vines that he had been at the library that morning because he was researching how to apply for a civil service job. Vines had never heard Harry talk about the library before. He figured it was just Harry puffing up, since he loved placing himself in the middle of anything eventful. Vines had developed a habit of fact-checking Harry, so he asked him details about the library — simple things, like where the entrance was. Harry had no idea. That convinced Vines that Harry was fibbing. He decided that Harry must have seen fire trucks downtown and decided it would make interesting conversation to say he was there.

Terry Depackh, one of the investigators of the library fire, told me not long ago that the case was unusually exasperating. The leads all fizzled; investigators didn't have any useful evidence or eyewitnesses. Nor did they have a motive, although Depackh leaned toward the assumption that whoever had started it was probably "on the pyro side." The librarians' description of the coffeemaker trespasser was the only sighting of a potential suspect, but it wasn't really useful. All the librarians could say with certainty was that someone had been seen somewhere he didn't belong on the morning the fire began.

A month after the fire, a woman named Melissa Kim called the tip line and said that her brother's roommate looked just like the man in the composite sketch. She also said that the roommate, Harry Peak, told her brother that he had been at the library at the time of the fire. She said Harry had recently applied for a job at the Santa Monica Fire Department but had failed the exam. Depackh thought the tip sounded interesting, and he passed it to Joe Napolitano, a retired investigator who was helping with the case. At first glance, Harry Peak didn't look promising as a suspect. There was nothing connecting him to the library. He seemed like just another one of the thousands of young men who churn through Los Angeles, job-hopping, tumbling from one apartment to another, a little feckless and starry-eyed, lifted by the continuous supply of hope and sun. But Napolitano was intrigued by the fact that Harry had told someone he'd been at the library that day, as well as the fact that he had applied for work as a firefighter. As with Glendale's notorious John Leonard Orr, firefighter arsonists do exist, and it is a stubborn and bewildering problem in the fire community. About one hundred of them are arrested every year, according to *Firesetting Firefighters — The Arsonist in the Fire Department,* published by the National Volunteer Fire Council in the 1990s. Although Harry wasn't a firefighter, the tip suggested that he had expressed interest, and might have been driven to do something vindictive because he hadn't been able to pass the exam. He also fit the profile of the typical firefighter arsonist, who is usually a white male between the ages of seventeen and twenty-five.

The arson squad decided to put Harry under surveillance. Harry noticed that he was being watched. Instead of being upset when he spotted the investigators sitting in a car outside his house, he chatted with them and brought them coffee and dough-nuts. The situation must have felt unreal to him, a scene in a bizarre movie in which he was the star. It must have seemed like something he could charm his way out of, which he was good at doing.

Ten days after Melissa Kim called the tip line, her mother called Napolitano. First, she asked if the thirty-thousand-dollar reward was still being offered. When she was told it was, she said that she had visited her son recently and had seen Harry Peak, and she'd noticed that he had cut his hair and shaved his mustache, as if trying to change his appearance. She added that the day after she visited, Harry had called her, shouting "he was not a firebug" and that "just because he was in the library the day of the fire and looked like the composite didn't mean he set the fire."

Napolitano decided it was time to question Peak. He and Terry Depackh went to Peak's house in Hollywood for the interview. Harry told them he was nervous, that he was worried that he was being viewed as a suspect. Depackh asked where he had been on the day of the fire, and Harry said he had been at the library. He said he had been downtown doing an errand for Martinet and was looking for a place to have breakfast. He'd seen the library and decided to go in because it was such a beautiful building. He had spent about a half hour walking around admiring it. Between ten and eleven A.M. he'd smelled smoke and heard someone yell "Fire." In his rush to get out, he had bumped into an elderly woman but had stopped to help her up and then walked her out to the sidewalk. He said when he was outside, he saw a Superior Court judge whom he knew, and they stood together and watched the building burn.

After he finished, Harry told Depackh and Napolitano that he bet the person who started the fire hadn't intended for it to get so big. The investigators took down his statement and noted the discrepancies. No one had smelled smoke when the fire began because there was no smoke for at least a half hour after the alarm, and no one had yelled "Fire" because there'd been no visible fire until the building was evacuated. Depackh then asked Harry if he had recently cut his hair and mustache. Harry hesitated. He was someone who preened and fussed over how he looked, and took special pride in his blond hair, but he told the investigators that he simply couldn't remember.

16.

Hollywood Babylon (1975)
By Anger, Kenneth
812.09 A587

How to Draw Buildings (2006)
By Beasant, Pam
X 741 B368

In Commemoration of the Greatest Engineering Triumph of the Ages and Most Wonderful Accomplishment of Human Endeavor in All History: The Building of the Panama Canal, the San Diego Panama-California Exposition Opens Wide Its Portals and Invites the World (1915)
Folio 917.941 S218-4

God's Drum and Other Cycles from Indian Lore: Poems by Hartley

After Charles Lummis was pushed out of his library job, the Human Encyclopedia made an unsuccessful pitch for the position. The board instead opted for a quiet, tender-faced librarian from Missouri named Purd Wright, who tidied up the wreckage left in Lummis's wake and then resigned after just eight months for a job at the library in Kansas City. His successor, who stayed in the post over twenty years, was Everett Robbins Perry, the head of the Astor Library in New York City. Perry was a small man with an imposing forehead and a penetrating gaze whose idea of leisure wear was a three-button suit and a four-in-hand tie. He was as imperturbable as Lummis had been tempestuous. "He is all business," the board noted after Perry's interview. "Listens well; doesn't talk much . . . the granite of old New England was in his foundations; imagination and creative spirit were not in his make-up." The board suspected that Perry had "no genius" for friendship and barely any inner emotional life but felt he would make an excellent city librarian. In fact, Perry was passionate, but his passion was exclusively for libraries, and he judged people by whether or not they shared his passion. The staff of the Los Angeles library adored him. They called him Father Perry.

By then, the city was a throbbing, thriving place, growing so fast that it erased and rewrote itself by the minute. The Southern California oil industry literally erupted in 1903 and soon led the country. The film industry began in 1910 with the production of D. W. Griffith's movie *In Old California* and grew by bounds. The city was a jumble, a mingle of roughnecks, starlets, immigrants, grifters, typists, cowboys, screenwriters, longshoremen, and ranch families, all streaming in, staking out a corner, mustering a livelihood or not, joining the fray. The expansion of the city was so rapid that it was unnerving. It had a quality of metastasis. The sunniness and vitality were ratcheted up so high that it had an undercurrent of weirdness, of something careening out of control. Even gleaming, glossy Hollywood had an undercoat of drug addiction, alcoholism, sex scandals, murders. A sense of desperation and solitude was welded to it. In 1920, former Ziegfeld girl Olive Thomas, who was married to actress Mary Pickford's brother Jack, died after overdosing on her husband's syphilis medication. In 1921, actor Fatty Arbuckle was arrested for the rape and murder of an aspiring actress named Virginia Rappe, who had been drunk and injecting morphine at the time of her murder. The following year, director William Desmond Taylor was found dead with a gunshot wound in his back.

Many people came to Los Angeles with nothing, expecting everything. Anything free was sought out. The library absorbed these newcomers. Book circulation in the Los Angeles system doubled and then tripled. In 1921, more than three million books were checked out — about a thousand books an hour. On an average day, ten thousand people passed through the library's doors. Librarians answered two hundred thousand queries a year. Often the reading areas were standing room only. The mix of library patrons was as assorted as the city itself. At the children's story hour, which was known as Joy Hours for the Wee Folks, "the petted darlings of prosperity rub shoulders with ragged urchins . . . The pampered child of luxury with her nurse comes to read the same stories as the little Russian or Italian girl who brings a grimy baby along to tend," according to the *Times*. During lunch hour, businessmen lined up against the walls, elbow to elbow, pinstripes to bow ties, flipping through journals and books.

A craze for self-improvement and reinvention thrived in this fresh new place conjured out of the scrubby desert. The library was part of that craze, since it offered the tools for fashioning a new self. In 1925, a man named Harry Pidgeon completed a solo sailing trip around the world, becoming only the second person ever to do so. He had gotten the building plans for his boat and most of his nautical knowledge from books he had borrowed from the Los Angeles Public Library. His boat, *The Islander,* was nicknamed *The Library Navigator.*

By then, the library had been operating in Los Angeles for almost forty years, and it reflected and inflected the city and world around it. In the year leading up to Prohibition, when the ban on alcohol seemed inevitable, every book about how to make liquor at home was checked out, and most were never returned. (The run on these books was probably prompted by a *Los Angeles Times* story, LIBRARY BOOZE BOOKS MAY BE THROWN OUT, which reported that if Prohibition was enacted, all of the guides to home brewing were likely to be destroyed.) The war came, and it found its way into the library, too. In 1917, the American Library Association formed its Library War Council, and Everett Perry was appointed head of the Southwestern Division. The council eventually collected six hundred thousand books to send to American troops overseas. The ALA offered other wartime programming around the country. Vowing to "fight Red delusions," it designed workshops about the dangers of bolshevism to warn patrons away from unpatriotic thoughts. As part of that effort, Perry directed his librarians to root out any books that "sing the praise of German Kultur." One librarian reported to him that she'd found the phrase "Kill the English" scrawled inside some German history books. The ALA commended the Los Angeles library for its war programs, especially for helping "Americanize" the city's many immigrants by encouraging them to read English and take part in library groups. In a newsletter article, the organization congratulated the library for hosting an event at which "a highly cultivated Jewish woman spoke [about] English literature to a large group of her own people . . . and these Jewish people are now busy reading the very cream of American and English literature!"

For some reason, the story ended with a list of strange, almost surreal details about the city's reading habits, such as the fact that Chinese people in Los Angeles were partial to Greek literature, and the city's firemen liked books about rabbits.

By this time, the library — and libraries around the country — had become an essential feature of the American landscape, a civic junction, a station in ordinary life. Everyone traveled through the library. In such a place, this crossroads, you might even find someone you had lost. People searching for missing loved ones sometimes scribbled messages in library books with the hope that the person they were looking for would see the message — as if the library had become a public broadcast system, a volley of calls and wished-for responses. Page margins were dappled with penciled pleas tossed into the wide-open sea of the library. "Dear Jennie: Where are you keeping yourself?" said one note written on a page of a book in the Los Angeles library in 1914. "I have searched three cities for you and advertised in vain. Knowing that you like books, I am writing this appeal in every library book I can get hold of in hope that it may come to your eyes. Write to me at the old address, please."

No one was quite sure whether this multiplying, spreading stew of a place was really a city. Los Angeles looked nothing like the old cities of the Midwest and the East, and its shape was spun out as if it had been created by centrifugal force rather than emerging from a hard center. The new city was comingled with the old ranchos. There were still orange groves downtown. It was the only major city in the country, and the largest city on the West Coast, without a stand-alone main library building. In 1914, Everett Perry arranged for the library to move out of the high-priced Hamburger Building to a less expensive building nearby, where the library shared space with a pharmacy and a grocery store. It was an awkward fit. In 1921, a bond issue for library construction was put on the city ballot. The campaign in support of it emphasized the humiliation of being a city without typical urban assets, a sore spot in a city that was trying to believe it was actually a city. "Grow Up, Los Angeles!" one pamphlet said. "Own Your Own Public Library and Take Your Place with Progressive Cities!" Another urged, "Mr. Average Taxpayer, pay fifty cents a year and remove this stigma from Los Angeles' name!" A short film showing the over-crowded reading rooms played in theaters around the city. A flyer supporting the bond issue stated bluntly:

A MASS OF REASONS WHY WE NEED A DECENT LIBRARY HOME

Because: Every Self-Respecting City Owns Its Own Library Home. San Francisco and Seattle make us look like a village with their own fine library homes, best proof of their culture and mental development. "Los Angeles," they can say, "hasn't advanced far enough to care for a first-class public library," while we hang our civic head with shame and mortification.

A local historian named Luther Ingersoll published a passionate letter supporting the building of a library. Titled "Our Public Disgrace," Ingersoll's missive begged the public to erase the "intolerable abuses" inflicted on all citizens by Los Angeles's inadequate library. He pitied librarians for being jammed into quarters "surrounded by codfish, onions, Hamburger steaks and Limburger cheese."

The bond issue was a success, passing

with seventy-one percent approval. But it raised only $2.5 million for library construction, which was a measly sum; the New York Public Library's building, for instance, had a $9 million construction budget. The bond issue wasn't even enough to buy the entire lot that had been proposed as the library's site. In 1923, Ballot Measure #2, to pay for the remaining land, was put before the voters. The city held a contest to pick a slogan in support of the measure. The entries included, for instance, "Hey Diddle Diddle / The Cat and the Fiddle / The cow jumped over the moon / But the library can't jump / So we voters must hump / To see that it has enough room"; but the winning slogan was the simple declarative "The library will belong to you / Keep it in sight / Vote 'Yes' on Two." The measure passed, and at last, Los Angeles had money to begin building its own library.

Like so much in Los Angeles, the library began with a reinvention. Most of the topography of downtown was crumpled and ridged by ranges of hills. The hills were once prized as landmarks. But as the city began to develop, hills were thought of as annoyances to be clambered over and built around, impeding the city's growth because

307

they were too steep to support large structures. Flat areas like Hollywood and Watts grew much faster than downtown, because of this knobby topography. The hills had developers stumped. In 1912, one business association proposed laying a pipeline from the Pacific Ocean to the center of the downtown, and using piped-in seawater to blast the hills away. Another suggested lifting the hills with hydraulic jacks and then knocking them over, or using a fleet of backhoes to chip them away.

The site chosen for the library was the block between Flower Street and Grand Avenue, bound by Fifth and Sixth Streets. It was on the southern flank of the Bunker Hill Ridge and was pitched so sharply that it was a designated topographical feature known as Normal Hill. It was too steep for something the size of the proposed library, so a clutch of steam shovels set upon it, scratching away until what remained was mostly level, with a lazy angle on the Grand Avenue side. (Eventually, many of downtown's other hills were also either scraped down or leveled off. Bunker Hill itself was lowered by sixty feet.)

The favored candidate to design the library was a New York architect named Bertram Goodhue, who had gained notice in California for designing San Diego's 1915 Panama-California Exposition, a sunny array of buildings with troweled stucco walls, terra-cotta roofs, and lavish decoration. The design was so popular that it inspired an outbreak of Spanish Revival architecture in Southern California and beyond.

Goodhue was slim and debonair, with a girlish complexion, a cresting wave of yellowy hair, and an air of impending tragedy. He was born in Connecticut and, at the age of fifteen, became an apprentice at a New York architectural firm. In addition to architecture, he excelled at book design and typography. He invented Cheltenham, one of the world's most popular typefaces; the *New York Times* used it as a headline font for decades. He was a workaholic and often spent fourteen hours a day at his drafting table. He was also pensive and neurotic, and suffered from inexplicable aches, unaccountable pains, and pervasive anxiety. He seesawed between bursts of ecstasy, which occurred when he was exposed to great art, and troughs of melancholy. His friends considered him mercurial and poetic. In his spare time, he enjoyed drawing intricate sketches of imaginary cities.

Goodhue's earliest buildings were neo-

Gothic churches and residences with spiky rooflines and elaborate stone latticework. His aesthetic began to change in 1892, when he visited Mexico and Spain and fell in love with the bright color and exuberance of the architecture. In 1902, he traveled to Egypt and the Arabian Peninsula and became fascinated by the domes and tile work of Islamic buildings. He visited California for the first time at the turn of the century. When he returned to New York, he told friends that he was enchanted by California and was eager to go back. Los Angeles, though, struck him as a strange place. In a letter, he described it as "a painfully big city wherein dwell practically no native sons of The Golden West, but a heterogeneous mob of movie actors and actresses and emigrants from Kansas, Nebraska, Iowa . . ."

Soon after he had finished his work on the Panama-California Exposition, Goodhue flew on an airplane for the first time, and the view from the sky transformed him. He was astonished by the power of bold, simple forms standing out of the distant landscape, and how profound they were even from a mile above. The airplane ride changed the way he thought about buildings. His next commission was the

Nebraska State Capitol. His design was much more streamlined and geometric than his previous buildings, featuring a low, wide stone base and a skyscraper tower. On the Nebraska prairie, it rose like a Machine Age monument, a limestone lighthouse. From the sky, it had a mighty presence.

Goodhue also began toying with the idea that a building should be a sort of book — an entity that could be "read." He wanted a building's form, its art, its ornamental surfaces, its inscriptions, even its landscaping, to connect in a unified theme that reflected the purpose of the building. Experiencing the building would be immersive. Everything about it would work together to tell a story about what the building was.

This kind of singularity of design and decoration is typical of religious structures, but it was rare for a secular building. Goodhue knew it was a complex task; instead of simply designing the form of the building, he would have to consider its interior, the land around it, the art hung inside it. He realized such a building needed a team working together. The architect would plan the building; a writer would develop the narrative theme; a sculptor would create the three-dimensional ornamentation; and an artist would be responsible for the color and surfaces. All of them would operate in service to the same concept. Goodhue had first begun exploring this notion when he developed the Nebraska capitol, and his team there was the prominent sculptor Lee Lawrie; an artist named Hildreth Meiere; and a professor of philosophy named Hartley Burr Alexander. In addition to being an academic, Alexander was a poet and a scholar of Native American culture and political thought. He coined the term "iconographer" to describe his role in the project.

The Nebraska State Capitol took ten years to complete. Goodhue's idea of incorporating visual and conceptual symbolism inside and out is essential to the character of the building. It was declared a great success and ended up influencing public buildings throughout the world.

By 1922, when he was hired to design the Los Angeles library, Goodhue had designed dozens of prominent buildings. He had won awards and dozens of important commissions. He had a happy marriage. He doted on his two children. He and his wife were popular; people invited them to parties and dinners all the time. Nevertheless, Goodhue was often gloomy and was obsessed with death and old age, which annoyed his wife. Work helped distract him from his morbid frame of mind. The library wasn't his biggest project, but he was exhilarated by it. He approached it with a kind of freedom he had never experienced before. He believed that its design could fuse everything he had learned and loved in the visual world into a monument to things he valued most: history, books, philosophy, design, aspiration, creativity.

He began sketching, with the idea of combining the fancifulness of Spanish Revival with a more modern silhouette. Thematically, he imagined the building as a tribute to the glories of knowledge — in effect, it would be a humanist cathedral celebrating the great intellectual works of civilization. Each lintel would tell a story. All the walls would carry messages. He asked Lawrie and Alexander to join him again as part of the design team. Goodhue sensed he was creating something that was even more profound than the Nebraska Capitol. He felt he was shedding all the conventions of his training and all orthodoxy of style. He wasn't even sure how to describe what he was doing. "My Gothic is no longer anything like historically correct," he wrote in a letter to an architect friend. "My Classic is anything but book Classic . . . at Los Angeles I have a Public Library in the same strange style, or lack of style." The building became singularly important to him. "I've come to take a deep personal interest in the success of this building," he told Everett Perry. "I promise to do something of which the city will be proud." He might have imagined spending time in the library himself someday. He loved California, and in 1920, he built a house for himself near Santa Barbara.

His first sketches presented a squat building on an enormous blocky base, squeezed down by a low lid of a dome. The Municipal Art Commission, which had to approve the plans, dismissed it as inadequate and "unimpressive." A newspaper article sniped, CITY TO GET DINKY LIBRARY ACCORDING TO PLANS ANNOUNCED. Goodhue was miffed but agreed to rework the drawings. By the time he produced his final version of the library, it had changed into something entirely different. The ornamental arched windows of the first sketch were now streamlined into stacks of rectangular panes. The blocky base was squared off, slimmed down, and broken up with ascending terraces, making a cubist assemblage of crisp, angled shapes with entrances on four sides. The squashed dome was gone. The top of the building was now an enormous but somehow delicate pyramid-shaped tower. The tower was covered in thousands of brilliantly colored tiles and crowned with a finial of a human hand holding an open flame, rising from a golden torch. The facade of buff-colored stucco was embellished with Lee Lawrie's architectural sculptures of thinkers, gods, heroes, and writers. Throughout the building were inscriptions addressing Hartley Burr Alexander's theme, "The Light of Learning." They included Plato's "Love of the beautiful illuminates the world"; French intellectual Blaise Pascal's "Thought is the Grandeur of Man"; and Alexander's own quote, which seemed to embody the spirit of the public library: "Books invite all; they constrain none." The building had a quality that was like a taste on the tip of your tongue that you can't quite explain. It was classic and symmetrical but had a hint of something foreign — maybe Persian or maybe Egyptian. It was fantastical yet as tidy as a toolbox.

The year 1924 was full of change and portent. The opening of King Tut's tomb and the first performance of *Rhapsody in*

Blue electrified art and design. Goodhue's building incorporated the feel of Egypt and the jazzy lyricism of Gershwin. The Municipal Art Commission loved his new drawings, so he returned to New York and began working intensely on the final plans. He hoped the library would be more than memorable. He wanted it to be exciting and even challenging; he hoped it would make the people of Los Angeles "sit up and scratch their heads." By mid-April, he was almost finished. He was about to turn fifty-five, and he planned to spend his birthday in Washington, D.C., at the dedication of his most recently completed building, the National Academy of Sciences' new headquarters. In spite of his predisposition to gloom, Goodhue was thrilled about his progress on the Los Angeles library. He was perhaps as happy as he had ever been.

On April 23, without any forewarning, and to the shock of everyone around him, Bertram Grosvenor Goodhue dropped dead of a massive heart attack. In spite of the library's importance to the city and the attention being paid to the project, there was curiously little news of his death in the Los Angeles papers, other than a single-column story in the *Los Angeles Times* with the

headline DEATH OF ARCHITECT OF LIBRARY DEPLORED.

17.

Toward a Literate World (1938)
  By Laubach, Frank Charles
  379.2 L366

Teaching the World to Read: A Handbook for Literacy Campaigns (1947)
  By Laubach, Frank Charles
  379.2 L366-2

Toward World Literacy: The Each One Teach One Way (1960)
  By Laubach, Frank Charles
  379.2 L366-4

Apostle to the Illiterates: Chapters in the Life of Frank C. Laubach (1966)
  By Mason, David E.
  379.2 L366Ma

I joined a conversation class in the Literacy Center. The teacher had a name that sounded Norwegian. The students went around the room introducing themselves and identified themselves as Korean, Chinese, Mexican, Ecuadoran, Taiwanese, Salvadoran, and Thai. The class began with an animated debate about the longest word in the English language. The teacher, Jorgen Olson, said the word was "antidisestablishmentarianism," but I wasn't sure that was true, having lost this argument myself in the past. As long words go, though, it would do. When Olson said the word, drawing it out deliciously, everyone but the Thai woman started laughing, and for the next few minutes, all the students in the room gave the word a spin. Olson then moved on to the next lesson. He pointed at the whiteboard behind him, where he had written CONFUSING WORDS in gigantic block letters. The first example he listed was the dreadful trio of "latter," "later," and "ladder." It was easy to take care of "ladder," but "latter" and "later" were a doozy, and even after many minutes of having their differences explained and examples given, "latter" and "later" were still hanging people up. Olson said he'd review them again later, and we moved on to something equally

319

confusing, the words "confident" and "confidante" and "confessor."

Between confusing words, the students told me their professions. They included housekeeper, dishwasher, computer repair worker, architect, student, and manicurist. One was youngish and a few were oldish, but most were sort of middle-aged. The class was being held during the school day, so there wasn't anyone younger than eighteen. The students were friendly and relaxed with one another. Some of the friendliest pairs of people in the room shared just a few words of a common language. Still, they managed the chummy ease of neighbors or coworkers. Outside of this room, there was a good chance they never would have met. When Olson had them practice out loud, they made outrageous goofs and mispronunciations without self-consciousness, and even the most fumbled efforts were cheered on by the other students, which seemed very touching to me. The conversation classes do have specific lesson plans, but they also function as an opportunity to practice talking in a setting where it doesn't matter if you have a faltering grasp of English or a heavy accent. "How was your weekend, Tina?" the Taiwanese architect asked the manicurist. He spoke formally, inching cautiously over the word "weekend." The manicurist, who was from El Salvador, beamed at him and said, "Okay." Then she started giggling and said, "I only say 'Okay' because I don't know how to say more."

Olson tapped the chalkboard and said, "Folks, here are a few more new ones I'd like you to try. Listen up. 'Shard.' 'Implicit.' 'Convulsive.' Again, 'shard, implicit, convulsive.' " A look of despair rippled through the room.

Like the people in the conversation class, about seventy percent of the library system's literacy students are people who are not native English speakers. The rest are native English speakers who read only at a third-grade level or never learned to read at all. Central Library has the largest literacy center in the system, but twenty other branches around the city have centers, too. They are run by the library and staffed by a group of almost six hundred volunteers.

The conversation class at the Central Library was held in a conference room in the Literacy Center, which is bland and beige, with the sanitized featurelessness of an orthodontist's office. I stepped out of the conference room while the conversation class wrestled with "convulsive," and I crossed into the main area, which has a few sofas and a few desks and several tutors on duty. I sat down next to Carlos Nuñez, a tutor who teaches a few of the conversation classes and spends the rest of his time meeting one on one with anyone who drops in needing help. He also has a few regular students he tutors weekly. Nuñez used to work at a call center, but then he injured his back and ended up on disability. He tried lazing off at home, but he was bored out of his mind and started shopping compulsively on QVC. He also ate a lot. That was when he decided he had to get out of the house. He liked the idea of being a volunteer, so on a whim, he called the library and offered himself. He now has pupils from France, Russia, Venezuela, Brazil, China, and even Galápagos. ("Can you believe *that?*" he said, raising his eyebrows in an admiring salute to Galápagos.) He has helped people understand their phone bills and school notices and tax forms. He has read personal letters to people who don't know how to read. Sometimes he's helped them write replies. He works two hours every week with a young man named Victor who was born in Mexico but was raised in Los Angeles and wants to apply for U.S. citizenship. Nuñez did all this while seated at a small desk arrayed with

The Civics and Citizenship Toolkit, a few literacy guides, and a recent copy of *Brides* magazine.

Victor was planning to come in that afternoon, so Nuñez stacked up some citizenship materials to be ready for him. As he was squaring up the stack, a young woman with long thick hair walked into the center, signed in, and then approached Nuñez. She told him that she was writing a research paper on Ernest Hemingway and didn't understand a sentence in some material she'd found. Her accent was rounded and musical, perhaps Caribbean. She took out a photocopy of the page in question. Nuñez read it and then explained it to her while she scribbled notes. After she left, an older Asian man appeared at Nuñez's desk and asked him what a sausage roll was. Nuñez was stumped. A few minutes later, a lanky, muscular young man wearing a Pep Boys jacket sat down at Nuñez's desk. Nuñez introduced him as Victor. He greeted me and then told Nuñez that he had been practicing since their last session and thought he had mastered the material.

Nuñez began quizzing him: "What did Susan B. Anthony do? Name a war in the 1900s. What is the supreme law of the land?" The questions were challenging.

Earlier, Nuñez told me that Victor suffered amnesia because of an accident at his job, so he sometimes struggled to remember answers. This day, though, he got almost all the questions right. When he wasn't immediately ready with the answer, he prompted himself by punching his fist into his hand, as if softening up a catcher's mitt. When they finished, Nuñez complimented him, and then Victor said he wanted to do it one more time. Nuñez began again. "What did Susan B. Anthony do? Name a war in the 1900s. What is the supreme law of the land?"

18.

Fishbourne: A Roman Palace and Its Garden (1971)
By Cunliffe, Barry W.
Series: New Aspects of Antiquity
942.25 C972

Occult Theocrasy (1968)
By Queenborough, Edith Starr Miller Paget
366 Q3

Lucy Gayheart (1935)
By Cather, Willa

Laika the Space Dog: First Hero in Outer Space (2015)
By Wittrock, Jeni
X 636 W832

After shaking off the shock of Goodhue's

death, his associate Carlton Winslow assured the city that he could finish the drawings and keep the project on schedule. Privately, Goodhue's team was shattered. Lawrie and Goodhue had been friends for thirty years. Before he returned to his work on the library, Lawrie devised a tomb for Goodhue decorated with carvings of his most important buildings, beneath a Latin inscription that read, "He touched nothing which he did not adorn." (The tomb is in New York City's Church of the Intercession, the first church Goodhue designed.) Lawrie also decided to include Goodhue on the facade of the Los Angeles library: he is above the building's southeast entrance, in a frieze alongside other luminaries in the world of typography and printing, including Johannes Gutenberg and William Caxton, the man who brought the first printing press to England. In the sculpture, Goodhue is sitting at a drafting table, leaning forward, eyes cast down, as if he is about to begin drawing.

On May 3, 1925, the library's cornerstone was laid. The concrete pour for the huge rotunda took twenty-one hours. At the time, it was the largest concrete pour in the city's history. The rotunda's chandelier, a massive bronze and glass representation of the earth and solar system, weighed one ton and proved so cumbersome to manage that winches were installed in the tower so the chandelier could be raised and lowered for cleaning. Some of the building's interiors were plain stucco. Other sections were loaded with ornament and artwork that took another several years to complete. There were sculptures on the banisters, sculptures in niches, and sculptures gazing down from the ceiling. Two huge black marble sphinxes flanked a main stairwell. In one alcove was the library's symbol — a sculpture of a torch known as the Light of Learning, which was repeated in a much enlarged size on top of the pyramid tower. In another alcove was a life-size figure of a goddess with colorless eyes and an imperious expression, known as the Statue of Civilization. The building had fifteen reading rooms arranged along its perimeter, and miles of open shelving, but the majority of the books were stored in four concrete silos, seven stories high, in the interior of the building. The shelves in the concrete stacks were made of steel grating that was touted as fire- and earthquake-resistant.

Goodhue wanted visitors to feel more than that they were in a pretty building. He wanted them to feel they were part of a three-dimensional meditation on the power of human intellect and the potency of storytelling. Even the garden was part of his plan. He called for it to be planted with olive trees, cypress, viburnum, and magnolia, all plants that might have been found in a classic Roman garden, which he felt would continue the experience of intellectual immersion. Among the trees were a variety of sculptures, including a fountain decorated with images of the great writers of the world, which was called the Well of the Scribes.

In June 1926, the building was completed, and on July 15, 1926, the new home of the Los Angeles library officially opened. Initial reaction to the building was praiseful but complicated. "This building comes as a distinct shock," wrote critic Merrell Gage in *Artland News.* "Like all creative art, it is disturbing: it leaves an impression that is satisfying yet mystifying. It follows no accepted order of architecture but through it strains of the Spanish, of the East, of the modern European, come and go like folk songs in a great symphony rising to new and undreamt-of heights in an order truly American in spirit." Another writer described the building as being "as frank and

The globe chandelier in the Central Library rotunda

open and honest as the eye of a little child. It looks one in the face and knows no fear or shame. It has nothing to explain and need make no apologies."

The dedication-day ceremony was a spectacle. More than one thousand children in costumes paraded around the building, led by a man dressed as the Pied Piper. Visitors mobbed the place. There was an air of elation, as if the library were not just a new municipal property but also a civic achievement, a communal wish that actually materialized. A pamphlet called "Like Stepping into a Story Book," distributed on opening day, captured the excited tone: "A magic castle in fairyland! Rich, beautiful colors.

Exquisite harmony of outline. An idyllic setting. A perpetual joy to behold . . . the mind of the visitor is attuned to the message of the poet, the prophet, the philosopher, the artist, the scientist . . . A story book building come true . . . because here is the home of our oldest and best friends — Books." The only objection to the new building came from a small group of people who maintained that the triangles and torch imagery in the library's design denoted something sinister. They insisted that Goodhue must have been a devil worshipper or a Freemason because he used Satan's symbols, and the library was an occult shrine. Their concerns were dismissed, but even today, a website called the Vigilant Citizen persists in making this claim.

The head of the library board was a local attorney named Orra Monnette, whose family became wealthy in 1906, when his father struck a vein of gold worth the equivalent of $131 million. Ordinarily, Monnette was soft-spoken and reserved, with country-club manners, but the new library moved him so deeply that his dedication address sounded like he was speaking in tongues. The text of his address was published later and formatted like poetry:

Life's players and actors present the
  following themes:
The Deepest Truths Which are the Hidden
  Mysteries of Life:
Man's Tragic Existence;
Urge of Keen Desire;
Hopes and Vanities;
Manifest Destiny;
Ages That Are Past;
Outline of History;
Life's Unwearied Travelers;
Toilers of Earth and Sea;
None Again Pass This Way;
And, these read like the Table of Contents
  to a Great Book and that Book is the
  "BOOK OF LIFE" — written by a Master
  Playwright, GOD! To the user, to the
  reader, to the student, to the scholar, in
  your study of this majestic play, this
  inspirational Book of Life, the Los
  Angeles Public Library is your exalted
  opportunity.

People surged in after opening day. Some
came with trouble in mind. Book thieves
prowled, snatching what they could. A few
enterprising con artists used the library to
flesh out elaborate schemes. In one swindle,
they posed as travel agents, using brochures
they'd created by cutting pictures of exotic

331

places out of library books to advertise trips that would never take place. The outbreak of criminality in the library was so alarming that a 1926 editorial complained, "Not only book thieves but other criminals infest the library. They are not readers, nor book borrowers, but come to talk over things and to lay plans for crimes, or to sell morphine, by appointment." At the end of the year, library security reported they had apprehended 57 "mutilators of books"; 105 people who had written in books; 73 who engaged in general bad behavior; 23 forgers; 8 people who were caught hiding books; and 10 who had switched their books' due dates. Sixty-three of the offenders were prosecuted, and six were "judged to have diseased brains" and sent for psychiatric treatment.

The new building wasn't completely finished. The rotunda was bare, and it took painter Dean Cornwell six years to complete the murals. Cornwell was a showman who worked out of John Singer Sargent's former studio in London, hired beauty pageant contestants to model for him, and suspended himself from enormous scaffolding while painting, which drew spellbound crowds. At the time, his nine-thousand-square-foot canvas was the largest such mural ever hung.

Library school had not prepared Everett Perry for his new role as steward of a significant piece of architecture with countless sculptures and carvings and fixtures and fountains. Sometimes he worried about them. In 1930, he wrote to sculptor Lee Lawrie for advice. "Dear Mr. Lawrie, Have you any instructions to give us as to the care and cleaning of the two Sphinxes and the Statue of Civilization?" his letter began. "I haven't the remotest idea of what should be done, if anything, but I imagine no water should be used." (Lawrie replied that Civilization required occasional dusting with a dry cloth.)

In the meantime, Perry still had to oversee the usual business of the library. Charles Lummis had urged his librarians to pounce on patrons. Perry instructed his staff to develop gentler habits, such as "Respect every request. Don't forget how to smile. Avoid snobbishness." He devised new notices for people who forgot to pay their overdue fines. The notices bore his genteel tone: "Dear [blank], A fine of [blank] is charged against your card, which has probably escaped your memory. Will you kindly call . . . within the next few days to clear this record? Very truly yours, Los Angeles

Public Library." The fines were humane, ranging from one cent for a soiled page to a nickel for overdue books. But if you drew in ink in a book or, worse, chewed on it — "chewed book" was an actual line item in Perry's list of violations — you had to pay to replace it. If you developed diphtheria, spotted fever, or the plague while you were in possession of a library book, you were required to inform the library, and the book had to be fumigated before it was put back in circulation, but the library covered the cost.

Three years after the glorious moment of the library's opening, the stock market buckled, and the Great Depression began. The crash came at what had been a proud and elevating time in Los Angeles: The city was galloping, growing, road-building, house-plotting, skyscraping. Its mainstays — movies and oil and airplanes — were strapping young industries that gave the city the luster of newness and youth and seemed immune to the sickness in the economy. But the sickness spread, and it came to Los Angeles, taking down businesses and factories and banks. Tens of thousands of migrants arrived in the city from the Midwest, where their farms had turned to powder after years of drought and deep plowing.

Before heading to California, they watched their planting fields in Oklahoma and Kansas blow away in dry gray clouds that darkened skies as far away as New York City.

Libraries were a solace in the Depression. They were warm and dry and useful and free; they provided a place for people to be together in a desolate time. You could feel prosperous at the library. There was so much there, such an abundance, when everything else felt scant and ravaged, and you could take any of it home with you for free. Or you could just sit at a reading table and take it all in. Or you might come to the library and something remarkable would happen, like, say, the day in 1938 when poet Carl Sandburg dropped by the children's story hour and played guitar and talked about Paul Bunyan. But overall, it was a time of sorrow and desperation, no matter what the library offered. On New Year's Eve in 1932, a man named Charles Munger threw himself into the pond in the library garden in an attempt to commit suicide.

After the stock market crash, book circulation rose by sixty percent, and the number of patrons almost doubled. According to the *Los Angeles Times*, many of these patrons had been "disgorged from flophouses." In the meantime, as tax receipts dwindled, the library's budget was cut by almost a quarter. Perry was determined to make the library just as effective as it had been with more money and fewer customers. He instructed his staff to cull books that seemed superfluous, including "books on spiritualism. Books on bridge. Cheap humor. Genteel poetry. [Books on] astrology, numerology, palmistry, fortune-telling." He published lists of recommended reading, which revealed the anxieties and preoccupations of the time. In 1928, one reading list called "The Jew in the Literature of the Last Decade" included books such as *You Gentiles; I am a Woman and a Jew;* and *Twenty Years on Broadway.* In 1931, under the title "The Unemployment Dilemma," the books recommended by Perry included *Layoff and Its Prevention; What's Wrong with Unemployment Insurance?;* and *Responsible Drinking.* The 1932 list included *Is Capitalism Doomed?* and an exhaustive inventory of books about war. People wanted so much from the library. They wanted it to solve things for them. They wanted the library to fix them and teach them how to fix their lives.

In a peculiar case of counterprogramming,

when many Americans didn't have work, CBS Radio launched a show called *Americans at Work,* a series of radio plays about different professions. There were episodes about toymakers, dynamiters, turkey farmers, and pineapple growers. One episode was about librarians. As the play begins, a young girl named Helen announces to her parents and her uncle that she plans to become a librarian.

MOTHER. Helen, it's ridiculous to think of your wanting to become a librarian. Why, that's just work for older ladies who need to help out a little bit.

HELEN. That's the whole trouble. That's what YOU think it is, and you don't know anything about it. I love books and I'd like to help other people love them.

FATHER, *to Mother.* That's what you get for letting the child keep her nose in books all the time. Girls shouldn't be bothered with book learning.

HELEN. Oh, Dad — how can you say such old-fashioned things! I do want to be a librarian, really I do. What do YOU say, Uncle Ned?

NED, *kindly, gently.* I say if the girl wants to be a librarian, let her. You know, times have changed. From what I can see, a librarian's got to be a right modern smart girl nowadays.

Men had been in charge of the Los Angeles Public Library since 1905, when Charles Lummis toppled Mary Jones in the Great Library War. At that time, about eighty percent of all American librarians were male. Within a few years, thanks in part to Andrew Carnegie's efforts, the gender balance in the profession teeter-tottered, and the number of male librarians dropped to twenty percent. Most women were employed as staff librarians and clerks, and they never advanced into management. Everett Perry's deputy director, however, was a woman named Althea Warren. She was an exception among female librarians, having previously held an administrative position as the head of the San Diego library system. Warren was from a wealthy, intellectual Chicago family. Her grandfather was a federal judge. She began her library career in her hometown, choosing to work at a branch in the poorest neighborhood in the city. While she ran the library system in San Diego, she also took care of her mother, who struggled with severe depression. In 1925, when her mother's illness became extreme, Warren decided to take a leave from the San Diego library. She bought a duplex near Pasadena and lived in one side of it and installed her mother and her mother's nurse in the other side. But her reputation was so outstanding that when Everett Perry heard she was in the Los Angeles area, he persisted until he convinced her to become his second-in-command.

Warren was big, with a strong chin and wild, wavy hair that she wore bunched up in a mess of a topknot. She had a good sense of humor; people liked being around her. She often described herself as an old maid, but in fact, soon after she began her job at the Los Angeles Public Library, she fell in love with the head of the Children's Department, a woman named Gladys English. In 1931, Warren and English moved in together and remained inseparable until English died in 1956.

Everett Perry's tenure began at a time when the Los Angeles Public Library was in its last days as a small operation squeezed into a rental space — when it was still a relic of the earliest version of Los Angeles, an outpost in the dust of the Southwest. Los Angeles was not a place you associated with books: It was a noisy gathering of pioneers figuring out how to prosper in its hopscotch of valleys and hills. The city and the library changed dramatically in those years. Perry was a link between the library's past and future. He championed Bertram Goodhue, so he is responsible for what the library looks like today. After the great excitement of guiding the library into its first permanent home, Perry was forced to navigate the first jolts of the Depression. He was steady and solid, even in the terrible upheaval of those years, but he was not a charismatic leader. Some of his predecessors outshone him; Charles Lummis, for instance, was an electrifying presence that glowed and sputtered in equal measure. Everett Perry was just what the library board had noted when he was first interviewed. He was "all business," "doesn't talk much," a man made of granite. But he loved the library, and the library staff and patrons loved him. In August 1933, Perry suffered a heart attack. At first he seemed to be recovering, but three months later, he died. The library staff was shattered. Perry would have been pleased to know that Althea Warren was appointed to take his place.

Warren was probably the most avid reader who ever ran the library. She believed librarians' single greatest responsibility was to read voraciously. Perhaps she advocated this in order to be sure librarians knew their books, but for Warren, this directive was based in emotion and philosophy: She wanted librarians to simply adore the act of reading for its own sake, and perhaps, as a collateral benefit, they could inspire their patrons to read with a similarly insatiable appetite. As she said in a speech to a library association in 1935, librarians should "read as a drunkard drinks or as a bird sings or a cat sleeps or a dog responds to an invitation to go walking, not from conscience or training, but because they'd rather do it than anything else in the world." Throughout her life, Warren published little tip sheets — "Althea's Ways to Achieve Reading" — to encourage people to find time for books. She approved of fibbing if it gave you an additional opportunity to read. "The night you promised to go to dinner with the best friend of your foster aunt, just telephone that you have such a bad cold you're afraid she'll catch it," she wrote in one of her tip sheets. "Stay at home instead and gobble *Lucy Gayheart* in one gulp like a boa constrictor." She was a reading evangelizer. She constantly looked for new ways to get books into the hands of the public. For instance, she thought it far too restrictive that children had to be in third grade or above to get library cards, so she opened library membership to any child who could sign his or her name.

Warren inherited a withered budget and a public who wanted more from the library all the time. Los Angeles in 1933 was only the fifth largest U.S. city, but the library circulated more books than any library in the country. To economize, Warren took measures that pained her. She cut back on hours when the library was open; she didn't replace staff who resigned; she closed some of the little book kiosks in hospitals and shopping areas; and she limited purchases of new books. She also was forced to shut down the library school that Tessa Kelso had established.

But she expanded services as much as she could when she could afford to. She established an advice line that parents could call to inquire if a particular movie was appropriate for children. (The staff invented their own rating system, which included such categories as "this movie would not be suitable for nervous children.") She expanded the main information desk. She also added a phone-in reference service. The reference service was extremely popular, and it was used in ways that no one at the

From left to right: *City librarians Mary Jones, Mary Foy, Harriet Wadleigh, and Althea Warren*

library anticipated. So many people called for help solving crossword puzzles that Warren finally forbade the librarians to answer those requests, because they hardly had time to answer non-crossword questions. In 1937, as part of a study of the Reference Department, the library compiled a list of what callers were asking, which included:

What Romeo looked like
Amount of milk produced in the U.S. in 1929
Negro slave writings of literary value

343

Statistics on the sterilization of human be-
  ings
Number of radios in Los Angeles
Type of work done in institutions for the
  feeble-minded
Number of Jewish families in Glendale
Burial customs in Hawaii
Average length of human life
Whether immortality can be perceived in
  the iris of the eye

One very hot Saturday afternoon in April 1940, sitting alone in her office, Althea Warren typed a letter addressed to "The City Librarian of Los Angeles on December 7, 1972" that she wanted opened by the future city librarian on what would be the hundredth anniversary of the library. She thought it would be interesting to leave a message, like a time capsule, for her successor. "You may be amused to know my troubles and hopes in your office thirty-two years ago," she began. "Thirty-two-year-old troubles are almost sure to be amusing." Warren mentioned that if by chance she were still alive when the letter was opened, she would be eighty-five years old, which at that time must have seemed nearly immortal. She wrote about how difficult it had been for her to inherit the library from the venerable Everett Perry, and how she felt like a "soft and shaking poplar tree" compared to Perry's "hard, primeval oak." She wrote about the contrast between the 1920s, when the library budget was lavish, and the cold shock of the stock market crash, when she was forced to cut salaries of library workers three times and could barely afford to order new books. The letter is by turns jolly and aching, full of the sober realization that because of her constrained budget, she was doomed to disappoint both her staff and the public. The public got less from the library than they wanted, and her staff was more aggrieved than she wished. She rued that she spent so much of her time on small matters — deciding whether to buy a new thermostat for the furnace in the San Pedro branch, finding money in the budget to buy paper towels for the washrooms — when what she hoped was to create a utopia of libraries across the city, staffed by librarians who were satisfied and proud.

The letter was also optimistic. It was clear that Warren believed the library would endure. She signed off, "My heart is with your work and you!" The letter sat in the office of the city librarian until its designated date, when it was opened and read by Wyman Jones.

In 1941, the United States entered World War II, and the library adapted. The one-ton chandelier in the rotunda was lowered to the floor in case explosions shook the building, and it stayed on the floor until 1944. To comply with efforts to darken downtown buildings at night, Warren announced that the library would close at sunset. But so many war workers asked to use the library at night that she reverted to original hours and even added later nights. To fulfill the municipal lights-out policy, she outfitted the library's windows with blackout curtains. Libraries throughout the city offered first-aid classes and sold war bonds. They distributed government information leaflets at the new defense information desk. Central Library's collection of international science material, including patent information from Germany and Italy, was especially large and was one of the few such collections on the West Coast. The army and navy consulted it regularly in an effort to understand what the Axis had in its arsenal.

Once American troops were sent overseas, reference librarians began receiving a new kind of call. Soldiers weren't permitted to say exactly where they were deployed, so they often put clues in their letters home, hoping to tip off their families as to where they were. The families, in turn, called the library for help deciphering. As one reference librarian noted, "We would be asked things like, 'Where in the world do men wear their hair brushed up straight?' or 'Where do people have rings in their noses?' or 'In which country do women wear full skirts and white aprons?' "

Late that year, Warren took a four-month leave of absence from the library to run the Victory Book Campaign, a nationwide drive to gather books for army reading rooms, military hospitals, and training camps. She appointed a director for the drive in each state and coordinated press releases and radio spots to encourage people to bring books to collection points. She enlisted the Boy Scouts and Girl Scouts to go door-to-door asking for books. By March 1942, the Victory Book Campaign had amassed more than six million books and begun distributing them to troops across the country and overseas — at the exact moment when the libraries of Europe were burning. That year, President Roosevelt gave the keynote at the American Library Association's convention.

"Books cannot be killed by fire," he declared. "People die, but books never die."

When the war ended, modern Los Angeles began. The bean fields and orange groves were plowed under and replanted with three-bedroom bungalows. Waves of soldiers returned, followed by waves of families who came to be near the burst of aircraft factories and electronic plants and oil drills. This was when Harry Peak's family pulled up stakes in Missouri and headed west, leaving their farm for the fresh chance that California seemed to offer. Los Angeles bulged and boomed, spread and stretched. If you were away for a few days, you might not recognize your neighborhood when you got back; such was the speed of growth. The library could hardly keep up. There were new communities asking for library branches in areas that had been nothing but tomato plants just a moment earlier, but there was no money to build them.

Warren led the library through the Depression, the war, and those first tumultuous postwar years, and in 1947, she decided she wanted to finally take the break she had planned before Everett Perry had lured her to the job. She was feted and celebrated before she left. She received hundreds of letters from appreciative patrons, including one from Aldous Huxley, a frequent library visitor, who wrote, "[I] must take the present opportunity of telling you how good I find the service at the library and what a sound selection of books you have built up."

Warren's successor was Harold Hamill, a young man with big ears and tufty blond hair and a second-cousin resemblance to *Gunsmoke*'s James Arness. Hamill, whose previous job was heading the library system in Kansas City, was a modernist. It was the perfect moment for someone forward-thinking to run the library, since technology was emerging, and uses for it in libraries were being invented all the time. Hamill embraced the innovations. He introduced a book checkout system called "photo-lending" that used micro-cameras to snap a picture of the book being borrowed; he also established an Audio-Visual Department, a first for the Los Angeles system, and began adding microfilm and microfiche to the library's collection.

In October 1957, the first Russian *Sputnik* orbited the earth. In November, the second *Sputnik,* carrying the space dog Laika, was sent into space. That same year, a German astronomer published a definitive catalog of planets and stars. Four out of the five Nobel Prize laureates in Physics and Chemistry that year were from countries other than the United States. Americans were terrified that the country was falling behind in math and science, so nationwide there was a renewed commitment to education, especially in those fields. It probably isn't a coincidence that the following year, the Los Angeles library loaned out more books than it had in decades, and the city's voters supported a $6 million bond issue to build twenty-eight new branch libraries.

Who was patronizing the library in 1957? A report from the time noted "an increase of use by professional artists and designers . . . FOREIGN DEPARTMENT: Displaced persons program has brought large number of Latvian, Lithuanian, Jewish, German, Russian people." The way the city had evolved was especially apparent in the makeup of visitors to the Science Department. No one asked for books on citrus or avocado farming anymore. While they were in great demand in the 1930s, books on how to prospect for gold now idled on the shelves. Instead, patrons wanted guides to prospecting for uranium, how to build computers, how to invent and patent new products. That year's recommended reading was a list of titles about atomic power. According to the department report, "The 'man on the street' as well as the specialist has an interest in science today." By 1960, though, the popularity of science books was matched by interest in books that offered what the librarians nicknamed "the cult of reassurance" — books about positive psychology, occultism, witchcraft, Dianetics, and Nostradamus.

A stand-alone children's department had been part of Central Library since the Goodhue Building was built. Until 1968, though, there hadn't been a department for teenagers. The concept that the years between twelve and nineteen form a distinct phase of life barely existed until the 1960s. By 1968, the library had acknowledged the existence of teenagers. The new Teen Department provided books and also hosted events — folk sing-alongs, judo classes, rock concerts — in hopes of attracting young people to the library and making it feel like a community center more than just a book depository. After a time, sing-alongs gave way to the less innocent aspects of teenage life, and the department began offering programs on sexuality, suicide, drug abuse, gangs, and runaways.

19.

The Complete Idiot's Guide to
Parenting a Teenager (1996)
  By Kelly, Kate
  370.16 K29

Su hijo adolescente: Cómo com-
prenderlo y relacionarse con él
(1989)
  By Davitz, Lois Jean
  S 372.1 D265

Il Pianeta Degli Adolescenti: I
Giovani D'oggi Spiegati Agli
Adulti (1998)
  By Burbatti, Guido L.
  I 370.16 B946

Dear Distant Dad [videorecord-
ing] (1992)
  VID 301.57 D2855

The film *Pleasantville* is about two siblings who are trapped in a 1950s television show about a suburban town that seems perfect but is actually sexist and racist and oppressively conformist. The movie, released in 1998, was written, directed, and co-produced by Gary Ross, who was the president of the Board of Library Commissioners in Los Angeles from 1993 to 1996. When *Pleasantville* was released, Ross made the premiere of the film a benefit to help pay for a new, larger teen department. A corner on the second floor, previously used for the Music Department, was designed with a big circular communal desk and splashy graphics, beanbag chairs, and lots of nooks and crannies. You would not mistake it for any other part of the library. Teen'Scape was inaugurated in March 2000 with a party that featured an appearance by actor Anthony Stewart Head, who played the librarian on *Buffy the Vampire Slayer.*

When I visited Teen'Scape recently, the librarian on duty was a slim, composed young woman named Mary McCoy who was wearing cat's-eye glasses and a slightly choppy haircut. Before she became a librarian, McCoy played in punk bands. Punk rock's loss was the library's gain. McCoy gravitated to the teen department because she has an affinity for young people, and they are drawn to her. She is cool enough to be a confidante, but she isn't a pushover. "I don't let them get away with anything," she said. "For instance, I saw kids here this morning, and I knew it was a school day, so I just gently asked why they weren't in school." It turned out school was in the middle of a lockdown drill, so they were killing time at the library. If they'd been cutting class, McCoy would have given them a not-so-gentle nudge back to school.

Being a teen librarian is a slight misnomer. The librarians in the department view themselves as a hybrid of unofficial advice-givers, part-time disciplinarians, and homework coaches. They act in loco parentis for many kids who get scant parenting at home. "They're my kids," one of Teen'Scape's librarians told me. The tug to parent them outside the walls of the library is mighty. "It's a fine line," McCoy said. "You mostly have to avoid it. But sometimes you act on your conscience. We had a girl here who was undocumented and really needed help. All the department librarians chipped in and bought her a bus pass and little things to help her."

Just then, a girl with black eyeliner winging skyward approached the desk holding a

354

bag of Cheetos. "Are you allowed to eat in here if you're not using the books?" she asked, looking anxious. McCoy said that eating wasn't permitted. The girl sighed and then walked over to shelves of manga books, jiggling her Cheetos bag. Some kids will check out twenty or thirty manga books at a time. The manga bookshelves took up most of one wall and ended at a bulletin board covered by an illustrated poster that read: "Looking for Your First Job? What to Wear: Baseline Casual, Boardroom Attire. How to Tie a Regular Tie Knot."

The department used to fill with teenagers who came to use its computers. Now many of them have computers at home or can use their smartphones to go online. They still come to Teen'Scape, but these days they come to make use of the free printers, or just to hang out somewhere away from their parents. The department has thirty thousand books, scores of board games, the newest version of *Guitar Hero,* and other teenagers. As a result of that last offering, there is a fair amount of horsing around. The two things that McCoy finds herself saying the most often are "Hey, watch your language" and "Hey, not so close on the beanbags." Lately, closeness on the beanbags had occurred more frequently than McCoy liked, and she sensed that the people being touched weren't always happy about it, so she arranged to present a workshop for kids on how to identify healthy relationships. It was scheduled for the afternoon I was visiting and would be conducted by a social service agency called Peace Over Violence.

Another Teen'Scape librarian named Teresa Webster had just arrived for her shift. She checked in with McCoy, who reminded her about the workshop. Webster nodded and then said, "You know, we have to get someone to come and give a talk to these kids about politics. One of them just asked me what a Republican is." Webster and McCoy both shook their heads in amazement and then burst out laughing.

The three Peace Over Violence volunteers walked in carrying an easel and placards and a welter of handouts. McCoy went around reminding kids that the workshop would start soon. It was being held in a section of the room where the television happened to be. A wiry boy wearing small hoop earrings had just fished a video controller out of a bin and looked crushed when McCoy told him he would have to wait to use the television until the workshop finished. He stood frozen, as if he couldn't quite absorb the news. "You mean . . . ," he said after a moment. "I can't . . ." McCoy nodded with great sympathy, and he finally put the controller away and wandered off. Several girls settled on the beanbags nearby. One cuddled with her boyfriend and kept squealing and smacking him playfully on the arm. In the farthest corner, almost out of the room, a lone figure sat in a broody slump, with a hood pulled up and winched so tightly that it obscured his or her face; it was impossible to tell if the person was a girl or a boy. The volunteers walked around greeting the kids, including the hooded one at the far table, and passed out a workbook titled *Teen Power and Control Wheel.* Mary McCoy hovered nearby.

One volunteer came to the front of the group, introduced herself, and began by asking if anyone in the room could think of an example of an unhealthy relationship. The girl cuddling with her boyfriend stopped and called out, "Rihanna and Chris Brown!"

"Doesn't have to be *stars,*" said the girl sitting on the beanbag next to her, sounding disgusted.

"I love Rihanna!" someone else said.

"Okay, okay, that's a good one," the volunteer said. "Anyone else?"

A small girl toward the back of the room

said, "It's . . . someone gets mad and hits you?" and "Uh-huh" rumbled around the room. After talking for a few minutes and reviewing the handout, the group read a depressing poem called "David Brings Me Flowers," which laid out the excuses that girls make for abusive boys. The mood in the room downshifted; the kids sat straighter and stopped whispering and cuddling and wisecracking.

I tiptoed out as the workshop continued and stopped once more at the desk before I left. The librarian there told me that his name was Russell Garrigan and he had worked in Teen'Scape for the last seventeen years. I asked him if he enjoyed the job, and he said, "Well, my hero is Albert Schweitzer. He said, 'All true living takes place face to face.' I think about that a lot when I'm here."

As I got ready to leave the library for the day, I decided to make one more stop, in the Children's Department, a dreamy room with dark wood, muted murals, and book-shelves that are about the height of a privet hedge. I walked in behind a teacher who was leading a fifth-grade class and repeating "Please use your library voice," in the monotonous tone of a mantra. Story time was under way to the left of the big wooden information desk; a librarian was leading a group of about two dozen children and a dozen adults in the "Alphabet Song." There was an eddy of ceaseless circular motion. A girl wearing a "Keep Calm and Rock On" onesie was hugging a tiny boy in a Batman shirt. A child in a tutu was trying to stand on her head. A boy with a Mohawk haircut toddled over and stared at her. When the "Alphabet Song" got to Z, the librarian segued into "Head, Shoulders, Knees, and Toes." The children brought their own interpretation to the song — "toes, floor, ears, nose," for instance, or "hands, hands, hands, hands." The head of the Children's Department, Madeline Bryant, had told me that preschool story time used to attract three or four kids at most, but over the last few years, young families have been moving back to downtown Los Angeles, and now a story time audience of thirty is typical. As an experiment, she recently offered an infant story time, and it was so popular that they experienced serious stroller-jam.

Diane Olivo-Posner, whose job title is associate director of the Exploration and Creativity Department, was behind the information desk when I walked in. Her eyes were damp, and she was fanning herself with what appeared to be a letter.

"The department," she said in a choked voice, "the department got a letter from Mo Willems! *Mo Willems!* Can you believe it? *Don't Let the Pigeon Drive the Bus!* is one of my favorite books. Oh, I think I'm going to cry."

A little girl who looked about four years old came up to the desk and handed Olivo-Posner a sheet covered with random scribbles. "This is for Miss Linda," she said, shaking the paper. Olivo-Posner took it and told her the drawing was very nice. The little girl dragged her foot across the carpet for a moment and then said, "Will you give it to Miss Linda? Do you know Miss Linda? Where is Miss Linda? Can I borrow some crayons now? Do you know dinosaurs? Tell me the alphabet? Are there scary stories here at the library? Not with ghosts, just scary?"

20.

Helter Skelter: The True Story of the Manson Murders (1974)
  By Bugliosi, Vincent
  364.9794 M289Bu

Criteria for a Recommended Standard, Occupational Exposure to Hot Environments: Revised Criteria (1986)
  613.6 C9345

Riots, U.S.A., 1765-1965 (1966)
  By Heaps, Willard A.
  320.158 H434

Word and Image: History of the Hungarian Cinema (1968)
  By Nemeskürty, István
  791.939 N433

In 1966, the coffeemakers that librarians

used in their workrooms were banned from Central Library. The wattage used by coffeemakers — more than a blender, less than a toaster — was simply too much for the library's weak wiring. It was one of many measures taken in the 1960s in deference to the building's fragile electrical system. In the book stacks, seventy-five-watt bulbs were replaced with forty-watt bulbs, the type usually used in ovens and refrigerators. The smaller bulbs cast a crepuscular half-light, making it almost impossible for clerks to find books on the shelves. Flashlights and miners' hats were in high demand.

By the mid-1960s, Central Library was just middle-aged, but it had the aches and pains of an elderly building. City Councilman Gilbert Lindsay, whose district included Central Library, liked to refer to it as "that piece of junk." *California* magazine described it as "an architectural flapper" that was a "functional flop." The fairy-tale building of 1926 had become shabby and adulterated. Some of the sumptuous mahogany panels had been painted over; the fanciful bronze reading lamps with their honeyed light had been replaced by plain fixtures with fluorescent tubes. According to *The Light of Learning: An Illustrated History of the Los Angeles*

Public Library, published by the Library Foundation in 1993, file cabinets and desks were everywhere, often pushed up against some of Lee Lawrie's finest sculptures and carvings. No one seemed to be the steward of the building. Decisions about it were made willy-nilly. A business manager ordered Julian Ellsworth Garnsey's *Ivanhoe* murals whitewashed because he found them dreary. (Someone managed to intercede in time to save them.) There were far more books than shelf space, and the overflow tumbled into the stairwells and corners. A beautiful fresco titled *Bison Hunt,* which was a 1930s WPA project, was painted over because it had been damaged by rain. Some of the murals were so dirty that they looked like dark abstract paintings; the human figures in them looked like rocks. (The layer of grime was so thick that it would ultimately protect them in the fire, like a Teflon shield.) Only two of the six entrances to the building were functional. Ornate bronze doors on the Hope Street entrance were replaced by industrial doors with panic release hardware. The original buff stucco on the building's exterior had been patched in places to cover water stains and graffiti.

Besides the cosmetic wear, the building's infrastructure was crotchety and failing. Not only were the stacks dark, they were leaky, and scores of books got soaked whenever it rained. In cold weather, the boiler was so overworked that the building engineer had to pour water on it three times a day just to keep it from blowing up. In the heat, things were worse. The library had walls as thick as a bank safe and very few windows, and some of them were wired shut to deter book thieves. There was no air-conditioning. Ventilation and cross breezes were mostly imaginary. When the temperature rose, a battalion of rackety old floor fans was brought out to push the hot air around; they took up almost all of the available electrical outlets. The library was in the midst of scanning its magazines and newspapers onto microfilm. When the floor fans were being used, there weren't any outlets left for the scanners, so the whole project had to be paused.

No matter how hard the fans spun, the heat in the building defeated them. The administration decided on a policy of closing the library when the temperature rose over 95 degrees — that is, when the inside of the building reached 95 degrees. At 94 and below, it was business as usual. More often than not, the radiators were raging even in the thick of a heat wave. They seemed to have a mind of their own that was unrelated to any thermostat. Patrons sweated. The librarians were miserable. They kept records of the temperature in their departments in order to document the misery and make a formal complaint. For instance, these appeared in the History Department's record of one beastly June:

6/3. Temperature 78°. in History Department. Building grossly overheated.
6/5. Temperature 81°. Building still grossly overheated. Patrons complaining.
6/6. Temperature 82.5°. Extremely humid and uncomfortable but heat on!!!!
6/10. Temperature 82°. Constant enervating heat
6/11. Temperature 90°. Smog like pea soup. Heat BLASTING!
6/18. Temperature 91°. RIDICULOUS CONDITIONS
6/19. Temperature 89°. HORRID
6/20. Temperature 88°. UNBEARABLE
6/21. Temperature 104°. It is totally ridiculous that people are forced to work under these conditions . . . terrible heat makes this a HELL! . . . This is outrageous.
6/22. Thermometer stolen.

Unfortunately, the library was aging

exactly when the mood in the city was for anything new, new, new. New neighborhoods, new buildings, and new roads bubbled up, while the old ones sagged under the pall of neglect and abandonment. In the postwar years, downtown became ratty and depopulated. The center of the city was no longer fashionable. Fancy retail bolted out of downtown to new shopping centers in Beverly Hills and Orange County and Brentwood, leaving downtown a hodge-podge of small, funky shops and storefronts that were spookily quiet after five P.M. For decades, buildings in Los Angeles weren't permitted to be taller than thirteen stories because of concerns about earthquakes. While other American cities sprouted their pinnacled skylines and distinctive towers, downtown Los Angeles remained squat and grounded. The ban against tall buildings was finally lifted in 1957. Nothing much happened at first; downtown remained stunted compared to most other cities of its size. As developer Robert Maguire put it, Los Angeles seemed destined to be a city "just ten stories high, all over hell and gone."

The 1960s were anxious times in Southern California. The white population was hurriedly decamping to the San Fernando and East valleys, stranding African Americans in the broken-down neighborhoods closer to the city core. If you were black, you had little choice but to stay in these de facto ghettos. Real estate in Los Angeles was earmarked based on color, in a brazen effort to keep white neighborhoods intact. In 1963, the landmark Rumford Fair Housing Act was passed. It was considered one of the most important advances in the interest of racial equality. But a group of unlikely allies — the John Birch Society and the *Los Angeles Times* among them — rallied behind a ballot measure in 1964 to reverse the Rumford Act, removing the protection against discrimination in buying a home. The measure passed by a margin of two to one — a rebuff of the civil rights movement and of California's self-image as progressive. It cleaved the city into unequal parts — the comfort of white Los Angeles and the pessimism and deprivation of black Los Angeles. Even the library became an arena where racial hostilities played out. Librarians began finding slips of paper tucked inside random books around the library. The slips were designed to look like cruise tickets on something called "Coon-ard Lines," offering, in vulgar terms, travel to Africa on a "boat shaped like a Cadillac with fins" featuring a watermelon patch, heroin, and "a framed picture of Eleanor Roosevelt." The tagline on the bottom read, "Ku Klux Klan, P.O. Box 2345, Overland, Missouri."

The police force in Los Angeles was mostly white, and in poor African American neighborhoods, officers were aggressive and sometimes brutal. One evening in 1965, a white police officer was patrolling Watts, a tough neighborhood southeast of downtown. He stopped a black driver on the suspicion of drunk driving. The stop turned into a confrontation and then into a convulsion of violence and fury. The upheaval lasted six days and ended only after the National Guard was called in. Thirty-four people died; more than a thousand were injured; forty-six square miles of the city were left in ruins. After Watts, there were spasms of violence of a different sort. The Manson Family murders, the shooting death of musician Sam Cooke, and the assassination of Robert Kennedy all seemed to signal that something was damaged and doomed in the nature of the city.

The library quietly fell apart in the blue stillness of downtown. In the wounded period after Watts, the city thinned out in the center and thickened on the edges. One of the many optimistic convictions punctured by the riots was the belief that books were good and true — that on the shelves of libraries, you could find all the answers to all the questions. Life now seemed juddering and inexplicable, beyond the reach of what we could ever know or understand. Gray paint covering a mahogany library wall is not the existential equivalent of the Manson murders or the miseries in a neighborhood like Watts, but they seemed to inhabit the same sour space of things falling apart.

In 1966, a city study known as the Green Report recommended that the Goodhue Building be torn down. The report advised replacing it with a building that would be twice as big as the current building, with an open interior and lots of parking. This proposed library would be more of a book warehouse than a traditional library, and it would no longer be in the bull's-eye of downtown but somewhere off the beaten track. The proposal had its fans. City Librarian Harold Hamill supported it, as did Councilperson Gilbert Lindsay, who said the city should "find some deteriorated ghetto skid-row land and put a great beautiful library on it."

Los Angeles seemed to always be moving toward the eternal future; it was a city that shed memories before they had a chance to stick. In 1966, no organized architectural preservation group existed in Los Angeles. To many people, the idea that there were historic buildings in spanking-new Los Angeles seemed like the punch line to a joke. But there were scores of meaningful buildings in the city. Some had fancy bloodlines, like the library. Many were examples of vernacular architecture that captured their time perfectly and were essential to the look and feel of the city. In general, old buildings weren't valued historically or architecturally or civically. The development potential of the land underneath them was paid more heed. Most old buildings went down without a fight; the haste to modernize knocked out many. The list of Los Angeles's vanished masterpieces included the turn-of-the-century Hollywood Hotel; the exotic Garden of Allah Hotel, built in 1927; Mary Pickford's classic Tudor mansion, Pickfair; and the Marion Davies Beach House, built in 1926 by her lover William Randolph Hearst. Across the street from the library, the Richfield Oil Company was headquartered in a spectacular art deco building with a skin of black and gold and a neon-lit oil derrick for its rooftop finial. When Richfield merged with Atlantic Refining and became ARCO, its executives decided the art deco building didn't project the sleek international image they wanted. The glorious old building was torn down and replaced by a skyscraper distinguished only by the fact that it was the thirty-second-tallest building in the city. "The [new] Richfield Tower celebrates the funeral of the future," Ray Bradbury said. "One can only wish for an earthquake to improve it out of existence."

The Goodhue Building — too small, too old, too decorative, too eccentric — seemed doomed until a group of architects, including Barton Phelps, John Welborne, and Margaret Bach, rallied people who were determined to save it. They knew the situation was urgent, and they managed to draw together a committed group. They were known officially as the Southern California Chapter/American Institute of Architects Library Study Team and met in office space donated by architect Frank Gehry. The team argued the building's case to the city's Cultural Heritage Board. After deliberation, the Cultural Heritage Board agreed with them, and designated the library Historic Cultural Monument No. 46.

Even in its sorry state, people used the

library. The reading rooms were often filled with patrons, and the line at the checkout desk snaked around the lobby. In the 1960s, Chicago had a larger population than Los Angeles. Los Angeles's library, though, was much more active: It loaned out 4.2 books per capita, compared to Chicago's 2.7. Maybe because it was a young library in a young city, Los Angeles was always looking to try new things. The Innovations Committee regularly brainstormed ways to make the library easier to use and more essential to the public, such as adding drive-through book returns and a child-care center. Another proposal suggested creating two different gathering places within the library. One would be called "Today Center," with material on current events and a stock ticker. The other would have an alternative emphasis and feature materials from "political activists, gay liberation, new poets, Third World groups, radical scientists." There would be a graffiti board and drop-in poetry jams, sofas and comfortable chairs for hanging out, and it would stay open twenty-four hours a day.

Even though the Internet and electronic media wouldn't appear for decades, you can sense, even in the 1960s, that librarians knew traditional book lending would not always be the institution's chief purpose. One innovations report advised presciently that the public be dissuaded from having a narrow concept of what a library was, because libraries were "increasingly moving in the direction of functioning as information centers as well as being repositories of book collections."

One feature considered critical to patron loyalty was a good reference desk. Central Library's reference department was called the Southern California Answering Network — SCAN — and it was popular locally and also nationally, since people on the East Coast who needed an answer after five P.M. Eastern Standard Time, when their local libraries were closed, could get ahold of SCAN for three additional hours. The SCAN librarians kept records of the requests they received, and they read like synopses of a play; each one seems like a snapshot of life that concluded with someone saying, "Let's just call the library!"

Patron call. Wanted to know how to say "The necktie is in the bathtub" in Swedish. He was writing a script.

Patron called asking for a book on liver

disorders for her husband who is a heavy drinker.

Patron wants to know origin of the expression "bear coughed at the North Pole." (Unable to provide answer.)

Patron call asking whether it is necessary to rise if National Anthem is played on radio or television. Explained that one need only do what is natural and unforced; for instance, one does not rise while bathing, eating, or playing cards.

Patron is a writer in Hebrew; wanted to create a pun between the word for *Zion* and the word for *penis.* We couldn't find a term for *penis,* but the word *copulate* is *mtsayen* which helped her make her pun with *tsion.*

Patron is an actor who has to impersonate Hungarian secret police. Wanted words pronounced. Found a Hungarian-speaking librarian who spoke to him.

Patron inquiring whether Perry Mason's secretary Della Street is named after a street, and/or whether there is a real street named Della Street.

Patron asked for help writing inscription for father's tombstone.

In 1973, the library even added a service called the Hoot Owl Telephonic Reference, which operated from nine P.M. until one A.M., long after the library was closed. Dialing H-O-O-T-O-W-L connected you to a librarian who could find the answer to almost any question. The Hoot Owl slogan was "Win Your Bet Without a Fight." Apparently, in the late evening, people all over Los Angeles did a lot of betting on trivia such as the correct names of the Seven Dwarfs. The service got a call every three minutes, adding up to about thirty-five thousand a year. Hoot Owl was a favorite target of conservative groups, who believed it catered to "hippies and other night people." But the library persisted, and Hoot Owl operated every weeknight until the end of 1976.

21.

Harry Peak after his release from jail

```
The Alibi (1916)
  By England, George Allan
  M


The Rediscovery of Morals, with
```

Special Reference to Race and Class Conflict (1947)
  By Link, Henry C.

The Devil Wins: A History of Lying from the Garden of Eden to the Enlightenment (2015)
  By Denery, Dallas G.

Garfield Gains Weight (1981)
  By Davis, Jim

As the investigation into the library fire zeroed in on him, Harry started rewriting his story over and over, each iteration a little askew from the one that preceded it. It was like reading a Choose Your Own Adventure book, taking a different path at each juncture. When ATF agent Thomas Makar interviewed him, Harry said he was downtown on the day of the fire and wanted to go into the library, but a security guard stopped him at the entrance and told him it was closed. He said he didn't know the building was on fire until he heard it on the news later that day. A few hours after the interview, Harry called Makar and said he'd misspoken, and that in fact he had never been in Central Library, ever. Four days later, Makar and another ATF agent named Mike Matassa interviewed Harry again. This time they put him under oath, hoping that would stop the slip and slide of his story. But the story slid. Harry told them he'd gone downtown that morning to do some sightseeing. At some point, he realized he had to call Leonard Martinet and needed to find a telephone. As he was driving around, he noticed a beautiful old building and thought it might have a phone, so he parked nearby. When he started to walk in, a black security guard — he made a point of mentioning the man's race — told him the building was closed; Harry got a few feet into the building before the guard stopped him. When he turned to leave, he bumped into an elderly woman. He helped her get steady on her feet, and then he escorted her out the door. As he recalled, the woman had thanked him.

When he was finished spelling out how he had spent that morning, Harry told Makar that he was very sorry about the fire and he hoped Makar would catch the arsonist. He said that he appreciated the importance of Makar's job, and that he'd recently applied for a job at the Santa Monica Fire Department, but he'd failed the written test. Makar took a Polaroid of him to show to witnesses. Harry was charming, friendly, cooperative. After Makar took his picture, Harry said he was happy to take a polygraph test. He seemed eager to have his story confirmed.

A few days later, Harry called Makar and said he wanted to postpone his polygraph test. They talked for a while, and then Harry confided to Makar that he'd made up everything he'd told him so far. He didn't explain why he had lied. The truth — at least what he was saying was the truth at that moment — was that he hadn't been anywhere near the library that day, and he had never been inside the library in his life. The morning of the fire, he was miles away, heading to Santa Fe Springs on the 101 Freeway. While driving, he was listening to the news and heard that the library was on fire. He could see smoke rising as he drove past downtown. Makar listened to him sympathetically and then wrote in his notes that, as far as he could tell, Harry was "an aspiring actor . . . and made up the story of having been at the library during the fire to make his life seem more interesting and exciting."

Harry finally agreed to take a polygraph

test on October 27, 1986. The examiner asked him the usual sorts of questions — if he was in the library the day of the fire; if he participated in the fire in any way; if he knew who had set the fire. Harry answered no to every question. Mike Matassa drove Harry home from the test, and they chit-chatted along the way. Harry complained to Matassa that he had gained a lot of weight recently and didn't like the way he looked. He said the problem was that he'd recently stopped using cocaine so he was hungry all the time and eating like a horse. Matassa made a mental note of this, remembering that when the security guard had been shown the Polaroid of Harry, he'd said it looked like a fatter version of the man who asked to use the telephone. Librarians who were shown the picture made the same remark: The man looked familiar, but they remembered the trespasser in the library having longer hair and being slimmer than the man in the Polaroid.

A short time later, the results of Harry's polygraph were released to the arson team. Using the physiological criteria of the test, the examiner concluded that Peak "was attempting deception when answering the relevant questions." With this, the investigators fanned out again, interviewing Harry's friends and roommates, his employers, and his parents, looking for something conclusive — a single thread of events or a motive that would advance the case from warm to hot. But none of the accounts of Harry's whereabouts that day cohered. In some details, they overlapped — the need for a telephone, the handsome fireman — but in many, they splayed far apart. He was there; he was not there. He was familiar with the library; he had never visited it. He smelled like smoke that day; he was odor-free. It was like looking at something through a kaleidoscope and seeing its pieces fractured and rearranged. The only constant among those interviewed was the opinion that Harry was a fabulist. "He finds it difficult to give a straight answer," one friend told investigators. "He doesn't know the difference between fabrication and truth." A former roommate said he'd kicked Harry out because of his compulsive fibbing. "It really got upsetting," he said. "He really couldn't control his lying. We couldn't stand it any longer. But he's a good person."

The problem with Harry was that he didn't just pick one lie and stick with it. He presented so many versions of the story that believing one meant disbelieving another; he produced a continuous coil of untruths, each contradicting the one preceding it, unlike a more typical single-track denial that at least was internally consistent, whether or not it was true. It was confusing and almost impossible to believe him. At best, you could believe what he said at a single fixed point in time, but just when you grew accustomed to that rendition of his truth, he produced another account that undid the one you had chosen to trust. For some reason, I felt a kind of affection for Harry Peak, for his blundering keenness and pure hunger for fame, but I could never find a moment when his stories stood still and I felt like I really knew who he was or what he believed.

Investigators went to see Harry's father at his job at Lockheed. He told them that he thought Harry was capable of setting fire to a vacant building, but he would never burn a library because he loved art and antiques. Harry was a good kid who was figuring out what he wanted to do with his life, he said. In fact, Harry had just told him he'd passed the entrance exam at the Santa Monica Fire Department and was on the waiting list for a job.

The fire began to feel like old, unresolved news. Stories in the Los Angeles papers took on a weary tone, droopy with stock phrases like "continuing investigation" and "ongoing inquiries." The only suspect who resonated with the investigators was Harry, but the evidence against him was like mercury: slippery, shape-changing, inconstant. In March, investigators decided to try a new approach. The response to the Polaroids stuck in their minds, as did Harry's comments about having gained weight. They got access to Harry's driver's license photo, taken two years earlier, when he was thinner and had long hair and a mustache. This was closer to the way he looked the day of the fire, before he cut his hair and shaved his mustache and put on his post-cocaine weight.

Eight library staff members who reported seeing a suspicious man the day of the fire were shown the new photo lineup. Six picked Harry's driver's license photo. The other two weren't able to identify anyone from the photos they were shown. Six out of eight positive identifications were enough to warrant another interview with Harry.

His story now took another turn. He told the investigators that he had never been in Central Library in his life. He said that on the morning of the fire, he'd hung out with two friends, whom he named and said would vouch for him. At ten A.M., he left Los Angeles and drove, by himself, to Santa Fe Springs. He went to his parents' house. No one was there, but he went inside. At some point, he called Leonard Martinet from his parents' phone. He was so confident of that fact that he said Matassa could check with the phone company to get proof of his calls to Martinet.

A few days later, General Telephone provided records of calls made to and from the Peaks' house in Santa Fe Springs the morning of April 29, 1986. No calls were made to Martinet's law firm from the Peaks' phone, nor were there any calls from Martinet to the phone.

A few days later, investigators interviewed Harry again, and this time his story pivoted entirely. He explained that the morning of the fire, he had spent time with two friends — different from the ones he'd mentioned previously. After hanging out for a while, he'd left his friends and headed to French Market Place, a frowsy collection of shops and small businesses in West Hollywood. Harry had plantar warts on his foot, and he had an appointment with his chiropodist, Stephen Wilkie, whose office was there.

After Wilkie treated Harry's warts, he closed his office, and he and Harry went for brunch at the French Quarter, a café in French Market Place. The Very Reverend Basil Clark Smith joined them, and the three men enjoyed a leisurely meal. While clearing the table, their waiter happened to mention that he'd heard the library was on fire. The only library Harry knew about was the Los Angeles Law Library, because he went there on many of his errands for Martinet. He assumed the waiter meant that the law library was burning, so he decided to call Martinet to let him know. This was the final version of his whereabouts on the morning of April 29 that he presented. He told investigators that everything else he'd said before had been a joke.

It is not easy to keep an accurate count of Harry Peak's alibis. Some were wholly new and self-contained, whereas others were tweaked and edited versions of previous ones. Investigators, doing the math, said that Harry had given seven different accounts of how he spent that morning. These included placing himself in the building, where he made a dramatic escape from the fire, or placing himself outside the library observing the fire, or in his car driving by, or in Santa Fe Springs, or, finally, at the French Market Place with the Right Reverend Nicholas Stephen Wilkie and the Very Reverend Basil Clark, elders of the American Orthodox Church, where Harry occasionally stayed. He was an equal-opportunity liar, telling contradictory variations of his story to investigators as well as to friends. He performed his fabrications not just to evade legal consequence; he lied to everyone; it was habitual. And he never stopped shifting his story. Months after his arrest, he told his ex-boyfriend Demitri Hioteles that he was in the library restroom that day, having sex with a stranger, and he absentmindedly dropped his cigarette in a trash can and the fire started. This story implicated him directly, and it even had the virtue of being logical: The fire had been an accident, and he fibbed to cover up that he was unfaithful. But the story was patently untrue. The fire never reached the library's restrooms. It remains a mystery why Harry would want to say he committed a crime when it simply couldn't have happened the way he described it. Sometimes I wondered if Harry could remember what the truth was or would have recognized it if he'd heard it.

After getting positive responses to Harry's driver's license photograph, the arson team was certain he'd started the fire. In a fifteen-point memo, they detailed their reasoning.

They cited the inconsistencies in his various alibis; his changed appearance; the selection of his photo by the library staff; and the fact that he'd failed the polygraph test. Also, he possessed firsthand knowledge of some of the day's events that he couldn't have known unless he had been there. For instance, he mentioned several times that he'd bumped into a woman. No news reports mentioned this incident, but it did occur — the woman and the guard on duty both confirmed it. It would have been impossible for Harry to know about the incident if he hadn't been present when she fell.

The investigators laid out their final comprehensive theory, including a motive. They believed Harry went to the library twice that day. He first arrived around seven thirty A.M., and the guard turned him away because the building wasn't open to the public. Then he returned around ten A.M., when the library was open, and he stayed for about an hour, which was when library staff noticed the suspicious blond man in inappropriate locations on the second floor. Investigators believed he started the fire because he was angry that the guard grabbed his arm and prevented him from going into the building earlier. He came back to burn the building down for revenge.

■ ■ ■ ■

Harry Peak was arrested at his house on a probable-cause warrant late Friday afternoon, February 27, 1987, and taken to the jail in Hollywood for questioning. He was upset, shaken, tearful. Despite the scrutiny he'd been subjected to over the previous several months, he seemed incapable of imagining that he was a real suspect and might be subject to a real arrest.

His arrest on Friday afternoon was intentional: That was normally a dead zone for news, and the prosecutors wanted to attract as little attention as possible in the hope that Harry would confess before they had to bring formal charges, perhaps even before he obtained a lawyer. He could be held in custody for seventy-two hours. After that he had to be either formally indicted or released. Investigators were hoping for him to confess because, in truth, their case was only circumstantial. There was no physical evidence or definitive proof that Harry had been in the library at all, let alone started the fire. Bail was set at $250,000, which investigators knew he would find difficult to raise.

The quiet around his arrest didn't last

long. First, Mayor Tom Bradley issued a statement of congratulations to the fire department — something that seems un- wisely premature, since Harry had not been formally charged, and Bradley probably knew the case against him was jerry-built at best. On top of that, two people in the fire department discussed the arrest on an unsecured radio channel that local papers monitored for tips. The story broke im- mediately. The *Los Angeles Times,* describ- ing Harry as a part-time actor and "errand boy," published with the headline FRIENDS SAY TALL TALES TRAPPED ARSON SUSPECT. Reverend Clark Smith, the last of Harry's alibis and the one he seemed to be sticking to most adamantly, provided a pallid defense of his friend: He told the *Times* that Harry didn't look very much like the police artist's sketch of the suspect, especially since he couldn't have grown a mustache if his life depended on it. Whether Harry resembled the sketch is a matter of opinion, but Harry's ability to grow a mustache is a mat- ter of fact. I recently borrowed several pictures of Harry from Demitri Hioteles, and Harry has a thick mustache in most of them.

What Reverend Smith didn't mention was that Harry couldn't have started the fire because he was sitting with him at the French Quarter. Smith only provided a version of the convoluted logic that made Harry's endless helix of confessions and denials so maddening: He said that everyone who knew Harry had laughed when investigators said he gave conflicting accounts of his whereabouts. You had to know Harry, Reverend Smith told the reporter, adding, "Harry always gives conflicting stories."

22.

Human Information Retrieval
(2010)
By Warner, Julian
010.78 W282

Food Safety Homemakers' Attitudes and Practices [microform] (1977)
By Jones, Judith Lea
NH 614.3 J77

Prisoner of Trebekistan: A Decade in Jeopardy! (2006)
By Harris, Bob
809.2954 J54Ha

A New Owner's Guide to Maltese (1997)
By Abbott, Vicki
636.765 M261Ab

The opposite of a sensory-deprivation tank might be to spend a Monday morning in the library's InfoNow Department. The phone rings with that weird blooping electronic tone all day long, and the staff of five reference librarians answer, ping-ponging from topic to topic so widely that just sitting among them and listening makes your brain feel rubbery.

"Monday mornings are busy," said Rolando Pasquinelli, the supervisor of the department. "Excuse me, hang on." He pushed a button on his phone and said, "Hello, InfoNow, can I help you?"

"I wanted to be a librarian since I was five years old," said one of the staff librarians, Tina Princenthal. "Hang on. InfoNow, can I help? Okay, okay . . . Did you say 'What's a cabana boy?' "

"We get a lot of repeat callers," said David Brenner, who was at the desk next to Princenthal's. "We have an older gentleman who calls regularly with questions about mythology, science fiction, World War I, that sort of thing. He also always asks about a few actresses and celebrities, asking me if I know what's going on with them. Actually, he asks about Juliette Lewis and the women in Pussy Riot."

The librarian beside Brenner, Harry

Noles, said, "Oh, and there's that guy who calls every few months to get updates on Dana Delany, the actress from that show *China Beach.*"

Princenthal hung up her phone and wrote something down. "Sometimes I'm amazed by what people call about," she said, tapping her desk with a pencil. "Once, a patron called to ask if it was okay for her to eat a can of beans that didn't have an expiration date. I mean, there is a website called *Still Tasty* that I use to check expiration dates on things, but I'm not going to take responsibility for a lady eating a can of beans!"

I said they all seemed to know a lot.

"I tried out for *Jeopardy!,*" Brenner said.

"I tried out and passed the test," Noles said.

"It was my first week of work!" Princenthal went on, still thinking about beans. "I told her what the average shelf life of beans was, but I'm hoping she didn't eat them."

"Yes, all branches are open today," Brenner said into his phone.

"Hello, yes, library cards expire every three years," Noles said into his phone, teasing the curly phone cord and letting it snap back.

"Last week a lady called and asked me how to sign a card for a baby shower," Princenthal said. "I mean, that's not exactly something to look up. I just said, 'How about . . . "Best wishes"? Or . . . "Congratulations"?' Just off the top of my head. I didn't consult any source. She seemed happy with that answer." She then added, "There are a lot of lonely people out there."

"We handle things in the department if possible," Pasquinelli said. He has been a librarian at Central for thirty-five years. His desk was a medium-size mountain range of papers and books and files and booklets. "We will refer things along if we have to. If someone calls and says, 'I want to know when Marilyn Monroe died,' we can do that here in the department, *boom!* But if they ask whether her death was a suicide, we send them to the Literature Department."

Princenthal hung up her phone and shook her head. "Why would someone call here and ask, 'Which is more evil, grasshoppers or crickets?' " she said to no one in particular. She took a deep breath and let it out slowly.

The phones stopped for a moment. The air vibrated. The phones started again.

"InfoNow . . . sure . . . okay, so I assume it's a British book?" Princenthal said. "Oh, the *hockey team* Kings. Not British kings."

She typed something into her computer. "Yes, several books in Sports. That's in Art and Recreation."

"I swear some people have us on speed dial," Brenner said, hanging up his call. "This woman — we call her 'Fur' — she calls for spelling and grammar help all the time. She says she's a poet. Sometimes she will call twenty-five times in an hour with editing questions."

"Not everyone has the Internet or knows how to use it," Noles said. "Hello, Info-Now?" Pause. "Say the title again? *Life-Changing Magic of Cleaning Up? Oh, Tidying Up.* I'll check. Just a moment."

"You're getting an error message on your e-media download?" Pasquinelli asked into his phone. "Hold on a moment."

"We get a lot of obituary questions," Noles said to me, "and a lot of etiquette questions. And actually, a lot of etiquette-in-obituaries questions. Hello, InfoNow, can I help you . . . Uh-huh. Sure. Can you spell that? C-e-l-e-s-t-e, last name the letter N, the letter G? Just N-g? Okay, just a moment."

"Are you saying Dylan is the author's first name or last name?" Brenner said, looking at his computer screen. "Okay, great. Just a moment, I'll get that for you."

"My friends think because I'm a librarian,

I know everything," Princenthal said to me. "We'll be watching the Olympics, and suddenly, they'll say, 'Tina, how do they score snowboarding at the Olympics?' Or out of the blue, 'Tina, how long do parrots live?' "

"Is the name of the book *The New Owner's Guide to Maltese?*" Noles asked, leaning toward his computer screen. He listened to the caller for a minute. "So are you saying *you* are a new owner looking for a guide to Maltese dogs?" Pause. With the phone tucked under his chin, he typed a few words. He read what popped up on his screen and smiled. "Okay, you're in luck," he told the caller. "We have both."

23.

Unionization: The Viewpoint of Librarians (1975)
By Guyton, Theodore Lewis
331.881102 G992

Parking 1956: Inventory of Off Street Parking, Downtown Los Angeles (1956)
388.3794 P2475-9

Richard Neutra: Mit Einem Essay von Dion Neutra, Erinnerungen an meine Zeit mit Richard Neutra (1992)
By Sack, Manfred
G 720.934 N497Sa

California's Deadliest Earthquakes: A History (2017)
By Hoffman, Abraham
551.2209794 H699

The tug-of-war over whether to renovate or replace the Goodhue Building went on for almost fifteen years. It included failed bond issues and feasibility reports and task forces; multiple proposals, such as one that suggested getting rid of a main library and just having branches; study groups; petitions; public hearings; and then more public hearings. Years were spent following the guidance of Charles Luckman, a controversial architect who was hired by the city to present a plan; he recommended developing a new building, and then recommended himself as the architect. One of the sharpest battles running parallel to the redevelopment debate involved parking at Central Library. There were only a few parking spots right near the library. Most staff members parked several blocks away and walked through downtown neighborhoods that felt perilous. The librarians began to agitate for some accommodation. What they proposed was paving the library's West Lawn and garden for staff parking.

Los Angeles's librarians — and most librarians around the country — are well organized, vocal, and opinionated. They unionized as the Librarians' Guild in 1967 and joined the American Federation of State, County and Municipal Employees in

1968. Many of the librarians I met had political or social service backgrounds and activist bents. I met several librarians who'd planned to join the Peace Corps but ended up in library school. One had expected to become a forest ranger but then became attracted to books. One librarian, writing in the union newsletter, referred to herself as a "librarian-priestess" and her employment contract as "her vows."

The librarians at Central considered themselves more than colleagues. As much as the idea of a work family can seem a little hackneyed, the library really does feel like one, with all that implies in terms of familiarity and fondness and gossip and conflict and longevity. The staff is generally united on the opinion that administration (usually) and the Board of Library Commissioners (almost always) fail to understand what it is like to be working in the stacks, dealing with patrons, day in and day out. There is special disdain for any city librarian who never worked on the floor, shelving books and handling patrons. When John Szabo was hired, a number of librarians reacted with pleasure to the discovery that Szabo had worked every position in the library, starting at the checkout desk, saying things like "He's a *real* library person," as distinguished from someone who is just a manager, with no real feel for the place.

The staff channeled opinions via the Librarians' Guild, which had a knack for coming up with lively demonstrations of those opinions. The Guild has organized sickouts and walkouts and protests over dismissals based on "insubordination." Once, the Guild released a live turkey at a Board of Library Commissioners meeting to illustrate its opinion of a budget-cut proposal. In February 1969, the parking problem was boiling. The librarians staged a sickout in support of the plan to pave the garden. The garden was integral to Goodhue's design, and Barton Phelps's group of architectural historians was committed to preserving it. But the staff's discontent was formidable, and while the larger issue of what to do with the library was stalled, it began to look like the staff was going to get a parking lot.

Architect Robert Alexander, who was the business partner of celebrated California architect Richard Neutra, decided to protest the proposed destruction of the garden. He chained himself to a rock near the Well of the Scribes and said he would stay there until the paving plan was abandoned. Barton Phelps and Margaret Bach's group filed a motion to preserve the garden, but it was overruled. As a final effort, the team suggested an alternative of placing expanded parking on an adjacent lot. According to Barton Phelps, the Board of Library Commissioners never even responded to the suggestion. The librarians' insistence won out, and the new parking lot was approved. Robert Alexander unchained himself from his rock, and within weeks, the West Lawn and garden were stripped of their fixtures and sculptures and fountains and plantings and were covered by a layer of blacktop. No one seems to know what happened to many of the garden sculptures once they were removed. The most significant one, the Well of the Scribes — Goodhue's monument to the great writers of history — is still missing. Over the years, several significant sculptures from the garden have been spotted in private homes. Other pieces were stashed in damp corners of the library's basement. Many are simply unaccounted for.

Not long after the garden was paved, City Librarian Hamill announced that he was retiring from his post and returning to academia. A national search was launched, and Wyman Jones was hired. He inherited a building with endless woes and no consensus on how to heal it. As a librarian, Jones was known as a builder rather than a programmer. He was even more eager than Hamill to bulldoze the Goodhue Building. But the plan to do so hit a snag when the Municipal Arts Commission announced that the library and its grounds were being designated as a work of art. Not long after that, the library was listed on the National Register of Historic Places.

The following winter, in 1971, the Los Angeles basin was bucked and broken, courtesy of the Sylmar Earthquake, which registered 6.7 on the Richter scale. The earthquake killed sixty-four people and cracked everything around it, from freeway overpasses to the Lower Van Norman Dam to the Veterans Administration Hospital in Sylmar. The aftershock pulsed under the library, giving it a hard shake. More than a hundred thousand books bounced off their shelves. Reshelving the books was so much work that the city put out an appeal for volunteers to help the library staff. The mayor requested emergency funds from Governor Ronald Reagan and President Richard Nixon to help restore Central Library and to renovate two branch libraries that were so badly damaged that they closed. That same year, the Los Angeles library system turned one hundred years old.

In 1871 a visitor to the Los Angeles Public

24

Babushka v seti [Grandma on the Internet] (2012)
  By Shuliaeva, Natal'ia
  Ru 510.78 S562

The Honest Life: Living Naturally and True to You (2013)
  By Alba, Jessica
  613 A325

Daily Activity Patterns of the Homeless: A Review (1988)
  By Reich, Shayne
  362.509794 R347

Madame Chiang Kai-shek: China's Eternal First Lady (2006)
  By Li, Laura Tyson
  92 C5325Li

In 1871, a visitor to the Los Angeles Public

Library published an essay imagining a future in which the library would be miraculously compressed into an object the size of a suitcase. Considering how physical, how insistently tangible, libraries are — their pounds of pages and bindings, the mass and fleshy bulk of books — such a notion must have seemed as preposterous as landing on Mars. Of course, with the invention of the computer and the Internet, that is exactly what has happened. The library has a large amount of material that isn't online, but the notion of much of it being pocket-size and contained in a small plastic box has been true for some time. Libraries saw the Internet coming and extended a hand. First they set up computer stations for public use; then they offered free Wi-Fi. Now at Central Library and many other libraries around the country, there are kiosks where anyone can borrow a laptop or tablet computer to use for the day, just the way she might borrow a book.

The Computer Center at Central Library is a large, long room with a line of utilitarian workstations and fifty-five desktop computers. It has a plain, workaday look, and all of the computers are in use almost all of the time. From the looks of it, if you didn't know you were in a library, you might think you were in one of those telemarketing call centers. Many of the people waiting to enter the library at ten A.M. every day head straight for the Computer Center, jostling each other as they pass through the lobby and down the escalators. As soon as the fifty-five computer spots fill up, there is a waiting list and a lot of grumbling. Aside from the grumbling, most of the patrons at least murmur "Good morning" to the librarian on duty as they walk in — even patrons who seem barely verbal or too damaged to care about social niceties like a morning greeting. Viola Castro, one of the librarians on duty when I was there not long ago, said of the patrons, "They do try to be very nice." Castro, a composed, square-shouldered African American woman, was dressed in smart clothes and looked like she worked in a bank. The other librarian on duty, Yael Gillette, had an open, cheerful face perforated here and there by piercings that wiggled a little when she spoke.

Castro said she'd worked at the library for seventeen years. "I was all set to be a paralegal and, well, I ended up here," she said, making a sound that landed between a laugh and a sigh.

"It's good to be here," Gillette said. "I ran a homeless shelter in Glendale for eight years before this. The library is definitely more low-key than that." She chuckled and added, "I have a wife and three kids, so I get enough drama at home."

At the Computer Center that morning were a few people who looked like students and a middle-aged man dressed in a fresh suit. Most of the patrons, though, looked like they were homeless or at least experiencing harsh living. "They're good people," Gillette said, "but we have our moments. It gets a little tough a few days before social security checks come, when they're down to their last bits. Now, when the patrons get frisky . . ." She pointed to a security guard who was in a spread-legged police stance near the entrance. He hitched up his belt and smiled at Gillette when he saw her pointing. "We've got our own guard now, full-time," she went on. "We just try to keep to the rules. Nothing extreme. But some rules they really don't like."

I asked what rules were unpopular, and she said, "Like, for instance, you can't dance or sing in here. Unfortunately, a lot of them do like to sing."

The Computer Center is muffled and dim, warm with whiffs of sourness, of body odor, and of the vegetal smells of dirt embedded in clothes that were advancing in the direction of compost. But it also had a pleasant, preoccupied feeling, somewhat disembodied, as each one of the fifty-five people was drawn away from the library and into whatever world he or she navigated to. I circled the room and glanced quickly at what was on the screen of each computer. Solitaire. A gossip website with a big story about Céline Dion. *The Flintstones.* A basketball game. A job-hunting site, Facebook, an online chess game. One man greeted me and told me he was working on his résumé. Viola Castro told me that some patrons do look at pornography, and the librarians leave them be unless it's child pornography, which isn't permitted. After she mentioned that, I got to thinking about a 1980 seminar for librarians I'd come across recently. Called "Sex at Central Library," it reviewed the library's policies on sexually related material. Included in it were books and magazines covering such topics as nude dancing, striptease, beauty competitions (filed under "Sports"), and kissing contests. The seminar couldn't have anticipated that someday you could sit in the library and dial up any version of sex you could imagine and many you couldn't.

As I was walking around the Computer Center, a man at a desk in the corner suddenly yelled, "Oh God!" It caused a worried head swiveling among the rest of the people at the computers, so I headed back to the desk. Castro waved her hand and said, "That's nothing, nothing, nothing. He does that every day." We chatted as everyone simmered down. She told me that she'd gotten a library card for each of her kids as soon as they turned three. Just then, a jittery young man wearing an Adidas sweatshirt came up to the desk and told Castro he was having trouble printing something. Castro got up and went with him to the printer, banged it a couple of times, wiggled a few things, and got it working again. She came back to the desk and whispered, "He's a little embarrassed. He was printing out a picture of Jessica Alba naked, and the paper jammed."

In the meantime, the security guard ambled over to the desk. "This is *nothing,*" he said. "You want drama? Come to the Hollywood branch. The other day, we had a lady there with a service wolf."

Gillette and I said in unison, "A *wolf?*" The security guard shrugged and said, "Well, maybe it was a dog. But it was as big as a wolf, I swear."

I rode the elevator downstairs, feeling

happy. I loved the elevator; it was wall-papered with cards from the old card catalog — those stained, dog-eared two-by-five-inch paper rectangles, always typed by someone who didn't have a firm strike on the keys, so the letters fade from black to gray, back to black. The artist who designed the elevator, David Bunn, must have had fun picking the cards to use. I was leaning against *Complete Book of the Dog; Complete Book of the Cat; Complete Book of Progressive Knitting; Complete Book of Harness Racing;* and *Complete Book of Erotic Art.*

I was on my way to meet David Aguirre, the head of security for the library. Chief Aguirre has a kettle-drum chest and a hearty handshake and a web of crinkles around his eyes when he smiles. He used to be the chief of security for the Los Angeles Zoo. He came to the library in 2006 and has forty-six officers reporting to him. Twenty-six of them are assigned to Central Library, and the rest are at the branches. "Here's the thing about library security," Chief Aguirre said as we began to walk around the building. "Library users are eighty percent male, and librarians are eighty percent female, so that's something to keep in mind."

According to Chief Aguirre, there are

about a hundred reports of trouble each week at Central. Many are what he called "property conflict" — that is, someone got something stolen. The epicenter of property conflict is the Genealogy Department, because people get so caught up in tracking down Great-Aunt Sally that they stop keeping an eye on their belongings. Another trouble spot is the Computer Center. Aguirre said it creates a lot of "time conflicts," meaning that someone overstays his two-hour limit at a computer and someone else gets pissed. In Religion, he gets a lot of complaints about people talking to God in overly loud voices. Aguirre walks the building once every hour, paying special attention to the restrooms and bike rack and garden. Usually, he encounters petty issues. Sometimes security officers find big surprises. A guard at the Jefferson branch found someone living on the roof a few years ago. On the roof at the Westwood branch, a guard discovered an elaborate shrine to Marilyn Monroe. Three times in the last six years, Aguirre found a dead person while on his rounds at Central. Most often the cause of death is a heart attack or a stroke. "Five years ago, we had a gentleman, a transient, die in Religion and Philosophy," Aguirre said. "He looked like he didn't have a dime in the world, but when we patted him down, we found twenty thousand dollars in cash in a piece of folded paper in his pocket."

One of the guards told me that his position at the library feels more like that of a psychologist or a priest than a security guard. The library security employees are Los Angeles Police Department officers. The library pays the police department over $5 million a year for their services. Their effectiveness has been sharply criticized from some quarters. After going undercover at the library for three months, an NBC affiliate ran a multipart investigative series claiming that "police officers [were] spending much of their time texting on their cell phones or talking, instead of patrolling," and as a result, Central and at least two other libraries had "rampant sex and drug use." The series was sensational and wrongheaded. Many of the cited incidents occurred on the sidewalks outside the library, which are the responsibility of city police. One thing the television story got right was the fact that the library has to manage the complicated issues that arise any time homeless or mentally ill people gather. Some librarians I spoke to at Central felt the reporters tried to sandbag John Szabo.

He didn't let the story faze him. "The most beautiful thing about public libraries is that they're open and free to everyone," he emailed me when I asked him about the series. "With that promise, there are unquestionably tough challenges that our library and public libraries across the nation face every day. Of course, they're not unique to libraries — they're big, complicated community-wide issues. And we're actually making a difference with programs serving the homeless and addressing health disparities."

Every day, many homeless people come to the library, and many hang out in the garden and around the sides of the building. Some are doing nothing that is concerning, but they look unkempt and seem erratic; the air around them can feel charged and nervous-making. I have seen people drinking and using drugs in the garden — not in the building — and if I had a young child, I would be upset to be near them. I have seen people drinking and using drugs in public throughout the city, in parks, on sidewalks, at bus stops. Every problem that society has, the library has, too, because the boundary between society and the library is porous; nothing good is kept out of the library, and nothing bad. Often, at the library, society's problems are magnified. Homelessness and drug use and mental illness are problems you see in every public place in Los Angeles. One difference is that if you see a mentally ill person on the street, you can cross to the other side. In a library, you share a smaller and more intimate space. The communal nature of a library is the very essence of the library, in the shared desks and shared books and shared restrooms.

The library's commitment to being open to all is an overwhelming challenge. For many people, the library may be the only place they have to be in close quarters with disturbed or profoundly dirty people, and that can be uncomfortable. But a library can't be the institution we hope for it to be unless it is open to everyone. I attended an international conference about the future of libraries a few years ago, and everyone — librarians from Germany and Zimbabwe and Thailand and Colombia and everywhere in the world — found the challenge of homelessness and the library exasperating, intractable, unwinnable. The public can come and go, but librarians are in the library all day, and their jobs include handling difficult and sometimes violent people nearly every day. The topic is bigger than libraries; it is a topic for society to solve. All libraries can do is try their best to manage it. On a reddit discussion of the NBC investigation, no one blamed the library for being a magnet for the city's most troubled people. The majority of the commenters blamed the police for not being more forceful and attentive. Referring to the NBC report, one person wrote, "This 'investigative' report just shows that homelessness is a problem. Not sure what the library has to do with it." Another commenter wrote, "I have news for everyone: This stuff doesn't just happen at the library. Welcome to L.A."

As he walked through the building, Chief Aguirre offered a crisp greeting to every single person he passed, including sad-faced men shuffling by with rickety carts full of shapeless dark things. "I love working with people," Aguirre said as we passed a man asleep on a bench. Aguirre tapped him lightly, and the man sat up, and Aguirre said, "Hey, buddy, no sleeping." He turned back to me. "I don't care who it is. I don't care if it's the mayor or if it's a transient. Anyone can empathize with someone else for two minutes, can't they?" Working the library detail is generally benign, although a few years ago, an agitated man stabbed an officer with a needle. The man had HIV/ AIDS, so he was charged with attempted murder. The officer never contracted the disease but will have to be tested for years.

The one thing Chief Aguirre dislikes about his job is when he has to tell people they smell. The library has rules to determine when that becomes necessary. Aguirre knows what an affront it is, no matter how bad your circumstances are. "It's sad, but we have to do it sometimes," he said, grimacing. "For the comfort of the other patrons, most of all." We rode the escalator down to the History Department and walked through. Glen Creason was at the desk and nodded at us. A woman in the Genealogy area was eating crackers, so Aguirre approached her and gave her a look. "You can't be eating in here, ma'am," he said.

"Oh, I'm not eating," the woman said, "I'm snacking."

"There's no snacking."

The woman looked aghast and said, "I thought you could snack!"

We strolled around the department, peeking down the rows of bookshelves to make sure no one was tucked away doing something untoward, reminding a few people to keep an eye on their possessions. There was nothing much of note. We were heading toward the door when a slight, high-strung, dark-skinned man buttonholed Aguirre and told him he'd seen someone sleeping in the men's restroom.

"Okay, thanks, we'll take care of that," Aguirre said to him.

The man started quivering. "It's actually two men, and it is homosexuality!" he said, his voice rising. "I'm willing to be a witness! It's white culture and Hispanic culture! It's a white male and a Mexican!" Aguirre glanced around the room. The other patrons were stirring as they heard the commotion. "Let's step into the lobby so we can talk more," Aguirre said, almost purring. The man followed him out but started bellowing as soon as we stopped walking. Aguirre pulled out his radio and called the senior security person on duty, Stan Molden. "Stan," he said into the radio, "we're going to be walking someone out. Come down to History." He turned back to the man and tried to direct him to topics other than race wars and homosexuality until Molden appeared at the top of the escalator. Aguirre, leading with his eyes, managed to point the man toward the escalator without him realizing it. It was almost balletic. Molden reached the bottom of the stairs and completed the pirouette, and the man rode up the escalator with him.

"No big deal," Aguirre said to me. "He's a regular. He'll lose his library privileges for the day, and tomorrow he'll come back on good behavior, especially if it's rainy. People don't want to lose their privileges here if it means they have to go out in the rain."

We finished making the rounds downstairs and rode back to the main floor. The guard at the desk handed Aguirre a report for the day, which listed six security issues, including removing the man from the History Department; a domestic dispute that erupted in the checkout line; and a stopped-up sink in the security office kitchen. "We also removed a male out of Level Four," another guard standing at the desk told Aguirre. "He was moving really slowly — I think there's something off with him."

Aguirre left for a meeting, and I began rounds again with Stan Molden. Molden is tall and lean and has a sly, sideways sense of humor. Earlier in the day, I watched as a man approached him at the security desk and rattled on in a panic for at least five minutes, describing a wallet he'd lost. Molden stared at the man impassively while he was talking, then reached under the desk and plopped down a fat brown wallet. "Would *this* be it?" he said as the man fell onto the wallet. "Brother, I don't know how you lost this," Molden said. "You've got everything but the kitchen sink in here."

Molden was born in Texas, but then he heard a song by the Beach Boys and decided he was meant to live in Southern California. As soon as he could head to Los Angeles, he did. He is well-known among the library staff for his skill on alto and soprano saxophone, which he has played occasionally at staff parties. His real passion, though, is juggling, which he taught himself by watching YouTube videos. He has worked for the city for thirty years — the first twenty, he did security at City Hall, and the last ten, he's worked at the library. "There are street people I've seen throughout all of those thirty years," he said. "It's sad. I get to know them pretty well." He told me that some years ago, he overheard a homeless woman tell someone she was sleeping on the street, and he decided to give her money so she could spend a few nights in a hotel. "I'm a bachelor. I had the money to spare," he said. "Believe it or not, I saw her about seven years later, and she told me she was doing better, and she wanted to pay me back." He shook his head in wonder. We took a turn through Art and Music. An elderly woman was at the desk, saying to the librarian, "I have nine kittens in my kitchen. Are you interested in a cat?" The librarian glanced up and waved at Molden, then turned back to the woman and said pets weren't allowed in the library. The woman sniffed with disgust. "Why is that? Cats are so much cleaner and neater than people!"

"I grew up in libraries," Molden said to me. "I love reading. My New Year's resolution is to read one hundred books this year. I just started the first one, a biography of Madame Chiang Kai-shek."

A man walking toward us signaled to Molden and then said, "Do you know how I can block someone on my daughter's Facebook?" Molden shook his head, made a few good suggestions, and then we left Art and Music and headed to the Business Department. "We have a lot of knuckleheads in here," he said, "and a lot of good people, too. And a lot of people just assume we know everything."

Molden will be eligible to retire in two years. He has no family and no obligations, but he does have a plan. Not long ago, he made friends with a man from Sri Lanka, and he learned a lot about the country from him. The man and his wife ended up moving back to Sri Lanka, but he stayed in touch with Molden and sent pictures of his house and neighborhood in Sri Jayawardenepura Kotte. Molden did research on the country and liked what he learned. When he retires, he plans to move there. "You can live really well there," he said. "It's very cheap. And it's beautiful." I mentioned that it seemed like quite a leap to move across the world to another country. He shrugged and said, "But I've seen the pictures, and I've read the books."

Trump Strategies for Real Estate: Billionaire Lessons for the Small Investor [electronic resource] (2011)
  By Ross, George H.
  E-Audiobook

Case Studies in Air Rights and Subsurface Tunnel Road Easements (0000)
  American Institute of Real Estate Appraisers
  333.01 A512-7

I Love You Phillip Morris: A True Story of Life, Love, & Prison Breaks (2003)
  By McVicker, Steve
  364.92 R967Mc

In 1973, more than fifteen hundred library

staff members signed a petition complaining that Central Library was a hazardous work environment. Shortly after the petition was delivered to management, the Los Angeles Fire Department cited twenty-six fire code violations in the building. Barton Phelps told me that he knew the building was dilapidated, but he was suspicious of some of the violations. "Someone was always leaving carts and boxes in the fire exits, and then somehow the fire department got called," he said. "It felt like they were doing it on purpose, to argue in favor of tearing the building down." The pro-teardown people and the preservationists were knotted up over how to proceed with fixing the library, but no one was budging, and each faction doubted the other's intentions.

One morning, a real estate developer named Robert Maguire came for a meeting at the ARCO offices. He stood by a window and looked down on the library and the shambles it was becoming. At that moment, he made a decision to do what he could to fix it. Not long ago, he described to me what that view from ARCO looked like: "A big horrible wall on Fifth street . . . a horrible narrow stairway that took you to the street above — really nasty. All the drunks were peeing down the stairwell." I wondered what he thought of the parking lot. "Oh, God, yeah," he said with a groan. "To sum up, you had a really interesting but ratty building with a really horrible parking lot. But still, I thought it was critical to protect it."

Maguire is one of the most successful real estate developers in the city. Many of his biggest projects were downtown. Like many people, including the architectural preservationists who had been so instrumental in keeping the library intact so far, Maguire hoped Los Angeles would develop a city center that actually felt like a city center. A blighted library in the middle of it wouldn't do. He was used to building new things, but he loved the Goodhue Building and was committed to the idea of saving and rehabilitating it. He also knew that ARCO, then a major corporate and philanthropic force in Los Angeles, favored saving the original building. Lodwrick Cook, the ARCO chairman, didn't want a skyscraper replacing the library and blocking his view, and Robert Anderson, ARCO's CEO, was a devotee of vintage architecture.

The sticking point was money. Economics favored the plan of sacking the old library, selling the land, and building a new one elsewhere with the proceeds. When downtown began percolating as a business district in the 1980s, the land under the library became more valuable by the minute; if sold, it probably would cover almost all the costs of a new library somewhere on cheaper land. Repairing and expanding the current building would cost close to $150 million. Bonds and fancy financing might pay for some of it, but that certainly would not be enough.

At that time, on the East Coast, people began tinkering with a new way of getting permission to put up buildings that were taller than what zoning allowed. Every city has height restrictions. Not every building is as high as it is legally allowed to be, but the building owns the rights to airspace above it, up to the permitted height. In the early 1960s, a Chicago developer first proposed the concept of air rights. Once the precedent was set, air rights became a salable commodity. For instance, if you had a building that was only seven stories high, which was the case with the Goodhue Building, and zoning would have allowed it to be sixty stories high, you could sell its "right" to fifty-three more stories to a neighboring building project that wanted to build higher than its allowance. Air rights withstood court challenges and were becoming a common instrument in urban development. No one, though, had tried it in Los Angeles.

It took eight years to orchestrate the sale of the library's air rights. By 1986, the transfer of the rights was approved, and the project was "going like mad," according to Maguire. His company bought the library's air rights for $28.2 million; he planned to use it to build two towering skyscrapers across from the library, one of which would be the tallest building on the West Coast. He also bought the land underneath the library's former garden to build a huge underground garage, with the hope that the old garden could be restored. Architect Norman Pfeiffer was hired to renovate the original building and design a new wing that would more than double the size of the library. At that moment, the Goodhue Building contained five times as many books as it was built to hold. The new wing would finally provide enough space for them. The original building would be polished and buffed — and returned, wherever possible, to the way Goodhue intended it. Everyone who advocated tearing down the old building accepted the fact that the Goodhue Building would endure.

The sales of the space underground and the air above raised almost two thirds of the money needed to restore and expand the library. The tobacco company Phillip Morris offered to pay the remaining third — with the intention of collecting a healthy tax deduction for investing in a historic building. The city council almost accepted the offer but, on second thought, decided it wouldn't look good to have Los Angeles Public Library financed by cigarettes. The remaining funds would have to come from somewhere else.

26.

---

*True Stories of Crime from the
District Attorney's Office* (1924)
 By Train, Arthur
 364.973 T768-1

*Tom Bradley's Impossible Dream:
The Educational Documentary*
(2014)
 DVD 92 B811To

In Praise of Litigation (2017)
 By Lahav, Alexandra D.
 347.90973 L183

*Hold Your Tongue!: The Layman's
Guide to Libel and Slander. A
Fascinating Exploration of the
Realm of Defamation, Including
an Analysis of Ideological,
Racial, and Religious Libels*
(1950)

Robert Sheahen is a criminal defense attorney in Los Angeles who has collected a stable of interesting clients, including the president of the Hells Angels; singer Rick James, who was accused of torturing a woman with a crack pipe; and the woman who was charged with giving John Belushi his fatal drug dose. Sheahen has a strong jaw, an intense stare, and a disarming way of making fun of himself. I never entirely understood how he first met Harry Peak, but their connection dated back to 1983, when Sheahen sent one of his investigators to find someone to testify for the defense in a murder trial, and somehow, the investigator found Harry. Even though Harry blew his testimony by talking to the jurors and saying he was an actor, his ingenuousness charmed Sheahen. He knew Harry needed work, so he hired him from time to time to run errands. Over the years, though, they fell out of touch, so Sheahen was surprised when Harry called, asking for representation in the arson case. "I knew the city had nothing on him, so I decided to take the case," Sheahen told me one day at lunch. "It was the kind of case lawyers call 'flam-

429

bono.' " He started laughing and waited to see if I got the joke. When I didn't, he said patiently, "That means you do the case for no money, but you know it will get you a lot of attention. Flamboyant. And pro bono. Flam-bono. Get it?"

Sheahen said he was stunned when he heard Harry's name in association with the library fire. "To be honest, I almost drove off the freeway when I heard it on the news," Sheahen said. "He sure didn't strike me as an arsonist." From the beginning, Sheahen believed that the city was over-reaching because the fire had happened almost a year earlier and the public was itching to have someone arrested. He wasn't bothered by the fact that Harry couldn't account for his whereabouts that morning, or that he kept reshuffling his alibis like a deck of cards. "Harry was just a little nuts," Sheahen said, putting his sandwich down. "He loved attention. He wanted to be famous."

Harry spent three days in jail before he was released. His family was mortified. "I never cried like that in my life," his sister Brenda told me. "I felt like people were staring at him like he was nothing but a gay motherfucker. Yes, he likes to make stupid comments, but that doesn't mean he did it." Brenda's own house burned down shortly before the library fire; she was living in a hotel at the time of Harry's arrest. Her fire was attributed to an electrical problem, but she was worried that someone might suggest there was a connection between the two fires. She was afraid it would be used against Harry, so she kept her distance from him, just in case.

After the paperwork for his release was complete, the jailers kept Harry cooling his heels for two hours, for no apparent reason, before they let him go. Sheahen believed they were just being vindictive because, like everyone in the city, they wanted to blame someone for the fire, and Harry was now that person. A scrum of reporters and camera crews waited at the door of the jail. Instead of looking downcast or remorseful, Harry walked out wearing a broad, bright smile. Maybe he was smiling nervously. Maybe it was a reflex for him, a burst of delight at being noticed, regardless of the reason. Maybe when he saw a camera, the aspiring actor in him couldn't resist smiling. Whatever his reason, the smile was featured in every story about his arrest, and it made him look brazen and shameless, like he had gotten away with something.

The local papers were ravenous for the story, especially after word got out that

Harry confessed the crime to several friends. Sheahen fended them off, saying Harry's behavior was dumb but innocuous, the equivalent of people who joke about bombs in airports and nothing more. "He likes to joke," Sheahen told the *Los Angeles Times.* "He made a few jokes he shouldn't have. He has a different sense of humor." Harry was a people pleaser, he added, and if it tickled his friends to have him say he was the arsonist, he would do it. Sheahen praised the investigators as "top people doing a top job." But this time, he said, they got the wrong guy.

According to Sheahen, Harry's day on April 29, 1986, started at nine A.M., when Harry delivered papers to a downtown courtroom for Leonard Martinet. At ten A.M., he went to a podiatrist appointment in Hollywood, followed by brunch with Reverend Smith and the podiatrist, Stephen Wilkie. As soon as he finished brunch, Harry drove to his parents' house in Santa Fe Springs and arrived there by eleven A.M. While this was orderly, it sounded to me like an impossibly tight schedule. Anyone who has spent time in Los Angeles knows that rarely, if ever, has anyone done a chore downtown and then made it to Hollywood in just an hour, and rarely, if ever, has anyone had brunch in Hollywood and then made it to Santa Fe Springs, twenty heavily trafficked miles away, in an hour.

In the end, the credibility of Harry's schedule didn't matter. On March 3, 1987, Stephen Kay, the assistant district attorney assigned to the case, held a press conference to announce that Harry would not be charged. "Though there is strong probable cause to believe the suspect is responsible for the Central Library arson fire," Kay said, "the admissible evidence is insufficient to warrant criminal prosecution at this time."

The fire investigators were livid. Dean Cathey, a fire department battalion chief who'd spent countless hours running the investigation, gave a statement to reporters after Kay's announcement. "We still believe Peak is the perpetrator of the fire," Cathey said. "There is no doubt in our minds. I believe a guilty man is going free." As reporters shouted questions at him, Cathey continued, "It's frustrating. We've expended five hundred hours internally on our investigation of this man . . . It's difficult on the investigators, and the people of Los Angeles are going to be wondering why we can't have this individual."

Kay did imply that if more evidence surfaced, Harry might still be charged, saying, "The case is not closed." But the investigation didn't advance after Harry was released. No new witness ever came forward, and no physical evidence was found. Nothing definitive linked Harry to the crime. There was also no hard proof of what had caused the fire; there was just an area in the stacks where investigators believed the fire began. The most powerful case for charging Harry consisted of the confessions he had made to a number of friends, but he'd unconfessed more often than he had confessed. Kay also acknowledged that Harry's confessions might not be admissible in criminal court. The investigators, convinced that Harry was the arsonist, found it hard to attack the case with fresh energy, to look for new suspects, when they were so sure Harry was their man. Once Kay announced he wasn't charging Harry, the momentum of the investigation thudded to a stop.

Many investigators suspected that Kay didn't pursue the case for other, strategic reasons. At that moment, the city's district attorney was in the middle of a sexual abuse case against the owners and staff of the McMartin Preschool, which expanded into being one of the longest and most expensive criminal trials in the history of the United

States. The city's case was beginning to disintegrate, and in the end, the jury came back with no convictions. The last thing the district attorney's office wanted was to lose another prominent case like the library fire. The wobbliness of the evidence against Harry was just too big a risk.

Harry walked out of jail and went back to his life. He looked for work with no luck. His sister Debra told me no one wanted to hire him because of his notoriety. "They'd say, 'Oh, aren't you the library fire guy?' And that was that," she said. Then, suddenly, the case was back in the news. At a press conference in January 1988, Harry appeared with his occasional employer Leonard Martinet, who was now representing him. To the assembled reporters, Martinet said, "It is hard to believe a totally innocent individual [like Harry] could . . . be beaten and imprisoned by government agents for the purposes of trying to extort a confession. It was a Gestapo technique." As a consequence, Martinet said, Harry Peak was suing the City of Los Angeles in civil court. Martinet said Harry suffered "soft-tissue injuries to the back and neck, requiring medical treatment . . . injury to his mind and shock and injury to his nervous system" during his three days in jail, and was "prevented from working, sustaining a loss of earnings and/or earning capacity . . . and believes he will be prevented from working for a period in the future." Harry sued the city for false arrest, slander, negligence, emotional distress, invasion of privacy, and assault and battery. The price tag was $15 million. He also sued arson investigator Dean Cathey individually for $5 million, on the grounds that Cathey slandered him when he told reporters that Harry was guilty. Harry was always short on money, so a civil suit that might bring him $20 million probably intrigued him. But I bet one of the things that pleased him most was that the complaint included the sentence "At the time of his arrest, Plaintiff was a part-time actor."

This development in the story perplexed me. Harry had been shaken up by his arrest, and might well have experienced rough handling in jail, but he simply didn't seem like the sort of person with the resolve to sue the city. The only thing that seems like Harry is that the suit was a way for him to revive the attention he had gotten when he was a suspect. Still, I sensed an invisible hand in the civil case. Harry knew a number of lawyers from his errand work. Did one of them encourage the idea of filing a civil suit?

Once the criminal case was dismissed, Robert Sheahen was no longer involved. But I wondered about Leonard Martinet, about whether he'd encouraged Harry to pursue the suit. Martinet was in and out of this story, always a day player, but I knew little about him and found little about him everywhere I looked. I tried tracking him down, but all I found were disconnected phone numbers, and one working number under his name in Palm Springs. I called repeatedly, but no one ever answered, and the outgoing message said the phone didn't accept incoming calls.

The arson team who investigated Harry was outraged by the civil suit, especially Dean Cathey, who sweated until he was assured that his union would handle the individual charges against him. The firefighters weren't satisfied to merely defend themselves and the city against Harry. A group of them approached a city attorney they admired named Victoria Chaney. She is now an associate justice in the court of appeals, but in 1988, Justice Chaney was in the civil liability unit of the city attorney's office and often worked with fire department staff. Chaney told me she'd been struck by how sure the investigators were that Harry was the arsonist. She reviewed their material and proposed a new tactic. Instead of waiting to see if the criminal case would be reinstated, she suggested suing Harry in civil court, just as he'd sued the city. In criminal court, a verdict has to be unanimous, and the evidence has to prove the case beyond a reasonable doubt. In civil court, a case only has to be proved by the preponderance of evidence, and verdicts are decided by a majority vote. The case against Harry could well have unraveled under criminal court scrutiny, but Chaney believed it would withstand the gentler prodding of civil court.

The fire department signed on, and Chaney began developing her case. The city would match Harry's demand for $15 million, and it would go a few million dollars better. Three weeks after Harry filed his lawsuit, the City of Los Angeles filed its cross-complaint in superior court, demanding that Harry compensate the city for the cost of replacing the library's destroyed books; the cost of repairing the damaged ones; the cost of the water used to extinguish the fire; the cost of fixing the damage to the building; and the cost of worker compensation for the firefighters who were injured on the job. The city was suing Harry Peak for $23.6 million.

27.

The Conservation of Books and Documents (1957)
By Langwell, W. H.
025.7 L287

The McDonnell Douglas Story (1979)
By Ingells, Douglas J.
338.78 M136IN

Salvage of Water Damaged Books, Documents, Micrographic and Magnetic Media: A Case History, Dalhousie Univ. Law Library, Aug. 1985; A Case History, Roanoke Virginia Flood, Nov. 1985 (1986)
By Lundquist, Eric G.
025.8 L962

After two years of being frozen, the books

were ready to be thawed, dried, fumigated, sorted, cleaned, repaired, and rebound. The aerospace manufacturer McDonnell Douglas, which had a division just south of Los Angeles, offered to try drying the first batch of twenty thousand books. The McDonnell engineers researched the nature of water-soaked paper and decided to use their space simulation chamber to defrost and dry. They placed a selection of books spine-down on an aluminum tray, and then flattened them with a rigid aluminum plate. The plated books were stacked six tiers high. The entire rig was secured with bungee cords and placed inside a forty-foot-wide vacuum chamber used to test satellites under different atmospheric and meteorological conditions. The temperature in the chamber was raised to 100 degrees, and the books were left inside it for five days. Then the air pressure in the chamber was dropped until it equaled the pressure found at 140,000 feet above earth. The pressure was increased and decreased in intervals, and the temperature was raised and lowered in wild swings. When the first small batch of books was run through the process, six hundred gallons of water seeped out.

The city scrambled for funds for the book salvage and divided the contracts between

Eric Lundquist's company, Document Re-processors, and a company called Airdex. The companies used different systems to achieve the same results. Document Reprocessors owned five vacuum chambers similar to the one at McDonnell Douglas that used intense vacuum pressure to remove the water through the process of sublimation. Lundquist estimated the chambers would draw off close to 250,000 pounds of water. Airdex, which was collaborating with NASA on the project, placed the books in a chamber that purged its internal atmosphere every twenty-five seconds, carrying away water vapor that evaporated from the books. Both of the systems took close to a week to dry a single book, depending on how wet it was. Book conservators estimated that the books' water content ranged from ten percent to one hundred percent — that is, some of the books were equal amounts water and paper. Book conservators like to argue over whether vacuum drying is better than dehumidifying for wet books. Eric Lundquist stamped "DR" in the books he dried because he was convinced his system was better than Airdex, and he wanted to compare them when the project was finished. He dared me to find one of his books and compare it to one of Airdex's. "Ours are *flat*," he said. "They look like they never got wet."

Once a batch of books was dried, it was shipped across town to the chief conservator, Sally Buchanan, who directed her staff to run each book through a checklist, which included questions such as:

Are the pages badly cockled?
Is the textblock swollen? Is it distorted, out of "square"?
Are the external joints and internal hinges strong?
Is the spine intact?
Are the endsheets solid?
Will the text open and close flat?

Buchanan told the library staff that it would take thirty-six months to rehabilitate the books and have them ready to be cataloged and returned to the shelves. "On the whole, the staff was pleased with what was salvageable," Buchanan wrote to Wyman Jones and Elizabeth Teoman. "Many books look good, but these are clearly ones which did not become very wet, i.e., tide lines from water up only an inch or two from the bottom edge . . . There are, however, signs of very active mildew on covers of a number of books." Buchanan said some books were hopeless. These were severely burned, or their pages were stuck together, or entire sections were missing; they were beyond hope.

Restoring the Central Library collection was the largest book-drying project ever undertaken. Approximately 700,000 books — 75,000 cubic feet of material — were wet or smoky or, in many cases, both. Up until the library, the largest book-drying project involved just 100,000 books. The pressure chambers chugged along for months. In the end, twenty percent of the books that made it through the drying process were in good enough condition to be shelved immediately. About thirty-five percent dried well but needed to have their bindings replaced. Seventy-five percent needed extensive cleaning or fumigating. All books with glossy paper, which became slick and sticky when wet, were completely ruined.

On June 3, 1988 — over twenty years after the Green Report suggested that the Goodhue Building be demolished — the restoration of the original building began, and ground was broken for the library's new wing. Until the work was finished, the library operated out of temporary quarters on Spring Street. The location didn't please anyone, but at least now that construction on Central finally was under way, it seemed tolerable for the time.

The new wing Pfeiffer had designed complemented the Goodhue Building without pretending to be the same vintage. The city had purchased the lot south of the existing building for the wing, which would be joined to the Goodhue Building's southern wall. Pfeiffer's design centered on an eight-story atrium. Even though the addition was massive, it wouldn't challenge the height of the original building, because four of its eight stories were belowground. Most subject departments would be relocated in the new wing. Book storage would no longer be in the stacks; it would be in an airy and sprinklered space in the new wing. Visitors to the library would travel up and down the eight stories of the atrium on a series of cascading escalators. The experience of passing through both buildings would be like walking through an eccentric playhouse and then tumbling over a waterfall.

28.

33 Revolutions Per Minute: A History of Protest Songs, from Billie Holiday to Green Day (2011)
    By Lynskey, Dorian
    784.491 L989

Fox Tossing: And Other Forgotten and Dangerous Sports, Pastimes, and Games (2015)
    By Brooke-Hitching, Edward
    796.009 B872

Passing Through: Groove-Oriented Chamber Music, Vol. 3 (2016)
    By Wolfgang, Gernot
    CD Classical Chamber

Knitting Without Tears: Basic Techniques and Easy-to-Follow Directions for Garments to Fit

There are a lot of surprising things in the library; a lot of things you don't think of when you try to imagine all of what a library might contain. For instance, the Los Angeles library has a huge collection of restaurant menus. Librarians Dan Strall and Billie Connor started the collection, and an ophthalmologist from Palos Verdes, who collected menus since 1940, donated most of them. The ophthalmologist used his menus as a running diary of his dating life: He wrote a note on the back of many of them, recording which of his girlfriends accompanied him to the restaurant. Besides the menu collection, there are other unexpected things. In a group of boxes in the Art and Music Department stacks, you will find the costumes, props, and large terrifying marionettes from the Turnabout Theatre Company, an adult puppet theater that flourished in Los Angeles from 1941 to 1956. There are collections of bookplates and fruit crate labels and sheet music covers and movie posters and the largest gathering of materials on bullfighting in the United States and, of course, Lummis's autographs. As soon as Xochitl Oliva, the senior librarian in charge of digitization, finishes cataloging them, the anti-war posters and pamphlets from the L.A. Resistance will join the library's ephemera. There are so many things in a library, so many books and so much stuff, that I sometimes wondered if any one single person could possibly know what all of it is. I preferred thinking that no one does — I liked the idea that the library is more expansive and grand than one single mind, and that it requires many people together to form a complete index of its bounty.

One thing I hadn't expected in the library was music. I knew there were books about music, as well as CDs and cassettes, but I didn't know the collection includes sheets of music to be played. One afternoon, I was hanging out with Sheila Nash, the senior librarian in the Art and Music Department. So far, my visit to Art and Music had been what I'd expected — the department was silent, almost slumbery, filled with people tenderly flipping pages of oversize art books, or lined up at the desk asking where they could find books on cello theory or protest songs or recent copies of *Bead & Button* magazine. The definition of "art and music" is generous, encompassing crafts, sports, games, gardening, stamp collecting, and dance. Its wide reach became so baffling that the name was changed not long ago to Art, Music, and Recreation.

Nash and her husband, Roy Stone, have worked for the Los Angeles library for a combined total of seventy-nine years. (Not long after I interviewed them, they both retired.) It was Nash's purse that Glen Creason and Stone had been looking for immediately after the fire, when they discovered that the Patent Room had melted. Nash and Stone are library people. Besides being a senior librarian, Stone had been the head of the Librarians' Guild for many years. He once confided to me that when he worked at a branch downtown, local drug dealers used to come to the library and ask him to help fill out their tax returns. He thought it was a perfect example of the rare role libraries play, to be a government entity, a place of knowledge, that is nonjudgmental, inclusive, and fundamentally kind.

Nash was on the phone, helping someone who wanted to know what year Dizzy Dean was born. She mouthed "He could Google it" to me and pointed at the mouthpiece of the phone, shrugging. Her desk was a mad mix, piled with a few copies of *Hollywood Reporter,* a book on the homes of the

American presidents, knitting instructions for little toys called Whimsical Woollies, a horse-racing magazine, a chess magazine, a recent copy of British *Vogue*.

When she finished delivering Dizzy Dean's birth date to the man on the phone, we headed back through the bookshelves and stopped beside a massive file cabinet. Nash pulled open one of the drawers of the file. Inside were dozens of orchestral scores, black notes prancing across eight staves. The department owns more than two thousand orchestral scores, and each one has the music for every instrument written into the piece. The scores are as thick as books. The library came into its first scores in 1934, when the founder of the Los Angeles Philharmonic, William Andrews Clark, Jr., willed his collection of 752 scores to the Music Department. The next batch was added in 1948, when the library bought an orchestral score rental library, and the collection has grown steadily since. The library also owns reams and reams of sheet music. The major donor of the sheet music was composer Meredith Willson, who donated his collection in the mid-1960s, soon after his play *The Music Man* was produced on Broadway and went on to be one of the most successful movies of 1962.

Musical scores are expensive. They cost anywhere from three hundred to nine hundred dollars per score, and each musician in an orchestra needs his or her own. Having a score for each musician can be an insurmountable expense, especially for small orchestras. Los Angeles is home to dozens of orchestras and music groups, such as the Los Angeles Doctors Symphony Orchestra, the Balalaika Orchestra, the Orange County Guitar Orchestra, the Inner City Youth Orchestra — the list rolls on and on. Los Angeles has more working musicians than any city in the United States. It also has one of the few libraries in the country that loans out musical scores. The coexistence of these facts doesn't seem like an accident.

Nash monitors the borrowing and returning of the music and is also the keeper of secrets. The classical music world is small and competitive. The Desert Symphony doesn't want the Armenian General Benevolent Union Orchestra to know what they plan to play for their winter season, and the Filipino American Orchestra doesn't want the New Valley Symphony Orchestra to know its plans, but at the same time, they don't want to end up all trying to sell tickets to the same program of Brahms's *Deutsches*

Requiem. Nash is the soul of discretion, and she will, with great subtlety, direct a chamber music group away from Igor Stravinsky's *Three Pieces for String Quartet* if she knows another chamber music group has just borrowed copies of it. She is also the soul of forbearance. Musicians appear to be incapable of remembering when their scores are due back at the library. Some of the music collection's clients have racked up as much as twelve thousand dollars in overdue fines. "Well, they're very artistic people," Nash said, squaring up a stack of Rimsky-Korsakov scores. "They seem to have a way of misplacing things."

29.

Manual of Procedures, Civil (1979)
By Association of Municipal Court Clerks of California
347.9 A849

Nitroglycerine and Nitroglycerine Explosives (1928)
By Naoúm, Phokion P.
Series: World Wide Chemical Translation Series No. 1
662.2 N194

The Mystery of the Fiery Message (1983)
By Farley, Carol
X

Odd Gods: New Religions & the Cult Controversy (2001)

On June 8, 1988, the City of Los Angeles, represented by Victoria Chaney, deposed Harry Peak in the matter of Superior Court Case No. 672658, which combined Harry's suit against the city with the city's suit against him. Justice Chaney spoke to me recently about the case. She said that, despite the ferocity of the city's claims against him, she found Harry very likable. When she met him, he was young and good-looking. There was something about him that seemed almost innocent; he wasn't worldly or hardened at all. But she also found him a little tragic. "He struck me as lost," she said as we sat in her office in the Federal Courthouse. "He had a sad child-hood. He drifted from job to job. He seemed like he was looking quite desperately for something." She said she didn't trust the Reverend Smith, who often accompanied him, dressed in his black cassock, wearing a jeweled crucifix. She knew a little bit about Smith, how he attracted forlorn men to his homemade religion. She assumed he had become something of a father figure to Harry.

In the new round of depositions, Harry's

testimony began adhering to a single time line different from the one he'd claimed when facing criminal charges. Harry now insisted what he'd said in the past about sightseeing downtown and delivering papers was not true. He said he'd spent the early morning of April 29 at home with his roommates. At ten A.M., he drove to Reverend Wilkie's office to get his wart treated. The treatment lasted close to an hour, and then he and Reverends Wilkie and Smith had lunch. As their waiter was clearing the table, he mentioned the library was burning. This was the first Harry had heard of it. He said that his statements about the fire later that night were jokes he'd told to amuse his friends. He said he'd made up everything he said about the fire — about having helped an old lady, about being carried out by a handsome fireman. "I was the center of attention of my friends, who believed me at the time," he testified, explaining why he'd claimed he started the fire. He said his only crime was naïveté, saying, "I did not imagine that I would get arrested as a result of this story."

Chaney next deposed Reverend Wilkie. After being sworn in, the reverend stated that his profession was podiatry, and that, along with Father Clark, he ran the American Orthodox Church, which was a small independent congregation. Father Clark helped Father Wilkie run his podiatry office and also worked as his driver, because Father Wilkie was in poor health and wasn't permitted to drive. Wilkie said he'd first met Harry Peak in 1984, when Harry had come to him for wart treatment, and he now considered Harry a friend.

Chaney asked Wilkie for more details about the day of the fire. He answered with essentially the same litany as Harry's: He saw Harry around ten, and they had a bite to eat after Harry's wart treatment. Suddenly, Wilkie keeled forward. Chaney stopped her questioning. "Excuse me, Father. Are you in pain?" she asked. "I notice that you're holding your chest."

Wilkie clutched his chest and then said in a halting voice, "Yes, a little bit." He paused for another moment and then said, "I took nitroglycerin a minute ago . . . five minutes ago . . . something. It helped. I'm . . . I'm . . . I would like to finish, please." Chaney asked if he needed a recess, and he shook his head and said he didn't want to take a break, because he was afraid he would fall asleep for hours if he rested. "Let's try . . . let's try to endure, please," he said, and then, collecting himself, gave more details of the lunch at the French Quarter. He said the waiter had told the men that the library had been "set on fire." When I read the deposition, those three words stuck out. At the point the waiter told them about the fire, no news source had yet described it as having been "set." At that time, the fire was still raging, and the news about it centered on the question of whether or not the library could be saved.

The city laid out its arguments about why it believed Harry Peak was responsible for the fire: His alibis were inconsistent. Several people identified him in a photo lineup. There were "triable issues of material fact" that pointed to his guilt. Once again, Chaney itemized what the fire cost the taxpayers of Los Angeles: $625,000 for sawdust and salvage sheets used to suppress the fire and protect books. Three million gallons of water, "exact cost to be ascertained." The cost of replacing or repairing more than one million books. Repair costs for damage to the building. Medical expenses for the injured firefighters. Central to the city's case was the assumption that the fire had an "unnatural" cause. Whether or not the fire was arson was never debated; investigators declared it arson, and their assessment was accepted as fact. As Chaney put it, the investigators "eliminated all accidental, natural, and/or mechanical sources of ignition . . . In other words, the fire started from an open flame, held in a human hand."

The case of the Central Library fire confounded me. As hard as I tried, I couldn't completely convince myself that Harry started the fire. He does fit the usual profile of an arsonist, which is a young single white male. But most arsonists who suffer from a psychological impulse to burn things begin displaying their compulsions in childhood. As far as I knew, and as far as any records indicate, Harry had never started a fire. He applied for a job at the fire department — or so he said — and perhaps he had more interest in fire than anyone realized. But lots of people apply to work in the fire department, and the vast majority of them are not pyromaniacs. Even though Harry only talked about being an actor, his interest in being a firefighter made a certain kind of sense. It was dramatic; it was heroic; it had status. His father's remark that he could imagine Harry burning a vacant building seemed just a clumsy way of saying that he considered Harry impulsive, capable of doing something irresponsible to a building of no importance, but not someone who would want to damage a beautiful, important building that was full of life.

The city now contended that it had uncovered a motive. Harry had gone to the library with no ill intentions, investigators believed, but he'd become upset when the security guard turned him away, and he'd started the fire in a fit of pique. The theory had some logic. But Harry's interaction with the guard seemed more trifling than provocative, and Harry didn't seem the type to react so strongly to a minor scold. But Harry had mentioned in his interviews that the guard who'd stopped him at the door was African American. Was it an idle comment, or did it imply something more? According to a 2015 survey, fewer than four percent of the people in Harry's hometown of Santa Fe Springs were black. When he was growing up, that number was probably smaller. Nothing else I ever heard suggested that Harry was racist, but I had noted that he repeatedly mentioned the guard's race.

If he were angry, it would have been easy to slip into one of the library's nooks and niches and then strike a match. Maybe Harry did it as a small defiant gesture, nothing more. Maybe he touched the match to a book without giving much thought to what might follow. Early in the investigation, Harry told agent Thomas Makar that he thought the person who started the fire didn't mean for it to get so big. Perhaps Harry wasn't the kind of person to set a building like the library on fire — but might he be the kind of person who struck a match when he was mad? I could imagine this: that Harry might have felt peevish because of the guard, and then each time a librarian stopped him, he got more affronted. He might have fingered a matchbook in his pocket with nothing specific in mind. But perhaps he found himself in a secluded spot, all alone amid the creaking piles of books and papers; Harry Peak, actor, always on the brink of being noticed but really always out of view, his image of himself getting a little more threadbare every day, his buoyant optimism unraveling, nothing happening quite as he'd imagined it and not at all like the version he bragged about to the people around him and even to himself. Maybe he let himself tear a match out of a matchbook and then flicked its rough orange head over the striker, and suddenly, he was holding the spurt of flame and feeling exhilarated by his daring, remembering in that moment the kid he had been, who always pushed things further and made more people admire him, and without picturing what would happen in the next minute or the next seven hours, he acted in that instant, almost in a disembodied state. Once he saw the flame take a bite out of a book and he realized it was out of his control, I can picture him rushing away, scrambling, the way you scramble when you've broken your mother's favorite vase — not because you feel bad about it but because you know you'll have hell to pay.

Judge Chaney preferred the theory that Harry started the fire intentionally because he wanted attention. In that regard, he was insatiable. But his usual tactic to get attention was to boast about something glittery, like saying he had gone drinking with Cher. He wanted to present a version of his life populated by famous people, superstars. Starting a fire in a public building didn't have the effervescence that his brags usually did. The fire wasn't glamorous. It was a gritty, ugly crime, decried by everyone in the city. Saying he started the fire may have placed him at the center of a news event, but it also would have made him appear, to many people, contemptible. Would he really have wanted that kind of attention? As Demitri Hioteles told me, "Harry got off on making people happy." The fire didn't fit

461

that; it was too dismal, too real.

But Harry did tell people he'd started the fire. He repeated the confession to investigators. If it was just a fib, why had he stumbled through his excuses, crisscrossing his alibis again and again? Why had he failed his lie detector test? Where was he, really, on the morning of April 29, 1986? If he wasn't at the library, how did he know details about that morning? And if he didn't do it, who did?

Some years ago, I read a story in *The New Yorker* that got under my skin. "Trial by Fire," by David Grann, was about a case in Texas in which a man named Todd Willingham was convicted of setting a fire in 1991 that killed his three children. The key evidence against Willingham was patterns left by the moving fire — what arson investigators call "burn marks" — in the family's house. A long-standing belief among arson people is that fires burn hottest where they originate. The charring on the house's wooden floors was darkest and deepest under the children's beds. There was nothing under the children's beds that could have started a fire spontaneously, so investigators believed that someone had set the fire intentionally. The only person in the

462

house that night besides the children was Willingham, who claimed he had been asleep at the time the fire began and that he had done everything possible to save his children. Eventually, Willingham was convicted, largely because the burn marks were interpreted as proof that the fire started under the beds. He was sentenced to death. After losing all of his appeals, he was executed in 2004.

Struck by Willingham's insistence on his innocence, a prominent scientist and fire investigator named Dr. Gerald Hurst had been asked by Willingham's family to reexamine the case shortly before the date of execution. Hurst began by trying to determine whether the fire truly was arson. Hurst believed that the analysis of where the fire started was wrong. Despite the heavy burn marks under the children's beds, he didn't believe the fire had started there. He inspected the house again. When forensic science was applied to all of the evidence, it showed that the accelerant on the front porch was probably from a can of lighter fluid used to start a small charcoal grill that had been knocked over by firefighters entering the house. A faulty space heater or wiring had probably started the fire inside the house. Flames had raced down the hall into the children's bedroom. The extreme burn marks under their beds indicated only that the fire had settled there for a while. Hurst's analysis was too late to change the outcome for Willingham, but it succeeded in raising great concern about the reliability of what we assume about fire.

As long ago as 1977, forensic scientists warned that the principles of arson investigation were mostly myth. If windows in a burned building were greasy, investigators assumed that accelerant must have been used and left residue on the glass. But modern buildings are filled with petroleum-based products that could leave residue on windows if they burn. Extremely hot fires were presumed to have been supercharged by accelerants, indicating arson, but scientists now know that the temperature of a fire is unrelated to its cause and to whether it was intentional or accidental. Burn patterns, which were central to Willingham's conviction, are more misleading than they appear. Scorch marks don't indicate where the fire started; they indicate only that at some point, the fire lingered there. Areas of the most extensive burning are not necessarily where the fire began.

The first scientifically based report on how to examine fires was published in 1992, six years after the fire at Central Library. Released by the National Fire Protection Association, the report debunked many assumptions about arson. It took special exception to the legal principle known as "negative corpus," often used as proof that a fire was set deliberately. The term "negative corpus" means, literally, lack of a body. It posits that an event is a crime if there is nothing to prove that it wasn't a crime. In the case of a fire, negative corpus means that if accidental sources are eliminated, the fire is deemed arson, even when there is no affirmative proof that it was arson. If there is no evidence of how the fire was started, it is assumed that the source of ignition was a lighter or matchbook that was then removed from the scene. It's like finding a dead body, ruling out the obvious causes of death like a heart attack or stroke, and then declaring it murder even though there is no positive proof that it is murder. This ignores the possibility that the death was caused by something natural that hasn't been detected.

Legal scholars and forensic scientists have challenged negative corpus for years. Shaken-baby syndrome is another theory that relies on negative corpus, with disastrous results. The logic behind shaken-baby syndrome works in a reverse spiral, just like it does with arson. If an infant dies and there appears to be no obvious natural causes, police used to assume that someone must have killed the baby by violent shaking, which leaves few discernible signs. The mysterious death would be attributed to an invisible method of killing, rather than to the possibility that babies are fragile and might die for biological reasons we don't always understand or might need a long time to discover. In the past, a number of parents and caregivers have been convicted of killing infants based on the illogical logic of negative corpus. Ten years ago, medical journals and legal analysts began to dispute the thinking behind shaken-baby syndrome and the legality of negative corpus. Many pediatricians and medical examiners who used to testify for the prosecution in the cases are now testifying for the defense, and many shaken-baby convictions have been overturned.

The National Fire Protection Association's report emphasized the danger of misinterpreting where a fire started, especially because point of origin is the key to any fire investigation. Every building contains items that could start a fire. If an investigator declares that the fire started in, say, the center of a warehouse floor or in the middle of a sparsely furnished living room — far from anything flammable — it leads naturally to the conclusion that someone started the fire.

But reaching this conclusion depends on knowing for sure where the fire began. In the majority of arson convictions that have been overturned, the point of origin was incorrectly identified. In the case of Todd Willingham, the difference between thinking the fire started under the children's beds and thinking it started on a porch next to a charcoal grill was the difference between life and death. In a 1995 case in Illinois, a man named William Amor was accused of setting a fire that killed his mother-in-law. The fire was so hot that it burned in a state of complete flashover for over ten minutes. Investigators still believed they could identify the point of origin in the room, even though what was left of it was a few sticks of wood and a burned floor. Amor was convicted of first-degree murder and aggravated arson and sentenced to forty-five years, based on the arson team's statement that Amor must have intentionally dropped a lit cigarette on the floor in order to start a fire. Eventually, his case was reviewed using more exacting science. In controlled studies, pinpointing a fire's origin in a blaze as hot as the Amor fire had an accuracy rate of between six and ten percent, suggesting it would have been nearly impossible to correctly establish a point of origin. Another study showed that a lit cigarette couldn't have started the kind of fire that destroyed the apartment. When studied more rigorously, the evidence used to convict Amor fell apart. After twenty-two years of incarceration, he was released in 2017.

Central Library had bad ventilation and ramshackle floor fans and sizzling light sockets and an extremely high "fire load," which is the measure of flammable contents per square foot. All of these possible causes of fire were dismissed because investigators determined the point of origin to be a small section of one of the stacks' bookshelves. Nothing on the bookshelf could have ignited spontaneously, so investigators concluded that the only possible cause of the fire was "an open flame, held in a human hand."

But what if the fire at Central Library didn't start where investigators thought? In 2011, a former firefighter and arson investigator named Paul Bieber founded the Arson Research Project, an organization modeled on the Innocence Project, that examines what it believes are wrongful felony convictions. The Arson Research Project does the same kind of work but concentrates its efforts on arson cases, especially ones in which someone was killed. Bieber likes to call himself a "forensic science nerd." His skepticism about arson investigation began when he worked on a 1997 case in which a man named George Souliotes was accused of triple-homicide arson. Investigators labeled smudges on the floor as pour marks from an accelerant, even though chemical analysis didn't find any evidence of accelerants in the house. Souliotes was convicted and sentenced to life in prison. Sixteen years later, after an examination based on the National Fire Protection Association's new recommendations, the marks were ruled out as evidence of an accelerant; there was no scientific basis for them to have been designated as such. No cause was ever found for the fire, and Souliotes was released.

"Souliotes was the case that exposed me to the errors in fire conviction and testimony," Bieber told me recently. "The point of origin was testified to with a certainty that science just didn't support." Bieber began to believe that many arson investigators' testimony consisted of nothing more than well-intentioned professional hunches. He didn't think investigators were willfully misrepresenting the information, nor were they wrong all the time. He believed the real problem was that they had the wrong foundation for their interpretations. Without science backing their findings, Bieber felt that firefighters' testimony should be considered ordinary observation rather than expert testimony, which is supposed to be analysis based on repeatable scientific methodology and is viewed by juries as having a special kind of authority.

Bieber suspected that many arson convictions were based on flawed investigations. The Willingham fire was one of the Arson Research Project's case studies. Bieber and his staff have reviewed dozens of other arsons since then. When they used scientific methods rather than the old dogma of arson, two thirds of the fires they studied turned out not to be arson. Many convictions had been made in error.

The statistics on misidentifying arson are alarming. Nationally, the rate is the same as what the Arson Research Project discovered in its cases: About two thirds of the fires that have been reexamined turned out not to be arson. The Exoneration Registry collects statistics about overturned felony convictions beginning with cases that were tried in 1989. So far, it lists fifteen hundred instances of overturned sentences. Thirty of those exonerations were arson convictions. Ten fires were arsons in which the wrong person was convicted. In the other twenty, scientists proved that the fire was caused by something ordinary, like a malfunctioning space heater. In these cases, someone was convicted of a crime that had never happened.

Bieber told me that many fire investigators think he discounts arson too quickly and is too critical of investigators' techniques. He understands that it is hard to find good evidence in fires. "It's very difficult to get around the site of a fire," he said to me. "And even when investigators get to the source, it's too hot to really get near it. Then water is dumped on it. Then shelves and furniture collapse, and the area is strewn with rubble. And you try to find evidence in there! It's crazy to expect that, and I'm telling you, people have been sent to prison for decades based on this kind of information." Bieber is on the extreme edge of arson theory, but his distance from the mainstream is shrinking as more investigators become convinced that the old way of studying arson is, as Bieber puts it, "bullshit."

I compiled a thick file about the fire at

Central Library, including reports from the Los Angeles Fire Department and the National Fire Protection Association. The reports described the path of the fire almost minute by minute. Reviewing files couldn't compare to actually examining the library, and Bieber warned me that it was impossible to draw conclusions from a study, but I still was interested in his opinion. Ever since I'd first spoken to him, I'd wondered about the investigation of the fire at Central. The fire took place in 1986, six years before the definitive NFPA guidelines were published. Ever since, the field has moved away from many of its long-standing suppositions and toward the hard-line, science-based methods the NFPA advised. The conventions of analyzing arson — about how to look at burn marks and fire temperature and concrete spalling and whether no obvious cause proved an obvious arson: assumptions that were passed on from one generation of arson investigators to the next — were upended. Jail doors were swinging open for people who, it turned out, really hadn't lit their houses on fire. Arson investigation had become a changed field in the time since the library burned.

I convinced Bieber to read the files on Central; I had been living in the world of

472

this fire and in the enigma of Harry Peak for over four years, and now, if I believed Bieber's analysis, there was the possibility that something would help it make sense. A few weeks later, he wrote me a long email: "Under the circumstances described in the report, an area of origin . . . more specific than the general area of the second floor of the Northeast stack is not reasonable. Suspicions based on a more specific area of origin are unreasonable." He said that from what he could tell, isolating the exact place where the fire started would be impossible, especially because it burned for almost seven hours, incinerating everything in reach. Bieber said he thought it reasonable to say the fire started somewhere in the northeast stacks, where firefighters first detected smoke, but determining an ignition point more specific was unrealistic. Within that large area were a number of items that could have easily started a blaze on their own without any human involvement. In conclusion, Bieber wrote, "After burning for two or three minutes past full-room involvement, where thousands of gallons of water have been pumped into the compartment, cement walls have been breached by jack-hammers, and the book shelves have collapsed on top of themselves in a big pile . . . figuring out exactly where a fire started is a fool's errand. Not to say people don't claim they can do it, but they can't."

Once investigators suspected arson, Bieber added, they began looking for evidence to support that suspicion and probably stopped looking at possible accidental causes such as wiring and coffeepots. They believed the fire was started by "an open flame, held in a human hand," and looked to confirm that. "At the end of the day, I have no idea what started the fire at the L.A. library back in 1986," Bieber wrote, "but neither do [the investigators]." When I told some of the investigators what Bieber had said, they dismissed it. "Only the gatherer of all the facts is in a position to opine as to the cause of the fire," said Ron Hamel, the former fire captain who had described the eerie colorlessness of the library fire, adding that anyone who didn't have access to witness statements and hadn't examined the scene wouldn't be able to have a professional opinion.

I called Bieber right after I read his email and asked him to walk me through his thoughts again. We talked about the fire for a long time, and he explained what he made of the case. He attributed Harry's confessions and clumsy alibis to quirks in his personality compounded by the fact that people under pressure often give false confessions and misstatements. If the fire department had provided any significant evidence, Bieber said, the district attorney certainly would have charged Harry. The city's refusal confirms that the fire department had only guesses and suppositions and a suspect who was a perfect target — someone intoxicated by attention. There was no malice or a desire to harm Harry, Bieber said, just a series of wrong assumptions and someone who was easy to blame. "At the end of the day, they're cops, and cops like to arrest people," Bieber said. "That's just the way it is."

As we were about to hang up, Bieber said one more thing: "In my opinion, it sounds like they got the wrong guy." He took a deep breath and added, "It also sounds to me like there isn't a guy to get."

30.

The Library of Tomorrow: A Symposium (1939)
By Danton, Emily Miller
020.4 D194

The Future of Library Service: Demographic Aspects and Implications (1962)
By Schick, Frank Leopold
027.073 S331

Libraries for the Future: The Los Angeles Public Library's Branch Facilities Master Plan (1985)
By Los Angeles Public Library
027.47949 L881Lo-4

BiblioTech: Why Libraries Matter More Than Ever in the Age of Google (2015)

In late winter, I spent a day with Eva Mitnick, the head of Central Library. The day I chose happened to be one of her last days in the job, because she'd just been chosen to head the new division of Engagement and Learning, which Mitnick called her dream job. The new division will handle the ways the library makes connections with the public, including its volunteer programs and summer reading and all services directed at new immigrants. Los Angeles is one of the first libraries to create this kind of service. Since it launched in 2016, many libraries around the country have modeled departments after it.

Mitnick is gangly but somehow manages to appear elfin, with a fine-featured face and dewy eyes. She has librarian blood. Her mother, Virginia Walter, worked for the Los Angeles library system for decades. When Virginia had to work a Saturday shift, she often brought Eva with her, so Eva grew up roaming the stacks and playing peekaboo at the checkout desk. Mitnick refers to herself as a "library brat" and says that many of the other brats she knew when growing up have ended up becoming librarians, too — and many of them are in the Los Angeles system. There weren't many moments in her life when Mitnick wasn't spending time in the library. After those Saturdays as a toddler tagalong, she started working here in 1987, when she was still in library school.

The day I arranged to spend with Mitnick was exceptional by Los Angeles standards, gray and rainy and dank. The rain didn't sprinkle down — it thumped, the nickel-size drops bouncing on the sidewalk, the kind of gushing drench you might get if you were wringing out a wet towel. As I drove to the library, I slalomed around garbage cans that had toppled over and were shooting down the hilly streets or were wedged against a curb or a parked car, their big blocky bodies damming the water and creating a foamy flume. I knew the library would be busy; whenever the weather is bad, people who live on the streets gravitate to the comfort of the reading rooms.

Mitnick was in her office when I arrived, nibbling on a dry-looking sandwich and staring at a webinar on her computer screen called "Rising to the Challenge: Re-Envisioning Public Libraries." More than one hundred other librarians around the country were logged on to the webinar, probably chewing on their own dry sand-

478

wiches. Mitnick had the volume turned down and was scribbling notes between bites. Running Central Library had been a change for her. She'd spent most of her first twenty-eight library years in various children's departments as a hands-on librarian rather than a manager. She recently returned to her roots in the Children's Department: In addition to running Central, she was now filling in as head of Teen'Scape and Children, because budget cuts and subsequent staff shrinkage had obliged the remaining librarians to double up on responsibilities. As the webinar continued, Mitnick pulled out a calendar and reviewed her schedule for the day, which included many events that were outreach-directed rather than book-directed. She started the day at nine A.M., meeting with Department of Health staff who were advising librarians from around the city on the harsher facts of having some of the city's estimated forty-five thousand homeless people among their clientele — facts like how to spot bedbugs and lice, and how to detect signs of tuberculosis. During that meeting, Mitnick ducked out for a minute to listen in on a seminar in the next room where librarians were being trained how to teach computer coding to children. She then dashed down the hall to check on a group of caterers who were arranging plates and glasses in the courtyard beside the Mark Taper Auditorium. Today at noon, the first class of Career Online High School was graduating, and the students and their families were invited for a celebratory lunch after the ceremony.

As soon as the webinar and her sandwich were finished, Mitnick and I went downstairs to a room just off the main lobby of the library. A line of people was winding from the door of the room all the way into the lobby and almost reached the checkout desks. Mitnick explained that this was a trial run of The Source — the gathering at the library of social service agencies from around the city that John Szabo had described when I spent the day with him. Mitnick and Szabo believed the advantage of The Source was that people could sign up for all the services they needed in the space of one large meeting room instead of traipsing from veterans' services in one building and food stamps in another and housing assistance in yet another. If all went well, Szabo and Mitnick wanted to host The Source at the library on a regular basis. Mitnick had noticed recently that people seemed to really like gathering at the library for things besides checking out books. She saw great turnouts for discussion groups and movie screenings, and recently, about two thousand people had shown up for a Maker Faire, a gathering of tech enthusiasts, tinkerers, and crafters.

The doors for The Source weren't open yet, but the long line seemed like a hearty endorsement. "Yes!" Mitnick said, pumping her fists. "I knew it! Everyone's here!" While she is a full-throated supporter of the library's role in social services, she has her limits. She told me that one of her greatest achievements as head of Central was eliminating what she called "the cubicles of sin" — the individual work carrels in each department that provided privacy for the users. The problem was that some people construed the highest use of privacy to be sex or drugs. "All sorts of terrible things were happening," Mitnick said. "And I just decided there was no reason to keep the cubicles. No one needs a private workspace in the library. And so they're gone."

Caseworkers from the social service agencies, food banks, and mental health organizations set up plastic tables in a big U-shape, so people would be able to move from one to the other, the way they would navigate a buffet line. Mitnick and I found seats next to a pierced and ponytailed caseworker from the Los Angeles Homeless Services Authority. He introduced himself as Hector. He lined up approximately forty ballpoint pens on the table next to a notebook swollen with intake forms.

"We're *doing* this," Hector said to Mitnick, smiling and tapping his notebook for punctuation. "This is really" — *tap tap* — "awesome!"

Once the room was ready, Mitnick motioned to Stan Molden, the security guard, who had held the line back as The Source was setting up. Molden nodded and stepped aside. The line bulged at the door and then began snaking around the room. I glanced over at Mitnick, who was smiling as she watched the line of people move in. "See?" she said, sounding excited. "See?"

There were so many people coming in, so eager for information, that I was pressed into service as a temporary intake worker. My job was to write down people's names and ask them basic questions about themselves and the benefits they were seeking. I was nervous. It's uncomfortable to admit, but I have always been scared of homeless people or, rather, scared of the air of menacing unpredictability I perceive around them. That feeling had deepened when a homeless woman slugged me in the chest as we passed each other in a crosswalk in New York some years ago. But the people moving from table to table were quiet and personable and patient despite the glacial progress of the line. Some were tidy, and others were in ruins of clothing that was so soiled it had taken on the sheen of leather. A woman with queenly bearing, carrying a tote bag the size of an orange crate, was my first intake. "I'm homeless," she said after telling me her name. "I might need a bus pass." She rummaged around in her bag and glanced up. She studied me and then beamed, saying, "Well, aren't you so pretty with your eyes and your hair!" She turned to the man behind her, who was in a battered wheelchair, accompanied by a grizzled dog wearing a service-animal vest. The dog looked bored. "Just take a look at her, Willis," she said to the man in the wheelchair, gesturing for him to look at me.

I finished registering them, sorry to have them move on. My next client was a good-looking man with silky dark skin. He was wearing a crew-neck sweater and slacks; he looked as immaculate as a dentist. He told me his name was David, and then I asked him the standard intake questions. The first was about current employment. One of the multiple-choice answers was "retired," which he found hilarious. Once he stopped laughing, he said, "I don't think 'retirement' would describe my situation. I'm not working. I do things. I sing in a barbershop quartet, which gives me satisfaction but no income." I asked the next question, "What is your immediate need?" and he replied, "My immediate need is for food."

He started laughing again and it was wonderful to hear, because he had a deep, rich, rounded voice — a movie star's voice, a narrator's voice. I asked if he had ever done voiceover work, and he said other people had suggested it to him, but he'd never pursued it and wasn't sure how. His appearance was so discordant with his situation that I continued talking to him, hoping he would tell me something about himself. He said he used to have a job and a house and even owned a second house as a rental property, but he had made what he described as "very bad financial decisions" and, one by one, lost all that he had. For the last five months, he'd been living in his car. The one part of his former life he clung to was a gym membership, so he could go somewhere to shower and shave. "I don't want to let myself go," he said. "I need to keep myself up."

The line was bunching up behind David, so we had to stop talking. Before he went to the next table, I recorded him on my phone saying a greeting and then a brief description of the weather. Between my next few intakes, I emailed the recording to a friend who sent it to people who hire voiceover actors. I suppose it was foolish to be so hopeful, but being in that room made me feel like anything was possible — that the unfathomable problem of homelessness could be solved, that a community of people with a common purpose could be drawn together and make everything work out. I fantasized that lightning would strike and that David would get hired for a great narration job on the strength of the phone recording, and everything that had gone wrong for him would go right. All the people who received the recording agreed that David's voice was magical, but none of them was hiring at the moment. They said they would keep him in mind. After I finished my shift at The Source, I never saw him again.

Mitnick and I talked about the future of libraries. She is an idealist. She thinks libraries are adapting to the world as it is now, where knowledge streams around us as well as being captured in physical books. Like

Szabo and many other library people who are eager for innovation, Mitnick sees libraries as information and knowledge centers rather than simply as storehouses of material. She is one of a large cohort of library people who believe that libraries will remain essential to their communities. By most measures, this optimistic cohort seems to be right. According to a 2010 study, almost three hundred million Americans used one of the country's 17,078 public libraries and bookmobiles in the course of the year. In another study, over ninety percent of those surveyed said closing their local library would hurt their communities. Public libraries in the United States outnumber McDonald's; they outnumber retail bookstores two to one. In many towns, the library is the only place you can browse through physical books.

Libraries are old-fashioned, but they are growing more popular with people under thirty. This younger generation uses libraries in greater numbers than older Americans do, and even though they grew up in a streaming, digital world, almost two thirds of them believe that there is important material in libraries that is not available on the Internet. Unlike older generations, people under thirty are also less likely to have office jobs. Consequently, they are always looking for pleasant places to work outside their homes. Many end up in coffee shops and hotel lobbies or join the booming business of coworking spaces. Some of them are also discovering that libraries are society's original coworking spaces and have the distinct advantage of being free.

Humankind persists in having the desire to create public places where books and ideas are shared. In 1949, UNESCO published a Public Library Manifesto to establish the importance of libraries on the United Nations agenda. The manifesto states, "The library is a prerequisite to let citizens make use of their right to information and freedom of speech. Free access to information is necessary in a democratic society, for open debate and creation of public opinion."

Even when it is impossible to establish libraries in permanent quarters, people want them, and librarians have accommodated. The first recorded instance of a bookmobile was in 1905, when a horse-drawn library wagon traveled around Washington County, Maryland, loaning books. The idea of bringing libraries to patrons caught on, and many libraries introduced book wagons modeled on the Maryland one. The earliest ones

Four of the Pack Horse Librarians ready for the day's work

focused on delivering books to lumberjacks, miners, and other workers far from a town library. In 1936, the Works Progress Administration established a Pack Horse Librarians unit to serve the mountain communities in Kentucky. Until the WPA lost its funding in 1943, this group of sturdy horsewoman librarians rode from village to village, delivering more than thirty-five hundred books and eight thousand magazines monthly.

In 1956, the federal Library Services Act funded almost three hundred bookmobiles to serve rural communities. These days, many public libraries have bookmobiles to serve areas of their cities that don't have branch libraries. The Los Angeles Public Library system doesn't have a bookmobile right now, but it has three book bikes that are dispatched to different neighborhoods around the city, carrying a saddlebag's portion of books. There are also private bookmobiles, such as Florida-based Bess the Book Bus, serving as mobile literacy programs. Sixty thousand Little Free Libraries, in eighty countries around the world, offer book exchanges — take one, give one — housed in wooden cabinets about twice the size of a birdhouse. They are part of the nonprofit Little Free Libraries Organization, but they are set up and run by any individual who is willing to put one of the cabinets in her front yard and fill it with giveaway books.

Worldwide, there are 320,000 public libraries serving hundreds of millions of people in every country on the planet. A large number of these libraries are in conventional buildings. Others are mobile and, depending on the location's terrain and weather, operate by bicycle, backpack, helicopter, boat, train, motorcycle, ox, donkey, elephant, camel, truck, bus, or horse. In Zambia, a four-ton truck of books travels a regular route through rural areas. In Cajamarca Province, Peru, there is no library building, so seven hundred farmers make space in their homes, each one housing a section of the town library. In Beijing, about a third of library books are borrowed out of vending machines around the city. In Bangkok, a train filled with books, called the Library Train for Young People, serves homeless children, who often live in encampments near train stations. In Norway, villages in the fjords without libraries are served by a book boat that makes stops along the coast of Hordaland, MØre og Romsdal, and Sogn og Fjordane counties all winter, distributing literature. Sweden has a book boat, too, and so do Finland, Canada, and Venezuela. Some mobile libraries focus on special communities and bring them material unique to their culture. Norway has a bookmobile that brings material in the Sami language to the nomadic Sami reindeer herders in the far north.

Animals power many of the mobile libraries around the world. Donkeys and mules are the most common library creatures. In the Magdalena Department of Colombia, a schoolteacher named Luís Soriano was worried that residents of the small villages in his province didn't have access to libraries,

The Biblioburro mobile library in Colombia

so he set up his own donkey-powered Biblioburro. On weekends, he rides one donkey, Alfa, and leads another, Beto, outfitted with saddlebags of books. After he crosses the province over the course of a month, Soriano heads back in the other direction to pick up returns. In the Nkayi District in northwestern Zimbabwe, donkey-drawn electro-communication library carts travel to remote villages with books and printed material as well as a radio, a telephone, a fax, and public access to the Internet. Kenya has a camel library that delivers books to nomadic villages in the regions of Garissa and Wajir. Sometimes the camels sit down when the villagers come to collect their reading material, their rough-furred bodies forming a kind of living berm separating the special space of the library from the wide-open fields.

In Los Angeles, the librarians I met were not the dour and discouraged personnel of a dying industry, but cheerful and eager individuals uplifted by the conviction that they were doing something important. I started going to library conferences to see if my impression of their optimism bore out, beginning in 2013 with the American Library Association conference, the biggest library conference in the world. The conference that year was held in McCormick Place in Chicago, a structure so huge that it seemed to have its own atmosphere and weather pattern.

Alongside tens of thousands of librarians and library supporters, I roamed through an exposition hall that had seven hundred booths and almost seven thousand exhibitors. The event was so populated that it felt like a new nation-state. The librarians were from Fort Collins and Painesville and Irvine and Oshkosh, from Anchorage and Austin and small towns in Tennessee. I knew there were librarians from Los Angeles here, too, but the crowds were so big that I never ran into them. The librarians wore flowered blouses or glittering READING ROCKS

T-shirts, or they had tattoos of books and Dewey decimal numbers. If they were wise, they were wearing comfortable shoes, or else they stopped at one of the Happy Feet inner soles booths, conveniently located at each of the hall's four corners, to edit their footwear. "Librarians have *pain,*" the northwest corner's Happy Feet salesperson told me as he fitted me with inner soles. "No one is on their feet all day like librarians are on their feet all day." I enjoyed the book displays, but I was really fascinated by the mechanical stuff, the gizmos and widgets a civilian might never realize that libraries need. A company called MJ Industries displayed a staggering array of sorting systems. ColorMarq shelving management promised "The End of Misshelved Books!" There were signs from ASI Signage Innovations, and automated checkout kiosks, and something called Boopsie for Libraries that asked the question "What's Your Mobile Strategy?" Interspersed among the manufacturers and mainstream publishers and niche publishers of, say, Christian cat books, were booths displaying single seemingly random books, such as *The Long Journey of Mister Poop* (illustrated, available in English and Spanish), and Young Revolutionary Publishing Company's lead (and perhaps only) title, *Memoirs of the Homosexual President: Told by the First Lady.*

Some months after my trip to Chicago, I went to Aarhus, Denmark, for a biannual conference called Next Library, an international gathering to "look ahead and explore the continuously evolving nature of the public library in the 21st century." That year's theme was "Rethink." It attracted several hundred librarians from thirty-eight countries who came, in part, to celebrate Aarhus's new central library, a building so fresh-looking and engaging that I really didn't want to leave it, and apparently, neither did anyone else. The building is a stack of concrete wedges on Aarhus Bay, and the space inside is soaring and open, with views of the water from the reading rooms. The bookshelves are in wide rows, adding to the feeling that the place contains more than the average amount of air and light. It is a loungey sort of library; there are big pillows everywhere, in case you want to lie on your stomach and read, and the main staircase, wide and gently sloped, has been adopted as a sort of indoor jungle gym for the infants of Aarhus. When those of us at Next Library weren't swooning over the new building or guzzling the very good coffee for sale in the library café, we went to sessions about innovation and engagement and outreach and learning. Some were talks, and others were participatory. I attended one session that involved building things with LEGOs. I never understood what that had to do with libraries of the future, but the worldwide headquarters of the LEGO Corporation were just sixty miles away in Billund, Denmark, so maybe the session organizers just wanted to make use of local products.

In every session, the point made was that libraries could do more and more while still being places of books. The possible ways a library could grow seemed, honestly, quite endless. Conference-goers were impressed that the Aarhus library has a marriage license bureau among its services. A Nigerian librarian told me that her library offers art and entrepreneurship training classes, and a librarian from Nashville described how the city library there just started a seed exchange and housed a theater troupe.

I often thought of how City Librarian Tessa Kelso would have felt at home at the Aarhus conference: Her suggestion in the 1880s that the Los Angeles Public Library should loan tennis racquets and board games would have fit right in. So many things at both Next Library and the ALA conference made me think of the Los Angeles librarians of the past whom I had come to know through my research. Charles Lummis would have reconsidered his opinion that librarians were dull if he'd joined me at the Librarians with Tattoos cocktail hour in Chicago. And Dr. C. J. K. Jones, the Human Encyclopedia, would have felt vindicated by the British Library and the Royal Library of Denmark's new "Wikipedians in Residence."

In Aarhus, I tagged along with Deborah Jacobs, the former Seattle city librarian, who is now running the Bill & Melinda Gates Foundation's Global Libraries Initiative. The foundation helps underwrite the conference, and Jacobs had been the person who urged me to come. She also happens to love Aarhus and mentioned that she was thinking of renting an apartment there when she retires. Jacobs is small and sturdy, with bouncy chestnut hair and a twinkly smile and a good laugh. She is also possessed of an iron constitution. In the weeks before we rendezvoused in Aarhus, she traveled to Nambia, Ghana, the Netherlands, South Africa, and San Francisco, and she didn't seem worse for the wear. Bill and Melinda Gates got interested in libraries long ago:

Supporting public libraries was one of their first charitable projects, before they even formed their philanthropic foundation. The effort began in 1997, with the goal of helping every American library get connected to the Internet. In 2002, after they completed their part in helping wire all the libraries in the United States, the Gateses decided to continue their engagement with libraries and to expand it internationally. The Global Libraries Initiative was founded in 2004. (The global and domestic programs merged in 2011.) One of its first projects was to help people around the world connect to the Internet at their local library. At that time, sixty-five percent of the world's population didn't have access to the Internet, which left them unable to get information online or develop knowledge of the digital world. In a sense, the Global Libraries Initiative designated libraries as the world-wide portal to the future, by making them the default location for free public Internet.

In the last twenty years, the initiative's goals have broadened beyond just wiring the world's libraries. It has awarded grants to international literacy organizations like Worldreader in developing nations, and has supported thirteen thousand libraries around the world, in such places as Botswana, Lithuania, Vietnam, Moldova, Jamaica, and Colombia, with funding for equipment and training for staff. More recently, Jacobs has steered the program's efforts toward educating librarians and connecting them to one another, especially in Africa, where librarians were isolated from one country to the next. She also wants to cultivate the next generation of what she calls "spark-plug librarians," whom she pictures guiding the profession in the future. She considers Los Angeles city librarian John Szabo one of the current spark plugs, but she's also thinking about the generation who will come after him. "We need to make sure there are strong people to step in when we're gone," she said to me recently, then added, "Wow, I almost choked up when I said 'when we're gone.' " At the time of our call, Jacobs was in South Africa, sitting in an office with Gertrude Kayaga Mulindwa, the former head of the National Library of Uganda, who is now a director at the African Library and Information Association and Institution. Because I wrote a book about orchid thieves a few years ago, Jacobs thought I would like to know that Kayaga Mulindwa is a passionate orchid collector, and when she travels to international library conferences, she has been known to tuck a few orchids in her suitcase and bring them home. "Is that illegal?" I could hear Kayaga Mulindwa saying in the background. "Deborah, I don't think that's illegal."

In 2014, the Bill & Melinda Gates Foundation redoubled its commitment to health and science issues and decided to prune programs that didn't fall into those areas. Rather than stopping it abruptly, the foundation gave the Global Libraries Initiative four and a half years to wind down so that the libraries and librarians it was helping would have time to adjust to the change. By the time the program ends in December 2018, the Global Library Initiative will have devoted twenty years and $1 billion to libraries and librarians and literacy programs around the world. The Next Library conference I attended with Jacobs took place in 2015, shortly after Jacobs had sent the email announcing the impending end of the program. The initiative and Jacobs are big forces in the library world. It seemed like every single person at the conference knew Jacobs, and many benefited from the initiative. Jacobs seemed pleased by the fact that most people reacted to the announcement not with panic or despair but with a bootstrapping determination to keep doing what they were doing, even without the

Gates's largesse. "We didn't build physical libraries the way Andrew Carnegie did," Jacobs said. "We encouraged and trained and connected librarians, and we helped communities develop. I'd say that's pretty good."

Still, everyone at Next Library talked about money and how there was never enough of it. The topic is such a constant in the world of libraries that it almost goes without saying that it comes up anytime more than one librarian is in a room. But just like the participants at the American Library Association conference, everyone I met at Next Library seemed excited about the future — even the people who ran tiny libraries in the basements of city halls in Polish villages or were barely breathing life into woefully underfunded ones in Kenya. It was like everyone shared the same great realization: that libraries have persisted, and they have grown, and they will certainly endure.

I stepped into another portal to the future when I visited Cleveland recently and toured the headquarters of OverDrive, which is the largest digital content catalog for libraries and schools in the world. If you have ever borrowed an e-book from a library, it is likely that you were borrowing it from the library's cache in the OverDrive mega-collection, which numbers in the multimillions. When Steve Potash founded it in 1986, OverDrive sold diskettes and CD-ROMs to publishers and booksellers. "That started to peter out," Potash told me, "and we saw where the technology was going." A few years later, the company executed what businesspeople like to call a "pivot" and reinvented itself as a gigantic collection of e-media. Essentially, the company created the concept of an e-book loan. At the time, libraries were sniffing around the business of loaning nonphysical books, but that would require more computing power and management than many had available. With OverDrive, they could just set up a membership and offer material for loan without having to do the daunting behind-the-scenes work. For instance, the Los Angeles Public Library's digital collection resides on a cloud run by OverDrive in Cleveland.

The first public library to give OverDrive a try was the Cleveland Public Library, which set up its e-book lending service in 2003. At the last count, more than forty thousand public and school libraries (and some academic and corporate ones) in seventy countries use OverDrive to handle the loans of their electronic media, which now includes audiobooks, music, and video, along with electronic books. The number is growing so fast that when I visited its headquarters, OverDrive had thirty-seven thousand member libraries and just a month later, when I called to confirm the number, it had risen by over eight percent. It might have seemed like a wild idea when it started, but within three years of its founding, Over-Drive had loaned one million books, and in 2012, it had reached a hundred million checkouts. By the end of 2017, it had reached the milestone of having loaned one billion books. On an average day, seven hundred thousand books are checked out through OverDrive. The company has been so successful that, a few years ago, the Japanese conglomerate Rakuten paid $410 million to acquire it.

I met Potash in the lobby of OverDrive's new headquarters, which is a stark, striking glass-and-concrete monolith perched on a grassy ridge west of downtown Cleveland, on the far side of a deep valley carved eons ago by what must have been a very impressive piece of ice. Unlike many people who have founded pioneering technology companies, Potash is a grown-up, and his three adult children — two daughters and one son — work at OverDrive with him. Potash is warm and rumpled, with a head of thick brown hair and a way of talking about the company that sounds parental and proud. OverDrive is essentially a technology company, but Potash has the manner of a library person rather than that of a technology person. He knew every Los Angeles librarian I mentioned, including details of their lives and histories. Before he gave me a tour of the building, for instance, we spent at least five minutes talking about Peggy Murphy, the head of the Catalog Department at Central, and Potash knew all about how Murphy had sneaked into the cage of dirty books at her first library job and read her way through them.

The lobby of the OverDrive headquarters is huge and high. A ten-foot-square screen that displays a world map dominates the center of the lobby. Every few seconds, a bubble pops up from somewhere on the map, showing the name of the library and the title of the book that had just been borrowed. The screen is mesmerizing. If you stand there for a few minutes, you will see that someone at a small library in Arles, France, has just checked out *L'Instant présent* by Guillaume Musso; that someone in Boulder, Colorado, has borrowed *Harry*

Potter and the Cursed Child by J. K. Rowling; and that in Mexico City, someone has claimed a copy of *El cuerpo en que nací* by Guadalupe Nettel. It feels like you're watching a real-time thought map of the world.

OverDrive may be the future of book lending, but that's not the same thing as the future of libraries. Libraries are physical spaces belonging to a community where we gather to share information. There isn't anywhere else that fits that description. Perhaps in the future, OverDrive will be where our books will come from, and libraries will become something more like our town squares, a place that is home when you aren't at home.

31.

Civil Procedure in a Nutshell (2003)
  By Kane, Mary Kay
  Series: Nutshell Series
  347.9 K16 2003

Great Careers with a High School Diploma: Health Care, Medicine, and Science [electronic resource] (2008)
  By Porterfield, Deborah
  E-book

AIDS, the Mystery and the Solution (1984)
  By Cantwell, Alan
  616.97 C234

Ask the Dust (1939)
  By Fante, John
  On shelf

505

In 1991, five years after the fire, it was finally possible to imagine a time in the not distant future when Central Library would move back to the Goodhue Building; the new wing would be open; things would return to normal. The Goodhue Building was still closed, but construction crews had power-washed the walls, shoveled out the soot, and put things right. On the adjoining lot, a huge hole had been dug to make room for the new wing. The rumble of construction equipment and the sharp chime of steel against steel rang through the blocks bounded by Grand Avenue and Fifth Street and Hope and Flower. A few miles away, the document restorers pressurized and vacuumed and groomed and babied each damaged book, then declared it either salvaged or hopeless. The number of books ready to go back on the shelves was growing. New books, paid for by the Save the Books campaign — which had reached its goal of $10 million — were starting to arrive. In March, the new wing was topped out. The interior work began, and in spite of the construction fencing and the saggy orange grid of Tenax barriers, the place was beginning to acquire the shape and dimensions of a library. Librarians began the process of cataloging the contents from scratch, merging the three collections — the books that made it through the fire unscathed, the salvaged ones, and the new books bought to replace the four hundred thousand that were gone for good.

The city's civil suit against Harry Peak, and his countersuit against the city, inched along — a deposition here, a motion there; a statement from the French Quarter waiter, a filing about damages from the city attorney — but nothing felt decisive. Rather than speeding toward a resolution, the case dawdled. It grew more bewildering. In his most recent depositions, Harry had altered his story yet again. He now insisted that he'd had breakfast with Fathers Wilkie and Clark before his wart treatment rather than after; he said they'd been in the restaurant at ten A.M., not noon. Father Wilkie altered his testimony, too, saying that he had another patient scheduled at eleven A.M., and that the patient had been a little late, and that he, Harry, and Father Clark left the restaurant and went up to his office a few minutes after eleven.

This new set of facts and times was hard to reconcile. The first alarm at the library sounded at 10:52 A.M., but it wasn't known to indicate a real fire and not just a false alarm until 11:11 A.M., when firefighters discovered smoke in the Fiction Department. Therefore, the earliest anyone knew that there was a fire at the library was 11:11 A.M. According to Harry's new time line, the waiter's mention of the fire would have occurred just moments after the alarm went off. This would have been impossible unless the waiter was listening to a police scanner; otherwise he couldn't have heard such an early report of the fire. In terms of Harry's guilt or innocence, the shift in time didn't matter. It was still the same alibi — Harry's claim that he was with Wilkie and Clark when the fire began. What mattered was that Harry's constant revisions made the truth about the day seem as unfixed as a drop of oil on water. Every time a coherent pattern formed, it almost immediately deformed and became unrecognizable, and what you thought you saw — a circle, a cloud, a face — dissolved into a murky swirl with no shape. I'm not sure why Harry thought changing this timing helped his alibi. Instead, it furthered my sense that his lying was an involuntary impulse, so automatic that he didn't weigh the lie's value before it flew out of his mouth.

In some ways, Harry seemed to be disengaging from the case. He was slow to respond to requests from the city attorney and made few motions of his own. His claim included medical expenses he said he'd incurred after being injured in jail, but he never responded when Victoria Chaney asked him to produce the names of the doctors who treated him and receipts for the bills he paid. Chaney asked Harry's lawyer to follow up on the request, and he said he would check on it. Months passed, and Chaney never received either a reply or a request for more time to get the information.

Perhaps Harry was distracted. He had a new boyfriend — "a nice man named Alan," according to Debra Peak. She said she couldn't remember his last name, but she knew he was well-off and that Harry wouldn't be hurting for money anymore. Keeping it a secret from his parents, Harry moved to Alan's house near Palm Springs. What a relief it must have been for Harry to find someone who loved him, and to get out of his tatty West Hollywood apartment and away from the passel of roommates. Maybe this was why his interest in the lawsuit flagged; he might not have wanted to think about the fire anymore. In his nice house, with his nice man, in the sunny languor of Palm Springs, he must have lost his appetite for the clawing and grabbing of Hollywood.

He was a flawed, self-destructive person who blundered through life, but perhaps he had begun to feel something close to contentment.

He told friends that he wanted a job that was more reliable than acting. After considering his options, he decided to become a medical assistant. The choice seems like a significant departure, but it offered a lot of what he yearned for. He could make people happy doing that job; he could feel heroic. He started the training program at a local school — Debra couldn't remember what it was called. She said Harry really liked it, although he had one complaint. When the students were learning how to draw blood, he said, they practiced on each other, using the same needles over and over.

In July 1991, the parties involved in the civil suit gathered for a status conference. Victoria Chaney hadn't seen Harry in months, and when he arrived at her office, she was stunned. Compared to the previous time she had seen him, he looked shrunken, dried out; his strong, sunny good looks were worn away. Even his glorious head of hair was thinned, and his skin had the sallow tinge of jaundice. His lawyer announced that he'd called the conference to request that the trial be expedited. He presented an affidavit from Harry's doctor that stated Harry was suffering from severe hepatitis and an enlarged liver and spleen, and "there is a substantial medical doubt that he will survive beyond six months."

Ten years earlier, in 1981, an immunologist at UCLA named Michael Gottlieb published an account describing a phenomenon he called acquired immune deficiency syndrome; Gottlieb's study is considered among the first documentations of AIDS. The disease's ascent in Los Angeles was explosive, brutal, and extensive. Its presence in the city was especially public. In 1985, actor Rock Hudson acknowledged that he was infected with the disease; that same year, Hollywood held its first AIDS walk, which drew thousands of marchers. Just a few months after Harry requested an expedited trial, Magic Johnson announced he was HIV-positive and retired from the Los Angeles Lakers.

Harry's family had never been comfortable with the idea that he was gay, and they would have been uncomfortable with the possibility that he'd acquired a disease through a homosexual encounter. The medical technician class was a convenient opportunity to explain away his illness.

Debra told me that everyone in Harry's class ended up with HIV/AIDS because of the shared dirty needles. First, she told me that Harry was the only one in the class who died; another time she said that everyone in the class passed away. It is possible for health care workers to acquire HIV accidentally, but it's rare. According to an article published in a medical journal in 2007, the worldwide count was 98 confirmed instances and 194 possible cases of health care personnel being infected accidentally. If five or ten students in a medical assistant program in Los Angeles all became infected with HIV/AIDS — especially if they became infected because of unhygienic practices in the program — the media surely would have covered it. But I never found any mention anywhere of such an incident, and to this day, I can't find anything to suggest that the story was true. When I asked Demitri Hioteles, he chuckled and said, "That needle story? I always knew that was bullshit." The irony is that when Hioteles and Harry were still a couple, Harry came home one day and asked Hioteles if he had heard about a new illness — some kind of gay cancer. Hioteles didn't believe him. "It sounded crazy," Hioteles told me. "And Harry was such a liar. I just thought it was another one of his stupid stories."

Harry grew weaker, smaller, sicker. After the conference with Victoria Chaney, Leonard Martinet petitioned the court to move up the date of the trial. The judge agreed, scheduling the trial for September 12, 1991. Martinet hoped there wouldn't be a trial at all and that the city would drop its suit and settle. He was correct in guessing that the city attorneys didn't savor the prospect of pitting the City of Los Angeles against a man dying of AIDS. The city's suit was mostly symbolic. Harry had no money and never would have been able to pay any portion of the damages. Chaney — and the firefighters — pursued the case to make a statement about responsibility, especially after the frustration of never having a trial on the criminal charges. But even in civil court, where the standards of proof are more lenient, there was no guarantee that the city would win its case. There simply wasn't any irrefutable evidence placing Harry at the library that day, and nothing connecting him directly to the fire. Considering how sick Harry was, the city could look vindictive and cruel.

At a conference a few days before the trial was to begin, the city made a surprise proposal, offering Harry thirty-five thousand dollars to settle the case. The amount was a pittance compared to the $15 million Harry had asked for, and a pittance compared to the kinds of settlements the city usually makes. Nevertheless, Harry accepted it. For the city, it was a great bargain. Trying the case, with its uncertain outcome, would have cost the city thousands more. The city's Budget Department drafted the check for thirty-five thousand, settling the case of the Los Angeles library fire — at least with regard to Harry's culpability — on October 2, 1991.

Harry spent his last days in Palm Springs. After that last meeting with Victoria Chaney, he never really left his house again, relying on Alan's attentions and finances for comfort. The settlement money must have felt like a windfall at first, but his medical costs gobbled it up in no time; the most basic medications for HIV/AIDS cost close to five thousand dollars a month. He had liver failure, hepatitis, and an enlarged spleen, followed by even more dismal consequences of the disease. "We were so close, we were like twins," his sister Debra told me recently. "The day before he died, I was incoherent. I just knew. I told my kid that we wouldn't see Uncle Harry alive again. I just had a premonition." On April 13, 1993, Harry Peak died in Palm Springs, California, of complications from HIV/AIDS. There was a private funeral service at Hope Country Church, a lovely little steepled building on a quiet street in Baldwin Park, about fourteen miles north of Santa Fe Springs, where Harry was raised.

32

The End of the Story: A Play in One Act (1954)
  By Thomas, Richard
  822 T461

The End of the Story (2004)
  By Davis, Lydia
  E-book

The End of the Story (2012)
  By Heker, Liliana
  Series: Biblioasis International Translation Series

This Is the End of the Story (2017)
  By Fortune, Jan
  E-book

January 1 is the day of the Rose Bowl Parade in Pasadena. The Los Angeles Public

Library always has a float in the parade. Every year, the parade has a theme. In 1993, the theme was "Entertainment on Parade," and the library float featured a giant bookworm reading a newspaper. One of the people riding beside the bookworm was City Librarian Elizabeth Martinez, who was appointed to the job after Wyman Jones retired in 1990. The newspaper that the bookworm was reading displayed a headline that said CENTRAL LIBRARY REOPENS OCTOBER 3, 1993. Robert Reagan, who was the public information director of the library from 1980 to 1998, said that publicizing that date at the Rose Bowl might have been tempting fate, but he believed they would really make it.

There was a lot still to do. As the date approached, the library held book-shelving parties, and hundreds of volunteers helped unpack two million books and place them on the new shelves. The parties were a little like the volunteer turnout after the fire, but in terms of mood, it was the mirror opposite, an occasion for optimism and renewal. "I like to work with books," one of the volunteers told a reporter who asked why she was giving her time. Then she added by way of complaint, "Today there were a lot of very young children getting underfoot and doing nothing. They slowed down the shelving." She paused and added, "But working to help open the library is personally very satisfying." Library administration, with help from ARCO, planned a spectacular opening celebration, featuring Brazilian folk dancers, Japanese drummers, flamenco performers, West African singers, Korean musicians, demonstrations by the cast of *American Gladiators,* and appearances by Spider-Man, Daffy Duck, and Bugs Bunny.

No one was sure how many people might come to see the library reopen after six and a half years. Maybe the city had grown used to the library being in its diminished state, stuck in its temporary out-of-the-way place; maybe the wonder of the Goodhue Building, the "magic castle in fairyland" that caused people to swoon when it opened in 1926, was gone for good. But the day of the opening celebration, it was clear that the whole city wanted to see the library. At least fifty thousand people danced with Barney the Dinosaur and walked through the rotunda and rode the cascading escalators to the bottom of the new Tom Bradley Wing, and more than ten thousand people signed up for library cards for the first time. Everyone enjoyed the spectacle of the entertainers. But as Robert Reagan put it to me recently, on that day in 1993, "the library was the hero."

The end of Harry Peak's case came with no clarity; in effect, it was more of an erasure than a conclusion. It didn't resolve the question of who had started the fire, or whether anyone had started the fire. Nor did it ever provide a final immutable version of how Harry Peak spent the day of April 29, 1986. It didn't answer whether he was or wasn't the human hand holding an open flame. I seesawed countless times in what I believed really happened, in particular whether Harry was involved. Every time I thought I'd settled on the version of the story I trusted, something arose to punch a hole in it, and I was back at the beginning. In the end, I had no idea what was true or even what I decided to believe. I finally accepted the ambiguity. I knew for sure that once upon a time, the Los Angeles Central Library suffered a terrible fire, and a fumbling young man was caught up in it. Beyond that was all uncertainty, the way life almost always is. It would remain a story without end, like a suspended chord in the last measure of a song — that singular, dissonant, open sound that makes you ache to hear something more.

I went to the library late one day, just before closing time, when the light outside was already dusky and the place was sleepy and slow. Central Library and the Bradley Wing are so big that when the crowds thin out, the library can feel very private, almost like a secret place, and the space is so enveloping that you have no sense of the world outside. I went down to History to see Glen Creason and find out how the indexing of the Feathers map collection was progressing. Then I roamed from department to department, just strolling through, and crossed the beautiful hollow rotunda, a gorgeous surprise every time I entered it, and then went up the wide lap of the back staircase, where the Statue of Civilization stared at me as I made my way. The silence was more soothing than solemn. A library is a good place to soften solitude; a place where you feel part of a conversation that has gone on for hundreds and hundreds of years even when you're all alone. The library is a whispering post. You don't need to take a book off a shelf to know there is a voice inside that is waiting to speak to you, and behind that was someone who truly believed that if he or she spoke, someone would listen. It was that affirmation that always amazed me. Even the oddest, most particular book was written with that kind of crazy courage — the writer's belief that someone would find his or her book important to read. I was struck by how precious and foolish and brave that belief is, and how necessary, and how full of hope it is to collect these books and manuscripts and preserve them. It declares that all these stories matter, and so does every effort to create something that connects us to one another, and to our past and to what is still to come. I realized that this entire time, learning about the library, I had been convincing myself that my hope to tell a long-lasting story, to create something that endured, to be alive somehow as long as someone would read my books, was what drove me on, story after story; it was my lifeline, my passion, my way to understand who I was. I thought about my mother, who died when I was halfway done with this book, and I knew how pleased she would have been to see me in the library, and I was able to use that thought to transport myself for a split second to a time when I was young and she was in the moment, alert and tender, with years ahead of her, and she was beaming at me as I toddled to the checkout counter with an armload of books. I knew that if we had come here together, to this enchanted place of stucco and statuary and all the stories in the world for us to have, she would have reminded me just about now that if she could have chosen any profession in the world, she would have been a librarian.

I looked around the room at the few people scattered here and there. Some were leaning into books, and a few were just resting, having a private moment in a public place, and I felt buoyed by being here. This is why I wanted to write this book, to tell about a place I love that doesn't belong to me but feels like it is mine, and how that feels marvelous and exceptional. All the things that are wrong in the world seem conquered by a library's simple unspoken promise: Here I am, please tell me your story; here is my story, please listen.

The security guards began arranging chairs and straightening tables while calling out, "Four minutes! Four minutes to closing!" The few of us here snapped our books shut and swept our belongings together and headed upstairs. In the checkout line, a heavyset man with three books under his arm began a jiggling, hip-wagging dance, and people stepped around him carefully on their way out the door.

ACKNOWLEDGMENTS

This book relied on the patience and generosity of dozens of people who gave me their time and their stories. My greatest thanks go to the staff at Central Library who were so welcoming and helpful throughout the many years I spent wandering the halls; a special tip of the hat to Glen Creason, John Szabo, Eva Mitnick, and Peter Persic, who never flinched when I returned with one more question. Thank you, Emma Roberts, for dragging out all those boxes of material. I'm also grateful to many former staff members who spoke with me, among them Helene Mochedlover, Elizabeth Teoman, Susan Kent, Fontaine Holmes, JoAnna and Robert Reagan, and the late Wyman Jones. The Library Foundation of Los Angeles, and in particular Ken Brecher and Louise Steinman, championed the project from the beginning, for which I am very grateful. I was helped by past and present members of the Los Angeles Fire Department, and in particular one very long-suffering woman named Jessica in the records department who humored my pleas to dig a little deeper and found material I had been told was long gone.

I owe a special thanks to the family of Harry Peak, and in particular his sisters, Debra and Brenda. Thanks, too, to Demitri Hioteles, who shared many memories of Harry and provided the portrait included in the book.

The Solomon R. Guggenheim Foundation, The MacDowell Colony, the Corporation of Yaddo, and the Banff Centre for Arts and Creativity helped make this project possible. I feel very fortunate for their support.

Huge thanks to Ashley Van Buren for her smart, insightful reads; for cheerleading along the way; for rounding up the photos; and for being a great friend. Julie Tate did the crackerjack fact-checking on a crazy deadline; thank you, Julie!

All my friends refrained from asking too often if the book was done yet, for which they have my undying gratitude. For handholding and carefully calibrated distraction, I am particularly indebted to, among others, Erica Steinberg, Christy Callahan, Sally

Sampson, Janet Tashjian, Jeff Conti, Debra Orlean, Laurie Sandell, Karen Brooks, Sarah Thyre, and all my merry crew of friends; I love you.

Thank you, Kimberly Burns, for your wisdom and enthusiasm.

Richard Pine, my forever agent: You're the greatest.

Chip McGrath, best boss, thanks for reading when this was a raw mess and giving me perfect advice and the greatest encouragement.

Thank you, David Remnick and Virginia Cannon, for giving me leave from *The New Yorker* to work on this. No one could ask for a better professional home or for better editors; when I realize I work with you, I keep pinching myself to make sure I'm not dreaming.

I work with the most wonderful group of people at Simon & Schuster. A huge thank-you to Carolyn Reidy, who made this all possible; Richard Rhorer, the associate publisher; Dana Trocker, the marketing whiz; Julianna Haubner, who knows how to get everything done; Kristen Lemire and Lisa Erwin and Beth Thomas and Patricia Callahan, who work magic behind the scenes; Tamara Arellano, who tweaked all the important tweaks; Jackie Seow and Lauren Peters-Collaer and Carly Loman, who made this book so beautiful.

And thank you, Anne Pearce! I'm so happy to do another book with you! Jofie Ferrari-Adler — editor extraordinaire, voice of wisdom, and sharpest pencil around — there are no words . . . ! Jon Karp, here we are on book number five! I am so lucky to work with you. Thank you, thank you for these many years of friendship, support, and inspiration.

It's a cliché to say "I couldn't have done this book without . . ." but in the case of my husband, John Gillespie, it happens to be true. He's simply amazing. He helped me plow through a huge amount of research material — and even though I could barely read his handwriting, I'd still be digging through those archives if he hadn't pitched in. He read every word I wrote — multiple times — and gave brilliant editing suggestions and reporting advice and boosted me whenever the task of writing this seemed too daunting. Most of all, he gave me support and love throughout, for which I am deeply and adoringly grateful.

To my son, Austin, who led me into this story and has endured me working long nights and weekends when we could have been playing Fortnite together, I love you.

Mom, I made a book for you.

Los Angeles, California
May 2018

NOTES ON SOURCES

The story of the Los Angeles Public Library and the 1986 fire required years of research and scores of interviews with current and past library staff, deep dives into the Fire Department's archives and the City of Los Angeles's court records, and a lot of digging through the musty boxes of material stashed in the library's Rare Books room. There I found a trove of information, including newspaper clippings about the library from the twenties; book lists from the thirties; paraphernalia from every decade; and countless, fascinating odds and ends left behind by the hundreds of librarians who passed through Central Library at some point in their careers. This material was essential to the writing of this book. I also found a great deal of valuable material in the many books and published papers about California and library history. Here is a selected list of those resources:

Books

Banham, Reyner. *Los Angeles: The Architecture of Four Ecologies.* University of California Press, 2001.

Battles, Matthew. *Library: An Unquiet History.* New York: W. W. Norton & Company, 2015.

Bradbury, Ray. *Fahrenheit 451* (Sixtieth Anniversary Edition). New York: Simon and Schuster, 2012.

Burlingham, Cynthia, and Bruce Whiteman, eds. *The World from Here: Treasures of the Great Libraries of Los Angeles.* New York: Oxford University Press, 2002.

Casson, Lionel. *Libraries in the Ancient World.* New Haven, CT: Yale University Press, 2001.

Davis, Mike. *City of Quartz: Excavating the Future in Los Angeles.* New York: Verso Books, 2006.

Ditzel, Paul. *A Century of Service, 1886–1986: The Centennial History of the Los Angeles Fire Department.* Los Angeles: Los Angeles Firemen's Relief Association, 1986.

Fiske, Turbesé Lummis, and Keith Lummis. *Charles F. Lummis: The Man and His West.* Norman, OK: University of Oklahoma Press, 1975.

Gee, Stephen, John F. Szabo, and Arnold Schwartzman. *Los Angeles Central Library: A History of Its Art and Architecture.* Santa Monica: Angel City Press, 2016.

Gordon, Dudley. *Charles F. Lummis: Crusader in Corduroy.* Los Angeles: Cultural Assets Press, 1972.

Klein, Norman M. *The History of Forgetting: Los Angeles and the Erasure of Memory.* New York: Verso Press, 1997.

Knuth, Rebecca. *Libricide: The Regime-Sponsored Destruction of Books and Libraries in the Twentieth Century.* Westport, CT: Praeger Publishers, 2003.

Palfrey, John. *BiblioTech: Why Libraries Matter More Than Ever in the Age of Google.* New York: Basic Books, 2015.

Polastron, Lucien X. *Books on Fire: The Destruction of Libraries Throughout History.* Rochester, VT: Inner Traditions, 2007.

Rose, Jonathan, ed. *The Holocaust and the Book.* Amherst, MA: University of Massachusetts Press, 2001.

Soter, Bernadette Dominique. *The Light of Learning: An Illustrated History of the Los Angeles Public Library.* Los Angeles: Library Foundation of Los Angeles, 1993.

Starr, Kevin. *Americans and the California Dream, 1850–1915.* New York: Oxford

University Press, 1986.

————. *Golden Dreams: California in an Age of Abundance, 1950–1963.* New York: Oxford University Press, 2009.

————. *Inventing the Dream: California through the Progressive Era.* New York: Oxford University Press, 1986.

————. *Material Dreams: Southern California Through the 1920s.* New York: Oxford University Press, 1990.

Thompson, Mark. *American Character: The Curious Life of Charles Fletcher Lummis and the Rediscovery of the Southwest.* New York: Arcade Publishing, 2001.

Ulin, David. *Sidewalking: Coming to Terms with Los Angeles.* Oakland, CA: University of California Press, 2015.

Wiegand, Shirley, and Wayne Wiegand. *The Desegregation of Public Libraries in the Jim Crow South: Civil Rights and Local Activism.* Baton Rouge: LSU Press, 2018.

Wilentz, Amy. *I Feel Earthquakes More Often Than They Happen: Coming to California in the Age of Schwarzenegger.* New York: Simon & Schuster, 2007.

Articles and Papers

Blitz, Daniel Frederick. "Charles Fletcher Lummis: Los Angeles City Librarian." UCLA Electronic Theses and Dissertations M.L.I.S., Library and Information Science thesis (2013).

Hansen, Debra Gold, Karen Gracy, and Sheri Irvin. "At the Pleasure of the Board: Women Librarians and the LAPL, 1880–1905." *Libraries & Culture Magazine,* vol. 34, no. 4 (1999).

Mackenzie, Armine. "The Great Library War." *California Librarian Magazine,* vol. 18, no. 2 (April 1957).

Maxwell, Margaret F. "The Lion and the Lady: The Firing of Miss Mary Jones." *American Libraries Magazine* (May 1978).

Moneta, Daniela P. "Charles Lummis — The Centennial Exhibition Commemorating His Tramp Across the Continent." Los Angeles: Southwest Museum (1985).

PHOTO CREDITS

535

Los Angeles Public Library Photo Collection

Jack Gaunt copyright © 2011. *Los Angeles Times.* Used with permission.

University of Kentucky Special Collections

Acción Visual/Diana Arias

ABOUT THE AUTHOR

Susan Orlean has been a staff writer at *The New Yorker* since 1992. She is the author of seven books, including *Rin Tin Tin, Saturday Night,* and *The Orchid Thief,* which was made into the Academy Award–winning film *Adaptation.* She lives with her family and her animals in upstate New York and Los Angeles, and she may be reached at SusanOrlean.com and Twitter.com/SusanOrlean.

The employees of Thorndike Press hope you have enjoyed this Large Print book. All our Thorndike, Wheeler, and Kennebec Large Print titles are designed for easy reading, and all our books are made to last. Other Thorndike Press Large Print books are available at your library, through selected bookstores, or directly from us.

For information about titles, please call:
  (800) 223-1244

or visit our website at:
  gale.com/thorndike

To share your comments, please write:
  Publisher
  Thorndike Press
  10 Water St., Suite 310
  Waterville, ME 04901